THE MAGIC BATON

Carnegie Hall, April 4, 1954

The Magic Baton

TOSCANINI'S LIFE FOR MUSIC

Filippo Sacchi

PUTNAM
42 GREAT RUSSELL STREET
LONDON : MCMLVII

Made and printed in Great Britain by Richard Clay and Company, Ltd.,
Bungay, Suffolk

Contents

Plates

CHAPTER I

The Gift

TOSCANINI's baton was a slender pointed stick exactly 20 inches long.

Today, to say that Toscanini's baton was a magic wand is a commonplace which is taken for granted. What is extraordinary, however, is that the word "magic" has been associated with him from the very beginning. He was, so to speak, born with it. As far back as 1888 an obscure journalist from Casale Monferrato used it to describe him when Toscanini was a young maestro of twenty!

Any attempt at explaining such an astounding career must involve postulating that there was something beyond reason, some strange magnetic power. One point to begin with: eight biographies of Toscanini have already been published; the last less than a year before his death. Eight biographies! Has any other celebrity eight biographies in his lifetime? And yet he was no creative genius like Verdi or Wagner, nor was he even a composer. Nor did he shine in high cosmopolitan society as did Liszt. Nor was there any question of scandal, as there was about Byron and Wilde. His life was never tragic like Verlaine's; he was never a Beau Brummell nor a Valentino. Even his divorce record is lamentable, not a single one! It might be understandable if he had gloried in self-advertisement and had deliberately encouraged his would-be biographers, but he abhorred publicity in any form.

We must visualize him in terms of the exceptional, use the concept of the phenomenal. Zweig, in the essay at the beginning of his autobiography, stresses the *phenomenal* quality of Toscanini's genius. According to him, Toscanini was the living representative of the Hero in the Carlyle tradition. After the Hero as prophet, poet, priest, writer, king, we have had the Conductor Hero: on the principle that great men are made from the same material but poured into a different heroic mould.

From every point of view Toscanini was a highly interesting phenomenon. He was, without doubt, one of the representative figures of our time. Representative in the modern sense of the word, with all the plastic and visual elements belonging to the spirit of the age. The latter being essentially physiocratic in character, the very conditions of any world-wide popularity imply some degree of publicity; hence the amazing success of people who are naturally photogenic, like actors or athletes.

The necessity for their continuous physical presence, as a condition of their fame, is such that all other celebrities, who may not and need not be handsome—politicians, writers, men of science, etc.—are forced to join in the scramble for publicity, try to make the headlines in newspapers, and get on television. Hence the invasion of magazines, revues, periodicals, and newsreels by ambassadors, generals, deputies, and financiers, all smiling and happy, either shaking hands, kissing babies, or signing important documents. In comparison with Churchill, Eisenhower or the Aga Khan, how insignificant are Trajan, Domitian, and Charlemagne; who had no methods of publicity other than having their heads stamped on their money; and Napoleon, who, poor fellow, had to be satisfied with printed engravings.

This physical popularity, this outstanding presence, was a fundamental feature of Toscanini's personality. Conducting an orchestra involves a considerable degree of physical effort; it is, in fact, a real *performance*. The conductor on his rostrum is the centre of all eyes, for as long as the opera, concert, or spectacle lasts—two or three hours—everything depends on his slightest gesture. Therefore, from the beginning to the end, he will be in perpetual motion. The violins or the trumpets may fade out in turn. The soprano, the tenor, the baritone may stop singing, sit down, or leave the stage. But the conductor is the only one who never leaves; he alone bears the burden throughout the performance. He carries the whole performance: showman and actor as well as conductor, he has to interpret the whole spectacle in his own inimitable manner.

It will naturally depend on the individual temperament of each conductor, as to what extent this theatrical element will be called into play. A certain faculty for miming is inseparable from conducting an orchestra, and it demands certain abilities and aptitudes: a gift for expression and movement and, in particular, a capacity for dominating, solely by virtue of a powerful personality.

There have been no conductors in the past, and very few contemporary ones, who possess the extraordinary prestige of Toscanini. His appearance on the rostrum was the signal for an immediate state of tension throughout a crowded hall. He had not yet moved a muscle. It was enough for him to gather himself together in a sort of inner concentration. He lowered the top of his large ovoid head, from which the hair was swept backward as if by an invisible wind, between his massive shoulders.

His arms were pressed rigidly to his body, the elbows bent at right angles, tensely ready to spring into action. This was enough to ensure a special silence, one might almost say an accumulation of silences, through which the first limpid sound flowed with the astral purity of a discharge through a vacuum tube.

There have been only two other men of recent years, belonging to the same class and generation, who have enjoyed a similar overwhelming popularity: Churchill and Shaw. With the difference that Toscanini never flouted any personal idiosyncrasies such as the painting, uniforms, and cigar of Churchill, or the beard, eccentricities, and epigrams of Shaw. Except at rehearsals, when he always wore a simple black alpaca jacket, in order to allow freedom of movement and diminish sweating, he was always dressed—even as a young man—in a correct manner; it might be called *bourgeois*, in keeping with his carefully brushed and parted hair and Edwardian moustache. On the rare occasions when he

granted an interview, he always limited himself to the indispensable minimum and said what he had to say as quickly as possible.

Even on the rostrum during a performance, his gestures were
always extremely simple, logical, and perfectly comprehensible.
The attack was made with a perpendicular movement from above
downwards. The signal to the violins a rapid parabolic movement of the baton. From time to time the left hand moved out-
wards, the thumb pushed out and the four fingers held nervously
tense; to mark an approaching change of mood, the hand expanded
and moved inwards—a reflex motion towards the zone of in-
timacy and reflection. A confidential, intimate gesture heralded a
special entry, one of those unexpected entries of new instruments
—delicate and refined sounds which sometimes emanate from an
orchestra with the nostalgic subtlety of a faint perfume stealing
into a room from the garden. Toscanini's left hand was more
essential to him than his baton for indicating changes in tone-
colour. He told his singers: "Keep looking at my left hand and
don't worry!" His imitative gestures were few; the undulating
movement of his wrists for the Rhine Theme (beginning of *The
Rhinegold*) or during the hurricane in Beethoven's Sixth Symphony, where the crashes of thunder are marked with a swift
rotation backwards of both arms, were the only examples of the
kind that I can remember at the moment.

The same clarity and order characterized his gestures. If you
watched carefully, an extraordinary regularity would be noticed,
which might almost have been called "topography". His gesticu-
lation developed instinctively on three planes which were separate
and distinguishable. One plane, which we will call low, was
roughly from the level of the groin to chest; another, middle
plane, went from the level of the chest to the chin; finally, a top
plane, from the chin upwards. This localization was by no means
casual, but corresponds to three different degrees of expression;
Toscanini's mimetic zones correspond to a determined order of
emotions, just as each part of the body, in certain systems of the
physicians of antiquity, corresponds to a determined pneuma, or
rather a determined functional disposition.

Naturally, these remarks are not meant to be taken too literally. His actions were not premeditated but unconscious, and therefore subject to all the fluctuations and improvisations of the instinct. Along general lines, however, he used the middle plane for expressing intense but well-defined emotions, strong and generous thoughts, luminous and profound passions.

Whenever Toscanini made a gesture which "laboured" along the axis of the shoulders, look to see, in the libretto if it is an operatic work, or in the page of the score if it is a symphony; you will nearly always find a word, a verse, a thematic coloration which led to this special order of the sentiments.

If his gesture rose to the top plane, if he moved upwards, there is an infallible alteration in the sphere of expression. We enter the plane of conflicting and vivacious emotions, of brilliant and mordant sonority, aggressive virtuosities, of glissandos, vertiginous runs, and showers of semiquavers. When, on the other hand, we descend to the lower registers of turbid and dramatic passion, the destructive urge of evil was expressed by gestures which were automatically and immediately transported to the lower plane. It is a curious point: Toscanini attacked his *fortissimi* not from above, but from below. During the Overture to *The Mastersingers*, the violent initial fanfare is carried up from below. Immediately after the final wild trill of the violins, the woodwinds gently murmur the theme of Eve's distress, which is followed by the ascending and precipitate movement of the bows; all this is expressed in the top plane. But when the brass breaks into the pompous fanfare of the Masters, we are back again in the lowest plane: violence is always earthy! Later, as the love-song develops, it leads us back to the middle plane; it is, you will remember, a love which has reached its bright culmination, a sane and chaste emotion, well-balanced between reason and the heart.

It seems futile to attempt to systematize Toscanini's mimetics in this fashion; it is rather like attempting to interpret a poem of Leopardi or Shelley solely in terms of logical analysis. If, however, one tried to interpret the movements of his baton as if they were tracing imaginary written words—i.e. a graphological interpretation—the distinctive characteristics were the extraordinary regularity and discipline, which reflected a complete mastery of expression.

The magical element in his interpretation is this absolute and unquestionable mastery; the magic is precise and exact, an enchantment realized by means of the infinitesimal calculus. We must attempt to explain the positive and scientific basis of his process of deciphering music.

Superficially, there is nothing more regular or carefully planned than a page of a score. Open one at random. There are thirty-two bands of very fine horizontal lines crossed by long, perpendicular dividing lines. Between them, hundreds of black dots are distributed, sometimes scattered, sometimes close together, and interposed with a capricious punctuation of asterisks, angles, tails, commas, and arches. The problem is to arrive at a result with all these different indications: to make music from them.

Actually, reading a musical score is about the most abstruse and complex operation that the human brain is called upon to perform. What, in fact, has to be done? First of all, every single column of notes has to be "added" at a glance, one after the other. An instantaneous total is registered. But this is only the beginning. Simultaneously with these vertical additions, you have to follow a whole series of horizontal additions, because the total sound of each column must be immediately carried over to the total of the succeeding columns, exactly like an adding machine. You have to carry over first the total of the single beats, then of the phrase—that is to say, of all its component beats— then carry over the preceding phrase on to the following phrase, and so on, in an infinite series of analyses and syntheses, through which you must clarify all the harmonic, tonal, and thematic links of the piece.

This is an enormously complicated mental process; exactly like a series of major mathematical calculations. With the further complication, however, that the operation must be performed at a definite "tempo" and at a definite rhythm because the result of the additions—i.e. the comprehensive effect—is determined by the speed with which the sounds follow each other. An *Adagio* must be deciphered at the tempo of an *Adagio*, and *Presto*, at *Presto* tempo, or the whole character of the piece will be lost.

There are thousands and thousands of people who are able to read a score, just as there are thousands of mathematicians who are able to make difficult calculations. Naturally, however, there are ways and ways of reading and of calculating. The degree of success with which an individual is able to penetrate, more deeply than others, into a profound interpretation of the single values will obviously depend on his capacity for analysis and synthesis. In this respect Toscanini is the Einstein of music.

An example of his immense capacity for deciphering, from my own personal observation: many years ago in Vienna I was fortunate enough to go to a concert with him. Toscanini had a box at the Konzerthaus, which he had kindly invited me to share. Mahler's Eighth Symphony was on the programme. The reader will remember that this is a composition constructed, technically, on a gigantic scale. Not only because there is also a chorus— many of Mahler's symphonies have a chorus—but because of its proportions; the score calls for two adult choruses of both sexes, and two choirs of boys. Further, the orchestra is disproportionately enlarged: besides the ordinary complement, there are parts for eight horns, four trombones, four trumpets, four flutes, four oboes, four bassoons, five harps, and three bass-drums; on top of all this, an organ, a grand piano, harmonium, celesta, gong, and even a mandolin! And, naturally, there are the soloist singers, also increased in numbers: three sopranos, two contraltos, a tenor, baritone, and bass.

We were alone in a box on the right of the hall. Toscanini, as the host, insisted on my sitting in the best seat facing the orchestra. He sat opposite me. The symphony starts with a colossal chord in E flat major followed immediately by the chorus with their imploring cries of "Veni, veni". I was fascinated and could not take my eyes away from the orchestra. This incredible mass of instruments and players arrayed on steps which almost reached the ceiling, the swift movement of the bows, the scintillating batteries of blaring brass, the hundreds of mouths opened to utter the mystic cry—these were a sufficiently impressive spectacle in itself.

It was only later, when, after the final paroxysmal appeal of the soprano, the orchestra suddenly subsides into the murmured prayer "Imple superna gratia", that I turned to look at Toscanini. His head was bent, his hands were folded over the programme on his knee and, as his back was turned away from the bright light which came from the orchestra, his face was so shaded as to be almost invisible. I stared at him and was astonished to see a sudden expression of pain flit across his face, as if he had been stabbed. He did not move a muscle, he might have been made of stone; repeatedly, however, I noted a contraction, a frown, a movement of the lips, which revealed that he was undergoing some painful experience, like a blow or a spasm.

That evening there were on the platform the full complements of five Viennese choral societies and an orchestra which was almost doubled in size. There were moments, as in the gigantic double fugue of the first tempo, in which cataracts of thousands of notes were poured out. He was following it all, note by note, as if he had the score open in front of him. Note by note, he was immediately comparing the sound produced with the other sound, with the perfect sound, which he was able to reconstruct in his mind; his interpretation was infallible and revealed to him every blemish and lack of balance in the performance. As he was fully aware of the slightest hesitation, of any delay or any premature note, of any lack of balance in the volume or in the architecture of the execution, each time he experienced a painful sensation, just as we feel a violent prick, a burn, or a dentist's drill approaching the nerve.

When we review Toscanini's career, which embraces a period of almost a century, we must interpret it as the result of an exceptional multiplicity of factors: an interpretation so intuitive as to be almost mediumistic, a complete knowledge of everything that is known about music, an inflexible capacity for self-discipline and for inculcating discipline in others. But, underlying all this, we must postulate the existence of a mysterious and inexplicable phenomenon: an ear, which allowed him to record and store up inside himself a number of sound vibrations, immensely superior to that of any other human ear. This was the magical element in his constitution. This could, to some extent, be inferred from the abnormal development of his auditory lobes. Behind the temples he had two pronounced prominences, almost like pads, like the earphones of a telephone operator. His ears themselves were extraordinarily fine, with convolutions like those of a seashell; they remained always fleshy and elastic, like the ears of a young man in his twenties. There is a popular superstition that plump ears are a sign of longevity. It is reported that Toscanini's mother-in-law, discussing him with her daughter, when they were still engaged, told her: "Look at his ears; he'll live to be a hundred."

Because his phenomenal gift was a personal one, it is ultimately inexplicable. Take for instance his rendering of the Fourth Movement of Brahms's First Symphony, and compare his recording of it with those by other conductors. He alone solves that bewildering rhythmical problem, of how to maintain the slow and solemn tempo of the chorale, and at the same time release the full whirling brilliance of the orchestral rush. Toscanini alone manages it successfully. How can it be explained? The record is there, it should be obvious; yet it is not. And if you had asked him the secret, he would have said, "There is no secret. I simply give the phrases room." That was his way, a simple formula, giving each note its own proper space and time and weight.

CHAPTER II

Youth in Oltretorrente

OLTRETORRENTE, as the name implies, is that part of the city of Parma which lies on "the other side of the river". The inhabitants on each side refer to the opposite bank as "Old Parma". Neither of them wants to be considered old, and both want to be new. This curious rivalry is an indication of the character of the citizens of Parma; odd, punctilious, and amusing.

It would be difficult to find two places so near to each other but so utterly different. The Parma opposite Oltretorrente is the aristocratic and residential Parma. The Farnese gave it its Roman stamp, its splendour, and its jesuitical element; the Bourbons plastered and painted it with French elegance and rococo ornamentation. Finally Marie-Louise added a flavour of Viennese and neo-classical grace. The end result is a city of distinctive character which still qualifies for inclusion in the category of Court cities by virtue of its monumental churches, its majestic palaces and its spacious streets and gardens.

If we compare ultrapontine Parma to the Court, Oltretorrente represents the plebs: Versailles on this side, the Cordeliers on the other. It is the suburb of the *sans-culottes*. From 1890 onwards, from the very beginning of Socialism in Italy, Oltretorrente has been known as one of the advanced strongholds of the movement. If it did not originate in it, Oltretorrente was involved in every episode of the interminable struggle from that time onwards, for the conquest of new political and trades-union rights, as well as every agitation, every strike, every parliamentary battle. There were times, during the first ten years of the century, in which the word Oltretorrente had the same ominous meaning to many Italians as Soviet or Cominform has today.

Barricade-building was its speciality. The speed with which barricades went up, at the right moment, in Oltretorrente was incredible; it was almost as if the inhabitants, when they married and set up house, had had their furniture made particularly suitable for erecting barricades. They developed a passion for barricade-making, which persisted even after modern armaments began to render barricades useless.

The last great epic of Oltretorrente took place in 1922, on the day of the March on Rome and the Fascist *coup d'état*. That morning Oltretorrente, in less than no time, was filled with barricades. There were barricades on the outer walls towards the countryside and barricades on the bridges. Particularly impressive was the barricade which blocked the Ponte de Mezzo, the bridge which leads from Oltretorrente to the centre of the city. After a day spent in alarms and skirmishes, the general in command of the town garrison ordered two cannons to be placed on the other side of the bridge, and declared that, if the barricade were not removed in half an hour, he would open fire. This was the signal for a mass exodus of the female population of Oltretorrente; those slender and hardy women, with their fiery eyes and mordant tongues, ranged themselves in front of the barricade. Half an hour later there was some commotion on the other side, the gunners could be seen running up, the cannons were being aimed. Then the word of command, "Fire!" and two terrific explosions which made the whole bridge tremble. The women, to show their contempt, applauded wildly.

All this has now been altered. Science has altered the technique of revolution, and the inhabitants of Oltretorrente, though they are still hot-heads, no longer erect barricades, but become members of the underground cells or work on factory committees. But when one looks at it, tumbling down to the river, Oltretorrente still seems to emanate from its walls a subversive aura reminiscent of 1848. This appearance of cascading is partly due to the broad bank of grass spreading down to the water and to the fact that the whole façade of the quarter seems to be elevated on black walls and buttresses, because the foundations have been uncovered by a deviation of the river-bed. In any case, I doubt whether one could find anywhere else a row of houses so heaped upon each other, so romantic and so proud. In fact, just like a barricade.

It was in Oltretorrente, one day in June of the year 1866, that a young man called Claudio Toscanini and a young woman called Paola Montani were married.

On the surface there was nothing to differentiate this couple from the thousands and thousands of couples all over the world who get married every day. They might have gone off for a short honeymoon or gone straight home, according to their circumstances. They probably spent a few days thinking of nothing except loving and enjoying themselves; then one morning they would put away their best clothes in the cupboard, dress in their old clothes, and go back to work. This would have been the beginning of the dull march of months and years. Later there would have been a child. Then, perhaps, another; the good would have alternated with the bad: a little good luck and a little bad luck; a little happiness and a little quarrelling. And so on, until their hair grew white and they were pensioned off; until the day in which one of them said goodbye to the other, and their life partnership was dissolved.

That morning, seeing the two newly-weds with their little procession of witnesses and relatives passing down the Borgo delle Grazie, the casual onlooker might have been justified in representing their future in this way. Nobody could have imagined that this young man was faced with a crucial decision; he was so handsome, so graceful, so dashing, complete with moustache and little beard; he was linking arms so proudly with his tall companion, with her glorious figure and her enormous black eyes—a decision which was to upset, completely, the prescribed course of the first week of marriage.

Claudio Toscanini was a follower of Garibaldi. It is a little difficult to realize now just what it meant in Italy in those years to

be a follower of Garibaldi. It meant being an exceptional, dedicated individual, marked by a special illuminating grace, destined
to unify the motherland and achieve honour and liberty for her;
a man whose fate was to exhaust himself in forced marches all over
the sacred soil of Italy, from the Alps to Sicily, from battle to
battle, bayonet fixed to rifle, until the day came when, his task
accomplished, he would be received into immortality with flags
flying and trumpets blowing. In short, to be one of Garibaldi's
men was a vocation, an individual destiny; it was to belong not
only to a company of adventurers but to an order of chivalry; it
was a dedication to priesthood and to the people of the whole
country. It incarnated that ideal of the "honest robber" which
was so dear to Garibaldi's heart: breaking the law to serve justice,
which has always been a conception extraordinarily attractive to
the Italian people, as their whole history shows. Hence the irresistible fascination of the followers of Garibaldi. There can hardly
have been a single Italian maiden between 1848 and 1870 who,
whether on a bed of leaves or on a feather mattress, whether under
rags or under a silken quilt, did not dream, at least once, of being
carried away by a devil in a red shirt, on a white charger, a devil
with bright blue eyes, the leonine locks, and the Nazarene beard
of Giuseppe Garibaldi.

Claudio Toscanini had already taken part in three campaigns.
He had followed Garibaldi in 1859, when, stifling his republican
ideals, out of generosity and love of Italy, Garibaldi had helped
Victor Emmanuel and Napoleon III. In 1860 Toscanini had
answered the call of the Thousand, probably fighting with the
dissident Garibaldini groups who had attacked the grand march
on Naples. In 1862 he had once more answered the call. This
time the cause was difficult, almost desperate. Garibaldi was now
the rebel, rejecting all appeals for obedience, riding roughshod
over all the plans of the King's Government; he had once more
set sail from Sicily and had crossed the Straits, scorching the air
with the burning order: "To Rome or to death!"

Claudio Toscanini was also at Aspromonte and was captured
with the others. His position was particularly serious, as he had

been called up as a conscript and assigned to the regular corps of Bersaglieri; and so his presence among the Garibaldini volunteers rendered him liable to the specific accusation of being a deserter. About three hundred of them were in the same boat. They were all condemned to death. Each morning a group of them was led off to be shot.

One day (very few of them were now left) they were ordered out. When Claudio saw a priest waiting for them, he thought: "Now it is our turn!" Instead of which the priest, after a mellifluous and unctuous preamble, informed them that His Majesty, in his infinite generosity and mercy, had deigned to spare their lives. That was all, however! The prison was a horrible building, evil-smelling and dark, which had once been a castle; the food was almost uneatable, so bad that Claudio contracted scurvy and lost all his teeth. The Garibaldini were shut up with common criminals, including the famous "Camorra" gang, the members of which were always having terrible quarrels followed by scenes of bloodshed. Finally, after three interminable years, they let him go. There is a delightful portrait of Claudio painted by a Parmesan painter, Affani, which shows him as he was after his return from Aspromonte. Claudio is bareheaded, with long rings of hair falling to the shoulders in the fashion of Garibaldi. His face is magnificently modelled, with a straight and finely chiselled nose, long almond-shaped eyes, bushy eyebrows nearly meeting over the nose; with his pointed moustaches and triangular beard, with an expression which is both gentle and virile, he looks half musketeer, half poet.

Soon after his release from prison at Aspromonte, Claudio returned to his trade as a tailor, met Paola Montani and decided to marry her. Meanwhile, the kettle was coming to the boil again. Austria and Prussia were at daggers drawn. The state of alarm was also felt throughout the peninsula. The hopes of the nationalist forces in every province were reawakened. The Garibaldini, of course, were at the head of the movement. In Parma the Garibaldi headquarters were already spreading rumours among their friends: "The General will soon be on the move!" Clandestine enrolments were being accepted, and Claudio Toscanini, incorrigible as ever, had been one of the first to put his name down. On his marriage day this was the great secret locked inside his breast. He said nothing to his wife; at any rate this is what Paola Montani always claimed. And that morning, when he walked along the Borgo delle Grazie with Paola on his arm, he knew perfectly well that shortly, in a week or ten days, or perhaps even in a few hours, someone would come to fetch him, would take him aside and, just like six years before, would whisper to him the General's watchword: "The merchant is leaving; ship the goods!"

Actually, the word came in twenty-four hours. And forty-eight hours after the wedding, Claudio Toscanini packed his old red shirt and his red beret, kissed his weeping spouse and said, like the soldier in the popular ballad, "Goodbye, my beautiful one, goodbye!"—away to war!

This time he was not gone for long. Whilst the Prussian troops were penetrating into Bohemia, after having hurled the Austrian armies back from the frontier, the Piedmontese troops, as soon as they had crossed the Mincio, committed so many mistakes, met with one ludicrous fiasco after another, that they managed to get themselves beaten with the utmost rapidity. They re-crossed the Mincio, and there, paralysed by the confused tactics of Victor Emmanuel, became completely demoralized, actually arousing the suspicion in Prussia that Piedmont wanted to betray it and come to an agreement with the enemy. It was only after Sadowa that the King's generals, seeing that the Empire was now in ruins, began to advance again as best they could. But the Austrian armies of the Veneto were already, spontaneously, falling back to the frontier. In any case, there was nothing more to conquer, because Francis Joseph, the old wolf, took it into his head to play a dirty trick on his old Piedmontese comrade-in-arms: he suddenly and dramatically surrendered the Veneto to Napoleon III and invited him to be the mediator between himself and the King of Prussia.

It was Garibaldi, once more, who played the part of the *enfant terrible*. Without worrying about the comic war being fought behind his back, he marched straight into the Trentino, which had always been his fixation. He fought five battles, one after the other, minor but tough engagements. It was in one of these that Claudio had the singular adventure (coming from Parma, he had been brought up on Verdi) of living a scene from *La Forza del Destino*, two years before it was written. You will remember in the third act, when, after the fight, the wounded Don Alvaro confides in Don Carlo the fatal secret of his love for Leonora. Well, Claudio's battle was over too. The drums were beating the assembly. Claudio was told that there was a wounded Garibaldini who was asking for him. It was a man from Parma, whose Christian name only was known, a name admirably suited to his role—Celeste. Claudio found him stretched out under a tree; he was mortally wounded. Celeste asked to be left alone with him.

In that solemn hour . . . no, the words were not the same, but there must have been the same background to that music, that sombre pulsation of those double-basses, when, his bleeding head leaning against his friend's arm, Celeste spoke to him. "Claudio . . . after . . . are you going back to Parma?"

"Surely, I think so," answered Claudio.

"Then you must do me a favour. . . . You must remember me to somebody. . . ."

"But, Celeste, you must rest now and not think such things."

"Promise me, Claudio. It is a woman. I've always loved her. Tell her."

"All right, if that is your wish. . . . What is her name?"

"Her name is Paola Montani. She used to live in the Borgo delle Grazie."

When he heard the name, Claudio turned his face away.

"But . . ." he stammered, pale as death, doing his best to control his voice, "and who is she?"

"We were engaged. Then we broke it off. It was all my fault. Then I left Parma. If she is still free, you ought to marry her, Claudio. She is a good girl. She's dead straight . . . and . . ."

His wound became so painful that he could not continue. He groaned and closed his eyes. Claudio was moved to tears.

"Ah, Celeste," he whispered in a broken voice, "if this will make you happy I'll tell you. Paola Montani and I are already married . . . we were married three months ago."

A faint, blissful smile flitted across Celeste's face and his head fell forward. He died that evening, and Claudio buried him.[1]

Verdi wrote *La Forza del Destino* two years after this incident. Certainly, the situation, and above all the sequel, were different. But there is an extraordinary similarity in the meaning and the atmosphere. It is true that a genius always works telepathically and uses themes which are "in the air" and are characteristic of the life of his period. In the years to come, every time that *La Forza del Destino* was performed at the Regio, Claudio, looking down from the upper gallery on Don Carlo bending over Don Alvaro's stretcher, could not help remembering the poor Garibaldini, Celeste.

Soon after there was a final rout at Lissa. The Prussian army was in front of Vienna. Then the news arrived that, at Nikolsburg, Prussia and Austria had come to an agreement, leaving Italy in the lurch. Nothing more could be done. In November even the Corps of Garibaldini was disbanded.

This was the fourth time that the good Toscanini came home to put away his red shirt. But this time it was different. This time there was a woman, his wife, who was waiting for him. He raced up the narrow steps of his mother-in-law's home and, when he saw his wife in front of him, was horrified. It was no longer Paola, but a shadow of Paola; no longer that beautiful full face, but drained of colour, the cheeks sunken in like an old woman's; no longer that proud gleam in the eye, nothing but a dull, listless expression accentuated by exhaustion. As soon as she rose to her feet and came towards him, he realized from the swelling underneath her apron and from her weight that she was expecting a baby.

The baby was born three months afterwards, on March 25,

[1] This conversation is not invented. Paola Montani told it to her daughter Ada, and Ada—a charming and distinguished old lady who died at Milan in 1955—told it to the author.

1867. Claudio gave his son a name which had never before been used in his family. He called him Arturo. He followed this precedent when it came to baptizing his other children, always choosing names which had not been in his family: Narcisa, Ada, Zina. The grandparents grumbled, the aunts and the uncles grumbled, but Claudio paid no attention; Arturo was to be the child's name and that was that. In any case, the family already knew that Claudio was eccentric.

Claudio Toscanini's trade, besides that of warrior, was tailoring. He was born, so to speak, among looms. His father had been proprietor of a cotton-mill in Cortemaggiore, with shops there and in Parma, and was relatively well-off. Claudio Toscanini's father was a highly efficient reproducing machine. He had already had three children, in rapid succession, from his first wife. But she, although still extremely young, must have had a premonition of what was in store for her, and removed herself in time by throwing herself down a well, where she was drowned. The second wife, Eligia Bombardi from Piacenza, was tougher. Grandfather Toscanini made her produce twenty-five children, three males and twenty-two females. Having renounced premature suicide, the poor woman became blind as a consequence of excessive child-bearing; then she was allowed to pass to her final rest.

Claudio was the last child. He came into the world in an absolutely extemporaneous manner, which was in tune with his character. One evening, during a service in the lovely fifteenth-century village church, Grandmother Eligia was unexpectedly seized with labour pains. The priest just had time to put the Host back into the tabernacle, to dismiss the faithful in haste, and bolt the door. A fine baby was born in the middle of the nave in candlelight, as the last clouds of incense were still floating over their heads. Claudio was kept at home up till the age of twelve. When he was between twelve and thirteen years old, in the course of a quarrel with his father, thinking that he had been unfairly treated, he lost his temper; he had a kerchief in his hand, which he flicked in his father's face. The kerchief may not have hurt, but the gesture was irreparable. Overwhelmed by remorse, the boy ran away just as he was and walked to Parma, taking refuge in the house of one of his half-sisters, a daughter of Grandfather Toscanini's first wife, the one who had thrown herself down the well.

So as soon as he came back from the war, Claudio resumed his old trade of tailoring, collected his wife, who had been waiting for him at his mother-in-law's, and set up house on his own account at number 13 of what is now called Borgo Tanzi. The house still stands. It is a slice of a house, crushed between other slices of houses; it has two floors, two windows per floor, a single chimney and a roof, a pipe from the gutter which runs down the middle of the discoloured and chipped plaster of the façade, and a small double entrance door at the side. When you enter from the street, you go through a narrow hall, or rather gut, in which you have to duck your head because of the beams, and which ends in a blind and melancholy little courtyard. The narrow staircase, of rough stone and with four flights, opens out of the middle of the hall. In these surroundings the modest nineteenth-century iron banisters seem almost elegant. On each landing there is a room opening out on the street side, and on the courtyard side a sort of store-room or attic with rough-hewn beams and tiny dormer windows through which no light penetrates. It was in the first-floor room that Arturo was born.

The circumstances were not exactly affluent. Claudio, it is true, exercised his profession of tailor. But it was already clear that he belonged to that interesting and pathetic species of mankind in which the excessive and almost heedless squandering of good qualities ends up by being an obstacle rather than an aid to social success. As soon as he encountered difficulties and things did not turn out as he wished, he made a sudden decision, with his usual impulsiveness, to move to Genoa with his wife and the boy, who was only a few months old.

Arturo, at first, was the reverse of promising; he was extremely delicate and succumbed to one illness after another. The sea air, instead of improving the child's health, made him worse; to such an extent that his mother, Paola, took him back to Parma and left him with his Montani grandparents. The family memories of Toscanini at that time are chiefly of his pitiful thinness. Arturo always seemed to be ailing, so they kept him on a rigid diet of soups and cereal paps. One day, when there was a plate of broad beans in olive oil on the kitchen table, poor emaciated Arturo, who was in the arms of one of his innumerable aunts, caught sight of the beans and, with an unexpected determination of which no one would have thought him capable, imperiously pointed his little finger towards them, wriggling his whole body and making it evident that he wanted some. "Oh, gracious heavens, he wants some beans!" exclaimed his scandalized aunt. "That would be the last straw!"

Grandmother Carolina, who was sitting on the other side of the table with her hands folded over her considerable paunch, reflected and said placidly: "But who knows why? Poor babe! if he wants beans give him beans. It's plain he's going to die, so why not let him have his little fling!"

So they gave him the beans. And the beauty of the story is that, whether because of the beans or because, at that precise moment, the course of his horoscope changed in the distant heavens, from that day onwards he improved in health and in a few days became a normal, bonny baby. There are two lessons in this story. First, the wisdom of grandmother Carolina, which is the ancestral wisdom of all grandmothers. And then, Arturo Toscanini's little finger, purposively pointed for the first time. There is no doubt this was the decisive gesture of his life, seeing that he has spent the rest of it pointing a finger from the rostrum at somebody.

Meanwhile, in Genoa, a sister was born to Arturo and baptized Narcisa. The arrival of a new baby, combined with certain obstacles which suddenly interfered with Claudio's affairs, and a misunderstanding with the family with whom they were boarding, made him change his mind again, in consequence one fine morning he suddenly brought his family back to Parma.

And so Arturo returned to and grew up in Oltretorrente. It is true that Claudio, after a short stay with his in-laws, had set up house in the old city. Arturo, however, always returned for certain parts of the year to his Montani grandparents and to his Serventi cousins. It is therefore legitimate to say that Oltretorrente remained the real background of his early childhood.

The world of little Arturo commenced roughly at the church of the Grazie, that delightful little baroque church, now a woodmerchant's store, which stands at the head of the Borgo of the same name and opposite which at that time there stood an enormous oak cross, a real cross of Calvary, which, many years after, was smashed to smithereens and burned by the red antiChristians of Oltretorrente. The walk down the Borgo led to the heart of the quarter, which was the angle between Borgo Santo Spirito and Borgo delle Grazie. At that time there was no little piazza as there is now; the space was occupied by the church of Santo Spirito, demolished many years ago. If one looks closely at the paving-stones of the piazzetta, the outline of the church can still be distinguished by an outline on the pavement. The priest was a certain Don Accorsi, a thin man, sickly and gloomy, who taught the children their catechism. On this side the little street which is now called Asdente was crossed by a great arch, and at the end of the street stood the workshop of the blacksmith, the florid Signor Zolesi, who specialized in repairing agricultural machinery.

Among the memories of everyone's childhood there is always noise and an artisan's workshop, the daily familiar noise which is the *leit-motif* for the humble symphony of childhood: "I hear the beating of the hammer, I hear the saw of the carpenter. . . ." During Toscanini's childhood the predominant noise was that of the blacksmith's hammer. Who knows how many times, mixed with the background noise, he may, in his imagination, have heard the hammer-triplet of Siegfried?

That part of the Borgo Tanzi on which little Arturo was born made the fourth arm of the crossroads. It was a street full of things to fascinate a child. First of all, just beyond the door of the Toscaninis' house there stood a yellow building which housed

the wax foundry of the Serventi, who were Grandfather's relatives. The Serventi cousins, proprietors of the wax factory, were
several brothers, the most important of whom was Signor Luca,
an extraordinarily hairy man with most imposing moustaches.
They were their own workmen and spread the wax over the garden, leaving it out at night to catch the dew. This whole branch
of the family was occupied in some form of wax-work, even to an
incredible female cousin who, right up to a short time ago, practised the speciality of making roses out of wax, which she
modelled with the greatest skill, complete with stalks, leaves, and
buds; everything except the perfume.

Further on there was another place almost equally marvellous,
the Bormioli glassblowers' workshop with its infernal fires, and
where even more stupefying and incomprehensible things happened. But, though Grandfather and several uncles worked there,
this was a less accessible zone, because it was almost next to the
Ponte Verde. It was the "no man's land" of the quarter. There,
in the remains of an old ruined medieval tower, lived another important and mysterious person, Pignoli, a mechanic of genius,
by whom the Bormioli had their moulds made. He and Centenari,
another mechanic who specialized in artesian wells and who invented one of the first rotary motors, represented the inventive
genius of the progressive century.

Arturo wandered through this world, in the poor quarter, as all
poor children wander and learn. Until a year or two ago, there
still lived at Salsomaggiore an eye-witness of those old days—
Medea Massari, who was almost part of the family, because she
had been sent to Papa Claudio's workshop to learn tailoring.

Arturo was a quiet and solitary little boy, but he liked to stop
and watch this and that, until he heard from above the usual impatient shout: "Arturèn!"

"He seemed like a little old man; he never made a noise,"
Medea recalled. "He was solemn and small for his age. He had a
small appetite and his mother always had to coax him to eat, but
he was obstinate and, once he had decided to refuse anything, it
was almost impossible to make him change his mind. He was not

an obedient boy. When he was told to do something, even if he
finally did it, he never said 'Very well', but went off without a
word, with a determined expression and his curly head."

Medea led him to take what may have been a decisive step in
life. She had noticed that little Arturo showed an extraordinary
interest, an almost morbid interest, in everything connected with
music. He had a raucous voice, hoarse and rasping (as it always
was). But if others sang or played an instrument, or if anything—
a toy trumpet or even an odd bit of iron—gave out a note, Arturo
was transported with enchantment. So Medea made him a sort of
musical instrument. She took a piece of the stalk of a corncob,
with the notches at the base of the nodes particularly well marked.
Then, with a knife, she cut two narrow fillets between the nodes,
which acted as chords. A piece of straw was inserted underneath
the fillets to keep them raised, and above the hollowed stalk underneath. Next she cut a small sliver of stalk and attached a thread of
garlic to both ends. Rubbing this apology for a bow to and fro
across the two chords produced a faint sound, thin and sweet. It
was an absurd contraption: a kind of violin for grasshoppers.
But when she gave it to him, the little boy's rapture was indescribable. Medea had never seen him so excited. From then
on, Arturo was always bothering her to make more of the little
instruments. Short as he was, he stood on his toes, with his arms
raised, to put the small instrument near his ear, the better to hear
the beautiful sounds. This was Arturo Toscanini's first personal
encounter with the Muse.

Medea had always thought that he was a boy who should be
encouraged to study, so she was not surprised when she heard
that Claudio Toscanini was thinking of sending Arturo to the
Conservatory. This decision was not made with a view to his
getting a higher education, but mainly for humble material reasons. The Conservatory of Parma was then not only a school but
also a residential college. It was reserved for boys from Parma
who had shown particular musical aptitude and ability. Curricu-
lum and board were free, thanks to an endowment made by
Marie-Louise. To have Arturo accepted meant to the Toscanini

family not only that the boy would be able to study and prepare himself for a profession without costing them anything, but, a far more important factor, that he would be fed and clothed for nothing for nine years as a boarder. This would relieve them of a not inconsiderable source of worry.

Medea had a last glimpse of Arturo, dressed in the boarder's uniform. Then, like the fairy godmother, she passed out of his life. Once, many years later, she saw him on the street in Milan, but was too shy to speak to him.

CHAPTER III

The Musical Beehive

THE Conservatory of Parma was then, as it is now, a part of the large building which, at one time, was the Carmelite convent. In fact, until recently it was usually called "the School of the Carmine".

These ancient monasteries are like the heads of some of the old characters in the novels of Balzac; there is no changing them without splitting them. Their framework is so characteristic, so strong, that it resists any alteration. You can modernize their façades, repaint them, make a new door here, close a window there, but you will not, unless you rebuild from top to bottom, succeed in suppressing their typical cellular structure which has arisen out of the need for ensuring, to all the members of the community, living quarters, which are perfectly uniform, separate and close to each other. Hence you have always a certain number of rooms equal in size, all in a row and served by a common passage-way. And, as it is convenient to have this passage-way covered, as a protection from the elements, and equally necessary to have it open on at least one side, to give the rooms more air and to provide a place for standing and walking up and down in the fresh air; hence the cloister, which, essentially, is a collection of cells around a courtyard, just as symmetrical as the alveoli of the beehive. This convent architecture is eminently suitable for housing a conservatory of music; the only difference being that there is a musical instrument, instead of a monk, in each cell. Even today, if you stand in the middle of the cloister on a hot morning during school hours, raise your head towards the

C

arches and listen, you will hear an indistinct pattern of sounds, a distant wave, consisting of murmurs and scrapings, rather like the buzzing of a mysterious beehive.

It was to this building that Arturo Toscanini presented himself in October 1876. He was destined to become the busiest and most determined worker which that musical beehive was ever to produce.

He was then nine years old. A photograph has survived from that time which shows him by the side of his little sister, Narcisa. It was taken the day he was confirmed. He is standing very straight, right foot on the ground, left foot on a block of wood, peculiarly like a rostrum. Arturo has his arm round the little girl's shoulders. Both of them are dressed appropriate to the occasion: full of tassels, lace, and flounces; the result of the combined efforts of the family. Arturo wears a little round hat, with the brim raised and a broad ribbon, like Nemorino's hat in the *Elisir d'Amore*.

The boy had to pass an examination before being accepted as a free boarder—there were also, besides the day boys, paying boarders at the rate of 12 Lire a month. He was prepared for this examination, it seems, by a tuba-player, Bonini, a friend of his father's. There is a family story, the authenticity of which cannot be guaranteed, that Arturo was not admitted without difficulty because of the hostility of the director, Giusto Dacci, who harboured an old grudge against Claudio Toscanini for political reasons.

In any event, the boy was admitted and assigned to the 'cello school—although his own preference was for the violin—under Leandro Carini, who was not a great 'cellist himself, but was quite an extraordinarily good teacher and a delightful man. Like most Parma musicians, he was an amiable eccentric. The story goes that he was in the habit of roaming the quiet Parma streets after nightfall and stopping to listen under the windows of his favourite pupils, to make sure that they were playing the piece he had set them as he wished it played.

Carini's department was on the first floor of the cloister, in room No. 27. Ferrari, Chierici, Del Campo, Diletti, all great 'cellists, owed their virtuosity to what they learnt in that room. And so the boy found himself, from the very beginning, in an atmosphere of highly disciplined study and an unusual degree of musical integrity. From this time onwards his life as a boarder was to be laborious and monotonous. Hour after hour throughout the twenty-four hours his time was mapped out, with the regularity of metronome beats.

His life was confined to the two cloisters; the lesser one enclosed by short, heavy columns; in the middle there was a bright green, but damp and melancholy lawn, dominated by an old clock, the rusty hands of which had long since ceased revolving and were eternally pointing to six. The other, the great cloister, was open to the sky. The prevailing colour was red—both columns and arches were red—and the wide expanse of lawn sparkled in the sunshine, as it was not, at that time, shaded by the four fir-trees which were later planted at the corners.

The time-table was the usual one for Italian boarding-schools. The pupils were called at seven; then came prayers, followed by breakfast, which consisted of coffee and bread. The classes began at eight. At twelve, lunch and recreation. At two, "solfeggio", and so on. At the end of the first course, Arturo's marks for 'cello were 21 out of a possible 30. He was not yet at the head of his class.

He was eleven years old when his little sister, Narcisa, died at the age of nine. It was a terrible blow to the boy, the first great sorrow of his life. Shortly before this another girl had been born to the Toscaninis, Zina. But she was too small to be a companion for Arturo, whereas Narcisa had been his companion throughout childhood. It was an even greater blow to his parents, especially his mother, who remained inconsolable for many months, during which her hair turned white. A year later she gave birth to another girl, Ada, who never saw her mother other than with white hair. Claudio must have mourned Narcisa with almost equal fervour, as he began to neglect his appearance, which he had never done before. He also allowed his beard to grow long, which made him look like one of the hermit saints in the sacred pictures.

This misfortune came at a time when the Toscanini household was breaking up. Claudio was ill-fitted to a humdrum and laborious existence. His small income was not sufficient to meet the expenses of a growing family. The gibes of his uncharitable neighbours embittered him still further. For the first time he began to neglect his home. All this in spite of the fact that he was an excellent tailor, who was then considered the best cutter in Parma; all the expensive shops in the city sent him work, or rather, they would have sent him work if he had been able to give any guarantee of finishing it. His habits were becoming more and more irregular. He had set up a little workshop, in which he employed a boy and two young girls, but he was never there. He spent more and more time at the café, playing cards or billiards; unfortunately he did not go to the popular cafés, but to the fashionable cafés frequented by the well-to-do, such as the Café Marchesi in the Piazza Grande, or Ravazzoni's, at the corner of the Borgo di San Quentino. He gambled, unfortunately, and when he was not gambling, he was arguing—usually about politics, which meant about Garibaldi. In the difficult years which followed the first attempts at creating a united Italy, there were never-ending polemics between monarchists and republicans, moderates and Garibaldini. Claudio adored Garibaldi, and so fanatical was he on the subject that at this time he spent most of his day, when he was not in a café, wandering the streets, hoping to find someone with whom he could pick a quarrel in defence of his idol. There is another family story on this subject. He left his workshop one morning to buy a skein of silk. Nothing was seen of him till two days later, when he returned with the skein of silk, but without his jacket. The paladin Claudio had probably been carrying on a private war of his own against an entire faction.

It is easy to understand why his tailoring became less and less lucrative. Often, after a whole week, during which they had hardly seen him, his three young workers waited for him until late on Saturday night, hoping against hope for their wages. Similarly, Paola had to wait for the housekeeping money. But, although her life was anything but easy, she was never known to complain, even to her relatives. She was as proud as Lucifer. She even went to the length of forbidding the children to say that they were hungry when they visited their grandparents. And woe to anyone who dared to utter a word of criticism against her husband!

Meanwhile, the invisible metronome continued to beat in the school of the Carmine, the sun continued to move across the cloisters, and ceaseless activity continued in the cells of the bee-hive. There was an infinite succession of scales, chords, modulations and "solfeggi". At the end of his second year, Arturo's marks for 'cello were no longer 21, but 27 out of 30.

Life inside the boarding-school was, on the whole, pleasant. The director, Giusto Dacci, was no brilliant scholar, although his *Treatise on the Theory and Practice of Harmony, Instrumentation, Counterpoint and Composition* is still sometimes used for teaching and is still in print. He was not a high-flyer, but he was a martinet, and attached such importance to the letter of the rules that he completely lost any sense of proportion; he made Arturo come back to school a whole month before the end of the holidays because he (Giusto Dacci) had met Arturo on the street in Parma without his uniform; the free boarders, according to the rules, were obliged to wear uniform all the time, even when they were away from school. He could be described as a decorative figure, with his soft blond beard, impeccable frock-coat, and gold-rimmed spectacles on a dignified nose. In spite of Dacci the boys enjoyed considerable liberty, thanks to the connivance of the two school porters.

A curious and eccentric couple, these two porters. One of them was called Mazzani and was said to belong to a good family, which had fallen on evil days. He had an enormous grey beard, which covered his cheeks. His good nature was inexhaustible. His serious expression never changed. As both of them were clowns, he was the sad-faced one, whereas the other, called

Colombini, was the cheerful one. He was short and stocky, with an enormous drooping white moustache and a great gilt chain across his waistcoat. He drank like a fish and was always more or less intoxicated by the evening.

There were about forty boarders. The food was, on the whole, not bad, though as monotonous as that of an orphan asylum, with too many soups and too much starch. The kitchen was, in fact, used, not only for the budding musicians but also for the foundlings, more commonly called bastards, who were housed in a distant wing of the convent.

Once a week, on Sunday between eleven and twelve, the relatives were allowed to visit the boys. This visit was somewhat of an ordeal for Arturo, because his mother never came to visit him. His only visitors were his aunts—Aunt Cesira, for example, or Aunt Ernestina. Arturo never understood why his mother failed to come, like the other boys' mothers. It was only much later that Paola confessed to her daughters that she had not visited Arturo because her clothes were too shabby. Instead, on Sundays and feast days Paola used to take her two little girls, Ada and Zina, to the church of the Cinque Piaghe, which was in the Borgo Farini (now turned into a large furniture shop), and to which the boarders also went every Sunday to hear Mass. In this way his little sisters met Arturo once a week. He was very good to them and, when he was taking more advanced courses and had to sell his wine ration to be able to buy music, or did their compositions for his more backward companions, he always kept back a few pennies to buy sweets for them.

The world has changed so much since those days that the story of the school seems faded and confused. Besides, very few eye-witnesses survive. But piecing together what memories we can find, it is possible to reconstruct, approximately, Arturo's life in that institution and arrive at some understanding of what those qualities were which differentiated him from his fellow-pupils. The first curious discovery we make is that, even then, he was animated by what was to remain the fundamental and dominant mainspring of his professional life: an innate and overwhelming urge to conduct. All boys have their hobby: football, mountain climbing, chess, or what have you. Arturo's passion was to gather a group of his companions and make them play music. It was not easy to persuade them, because boys, like soldiers, are disinclined to work in their free time. Further, it had to be done on the quiet, because one of Dacci's innumerable disciplinary idiosyncrasies was that the pupils should not play music out of school hours! This did not deter Arturo. He kept nagging his companions, as if playing together was as essential as eating or sleeping; so great was his insistence that they always ended by giving in to him. It was he who did all the preparatory work: getting hold of the music, rearranging it for the limited number of instruments at his disposal, and sometimes, when there was no score-paper, even ruling out the staves by hand. Thus Toscanini, even at this early age, showed evidence of possessing all those qualities which so distinguished him in later days: absorption in music, patience, assiduity, and attention to detail, as well as a gift for persuading and dominating others—even those most difficult subjects, his own fellow-pupils.

The boy undoubtedly made a great impression on his companions—they used to nickname him "Genius", much to his annoyance—and also on some of his teachers, for one of them, Pio Ferrari, the Professor of Harmony, was particularly fond of him. He impressed because of his exceptional musical gifts, which allowed him to grasp any technical problem, however abstruse, with great facility, and because of his infallible ear and astonishing memory. On one occasion he was taken to the Regio to hear *Carmen*. The next day, without even having seen a glimpse of the score, he wrote down what was then called a potpourri—a mosaic of the most beautiful passages. He also orchestrated it for his few instruments, reproducing melodies and colours with the fidelity of a gramophone. He had learnt to play the piano by himself. "That is why," he later said, "I play it so badly." The piano was a source of conflict with Dacci, another of whose manias was that the pupils should not be allowed to read music; one day when he caught Arturo strumming *Gazza ladra* on the piano, he punished him severely. "Who gave you permission to play it?" shouted the indignant director. He would not have believed that it was Rossini himself who had given him permission.

Even in the everyday life of the institution certain characteristics emerged which always remained with him. For example, he was an extremely meticulous and orderly boy. He was, to an extreme degree, scrupulous about personal cleanliness and neatness. Till recent years he cleaned his clothes and his shoes himself. He was sociable, did not object to being told risqué jokes, but practically never told them himself, and was thus already distinguished by an instinctive reserve and a basic seriousness of character. He was very obstinate. A tragi-comic story of minor importance illustrates this quality. In the morning the boarders cleaned their boots on a bench in the corridor outside the dormitory. One morning Arturo quarrelled with one of his companions, a certain Rastelli, a hot-tempered youth, who gave Arturo a blow on the head with a boot-brush. The wound bled a little. Arturo washed it and the incident seemed over. The next morning he had a temperature. The school doctor was called, examined him, prescribed a classic dose of castor oil, but before leaving spotted the scar on the head. When questioned, Arturo answered evasively, which made the doctor suspicious and he reported the matter to Dacci. The latter subjected Arturo to a lengthy interrogation. Arturo stuck to his story that he had hit his head against an iron spike. But when Dacci pressed him for exact details, the boy suddenly lost his temper, shut up like an oyster and would not say another word. Dacci threatened to shut him in the little closet which was used as the ultimate punishment, and not let him out until he confessed the truth. Still not a word from Arturo, who was then locked up in the closet on bread and water. Not a word. After two days, three days, five days, still not a word. Dacci was forced to confess himself beaten, and Arturo was set free and returned, triumphantly, to his companions.

His compositions in his last few terms were models of their kind. For obvious reasons, they were formal; but, even so, were considerably better than the compositions of the other pupils. There is, for example, a *Scherzo in G minor* for orchestra written by him in 1883–4 (*allegro scherzoso—meno mosso—primo tempo—prestissimo*), which, in the clear fluency of its texture, remotely inspired by memories of Mendelssohn, already shows an expert hand. The *Andante in E flat* (*andante—allegro moderato—andante*), composed in the same year, with a song reminiscent of Schumann. Still more complex and expert is the score of an *Overture in G* (*andante—allegro vivace—meno mosso—piu mosso*) which was written during 1884–5. The theme is faintly Wagnerian; in that particular year Arturo had, by chance, played as 'cellist in the orchestra of the Regio at a performance of *Lohengrin*.

Arturo presented these compositions at his final examination. His diploma, dated July 25, 1885, qualified him *alumnus emeritus* with the following marks: 'cello, 160 out of 160, with special mention; composition, 50 out of 50, also special distinction. The document is signed by Giusto Dacci in old-fashioned copperplate handwriting with a pompous flourish at the end.

Because of the brilliant results of his examination, Arturo Toscanini was given the first place for a prize presented by Legato Barbacini, instituted for the purpose of rewarding the most promising graduates. The total amount of the prize was 450 Lire (about £50), to be divided among three graduates. Arturo Toscanini received 200 Lire.

CHAPTER IV

Parma in his Blood

TOSCANINI received his diploma in July, 1885. That winter he accepted an invitation to play as instrumentalist at the Regio. To play for at least one season in the orchestra had been compulsory for the free boarders ever since the period in which both school and theatre had depended on the munificence of the reigning house.

The following year, 1886, he left Parma. Such was the fame of the Parma Conservatory that agents and impresarios from all over Italy were on the look-out for its promising pupils. Hence offers were bound to come from Bologna or Milan or even Buenos Aires. Instrumentalists from Parma had the same sort of reputation in the international world of music as had French cooks in the restaurant world.

What did young Toscanini take with him from Parma? He took his college uniform, an outfit of linen presented to each pupil at the end of the course, a pair of boots, and a black suit which he wore for playing in the orchestra. He also took a 'cello, which he had bought with his savings out of the 200 Lire of the prize and his salary at the Regio (1.50 Lire for the evening). . . .

But he also carried Parma away with him, the whole of Parma, which was in his blood and was the most important and precious part of his baggage. If this is not understood clearly, it is impossible to understand Toscanini. His life, his music, his temperament, his qualities, his defects, his generosity, and even his outbursts of temper belong to Parma. He was a true "Parmesan of the rock", not one of those who come from outside, "Parmesans from the air", who come from the surrounding country and bring with them the fresh air of the fields. These people ("of the rock") are hard and energetic, hot-blooded, with subtle brains and an accentuated disposition for at least three of the seven capital sins; theirs is a peculiar character, compounded of a lively sense of humour, enthusiasm, a love of gossip and argument, and, to some extent, a tendency to crazy exuberance akin to madness. They have big appetites—consuming steaming plates of *tortelli*, which are a round form of macaroni stuffed with cheese, or those formidable sausages which are the speciality of Parma, like the *culatello*, as red as roast-beef, or the *felino*, a mosaic of white-and-pink flesh, or their cheese, which is as delicate in flavour as it is hard in texture, or their dazzling white bread. They wash down their food with plenty of Lambrusco wine, which is light, refreshing, and has a natural sparkle.

Unfortunately this characteristic physical and mental zest has become gradually attenuated by the habits of modern life. But, when Toscanini was a boy, if a foreigner happened to be invited to a social gathering for the first time, you may be sure that the Parmesan who had introduced him would have been taken aside immediately by one of the other guests and asked: "What is this fellow interested in—politics, law, or the theatre?" Because these were, and still are to some extent, the three main interests of the inhabitants of Parma: politics, litigation, and music. If you consider them carefully, you will find that there is one element which the three have in common: eloquence.

The inhabitants of Parma not only have an exceptional appreciation of eloquence but they practise it among themselves day by day. It is doubtful whether the art or science of arguing has been exercised as conscientiously and carried to such lengths in any other city as it has in Parma. Parma has produced examples of great demagogues which, to this day, have never been equalled in Italy; men of torrential eloquence and legendary courage, like the famous Alceste de Ambris, the revolutionary with the eyes of an angel, or Corridoni, the trades-unionist who became an interventionist in 1914 and was killed in the trenches on the Carso.

The inhabitants of Parma idolized their barristers as much as they did their demagogues: Agostino Berenini, who was also a senator and minister; Amedeo Passerini, or that unique character Ildebrando Cocconi, whose knowledge of penal law was encyclopædic. He was a little man. Though inordinately addicted to drink, he realized his weakness, and when he was to plead in court was always accompanied by an enormously tall clerk, whose orders were to stop him, at all costs and even by physical force, from drinking more than a specified number of glasses. He was a magnificent orator, but his peculiarity was that often, in the heat of debate, he broke out into a spate of pure Parmesan dialect— the Demosthenes of Parma!

The supreme and poetic form of eloquence is singing; all the inhabitants of Parma are mad about singing. This leads us to what cannot be called a passion, but actually the religion of Parma: music.

Music, like any other religion, has its temple, and its temple in Parma is the Teatro Regio. This means Theatre Royal, and it will remain Royal, you may be sure, whatever form of government there may be, because music is royal—the only royal thing which is reverenced by this riotous and republican population. The Regio was Marie-Louise's masterpiece. Marie-Louise's role in the history of Parma cannot be ignored. Whatever the reader may think of Napoleon, Marie-Louise should have some claim to sympathy on the grounds of her services to Parma. Although she had been unfaithful to her imperial husband, she had learned something from him: he had communicated to her his passion for building. Throughout the rest of her life, Marie-Louise built and founded schools, colleges, academies, asylums, and institutions of every description.

The Regio was Marie-Louise's greatest masterpiece. Built, according to her instructions, by Nicola Bettoli, inaugurated in 1828, the Regio is one of the finest theatres in Italy. It is a theatre worthy of Milan, Florence, or Naples, with a sober and imposing façade, embellished by a portico enclosed by ten slender ionic columns. Renovated in 1954, the inside, which has four rows of

boxes and a gallery, still preserves its rigorous neo-classical character: a white-and-gold ellipse, as elegant as a chocolate-box and
with perfect acoustics.

Not content with creating the Regio, Marie-Louise founded
the ducal orchestra, which became the best orchestra in the world.
This was largely due to her choice of Paganini as director, who in
his old age had retired to his villa at Gaione, near Parma. The
part Paganini played in forming the ducal orchestra is not known,
but it is certain that the strings in that orchestra were more homo-
geneous, more irresistibly brilliant, than any other body of strings
before or since. A tradition of exceptional violin virtuosity was
created at the same time. So much so that in 1872, when Verdi
conducted *Aida* at the Regio, he was astounded, and declared that
he had not heard such strings in any other orchestra, and that the
strings of the Parma orchestra were worth twice those of any
other; twenty violins at the Regio were equivalent to forty violins
in any other part of the world.

It may well be that the great tradition, which owed its founda-
tion to Paganini, was indirectly responsible for a second musical
efflorescence in Parma. Giuseppe Verdi was not a Parmesan "of
the rock", strictly speaking; he was born at Busseto, which is just
outside Parma. It was he who originated a new kind of music—
drama which could only have been created in the appropriate
musical climate. Verdi and his work reflected the spirit of Parma.
He wrote *La Traviata*, *Aida*, *Otello*, and *Falstaff* at Busseto,
which, because of this, has become recognized as the birthplace of
opera.

In the period which interests us now—roughly between 1860
and 1890—in which the young Toscanini was born, grew up,
and was educated, Parma and the whole countryside around it
was living a rich, febrile, furious, and incredibly musical life. It
was a life which was not limited to a few privileged and cultured
people, but was shared by all classes of the population. At that
time, anyone who went for a walk, on a Sunday or an evening
after work, through the countryside between Enza and Arda,
past the farms of S. Ilario and S. Pancrazio and the hamlets of

Langhirano or Berceto, would have heard music wherever he
went: accordion, flute, cornet, and trumpet. There were innumerable small musical groups of three, four, or five amateur
musicians, playing the violin, the double-bass, the guitar, and the
instrument, popular at that time, called the terzino, which was
half-way between a double-bass and 'cello. These groups went
from farm to farm, inn to inn, village to village, each with their
speciality and bravura pieces, for which they were well known
throughout the region. Perhaps the most famous of these groups
was the Migliavacca trio, two violins and a terzino, composed of
Migliavacca in person, who played the violin and was blind, and
two others called Ferrari and Marchesi. Their *pièce de résistance*
was a "Migliavacca Mazurka", written by Marchesi's son, who
became and remained for many years prompter at the Scala and
the New York Metropolitan under Toscanini.

There were almost as many bands. Even villages often had a
school of music and all of them had bands, varying in size according to local resources. Naturally, the most famous was the Parma
band, conducted by an illustrious maestro, Fontana. In good
weather Fontana's band gave evening concerts. The star item on
the programme was the so-called "Midnight Serenade", a piece
for which the good Fontana had to preside over a whole series of
strategic manœuvres, like a general on the battlefield. While the
main body of the band stopped and played in the piazza, a group
of trumpets were moved to the top of a tower, others to the roof
of a house opposite, and one isolated cornet on the highest point
of the belfry. The climax of the piece was a solo on this cornet,
an extremely difficult solo, which finished on a high note—so
high and prolonged that it held the audience enthralled for fifteen
seconds. After which the whole band resumed playing together
amidst the delirious applause of the crowd. The entire population of Parma, men, women, old people, and children, went to
hear the "Midnight Serenade".

But even bands could not satisfy their unslakeable thirst for
music. Real seasons of opera were organized in the country
villages. They were short seasons of a single opera. Orchestra

and chorus were provided by the local musical society, amplified by a few outsiders. Only the principal parts—the prima-donna and tenor—were filled by singers from the city. The remainder were rustic and primitive singers in tiny theatres, or even in the hall of the communal council. If it was impossible to stage an opera in a theatre, it was performed in a church; in the villages around Parma, at that time, Mass and even funeral services were celebrated to selections from opera accompanied on the organ. They might be romantic arias like the *Virgine degli Angeli,* or choruses like the one in *Nabucco;* no one would be shocked even to hear love-duets in church—was it not Verdi's music, and therefore divine?

In this world which lived for opera and music, the Regio was an inviolable temple, dedicated to *bel canto.* The whole life of Parma was literally centred on the Regio. The fall of a ministry, a riot in Sicily, a war in Africa, were all brushed aside as of no importance when the poster announcing a forthcoming programme at the Regio came out. And when, a few days before Christmas, the wooden board appeared between the grand porticoes of what is now the town hall, announcing the performance at the Regio ("Doors open at 8.30"), the blood pressure of all the inhabitants of Parma immediately went up.

Every mother in Parma dreamt of seeing her child become a member of the chorus at the Regio. There were actual dynasties of choral singers at Parma, such as the Panighi, the last of whom died only a year or two ago. There were all grades of chorus singers, from high to low, first tenors, second tenors, baritones, bass, etc. There were also the "starters" who led the attack. They were tall and burly, often illiterate, but with natural voices. They formed a closed corporation and always frequented the same hostelries—Pirlino in the Via Imbriani, or dalla Cibia— where you would find the same sort of exclusive and picaresque atmosphere as you do in the cafés frequented by bull-fighters in Madrid or Seville. The most celebrated of all choral singers was Giuseppe Adorni, who came of a family of singers, an extremely ignorant man who could neither read nor write, but was unrivalled in his profession and with a greater knowledge of scores than most conductors. He sang Marullo and the Messenger in *Aida*. He crossed the Atlantic twenty-eight times to fulfil engagements in America. He went on singing till 1947, when he was seventy-four. He gave up singing altogether the following year, and promptly expired.

In Parma, in those days, opera was an element of domestic life, just as much as the Madonna, the sewing-machine, or dressmaking. The Toscanini family is an excellent example. Claudio Toscanini was a chorus singer at the Regio. His two apprentices, both the boy and the girl, went to the theatre every night to help dress the singers. His mother's family were all passionate music-lovers. The older members, grandfather and uncles, had very fine voices. Every Sunday there was a family reunion and they sang interminable choruses: Uncle Emilio, Uncle Giovanni, Uncle Carlo, Cesira, Esterina, who was the youngest and later married a brother of Pio Nevi, who was first trumpet at the Scala and director of the municipal band at Milan. Ada still remembers these occasions and has a vivid memory of herself at the age of three sitting at her brother's feet in his college uniform and shaking a boxful of buttons to mark time for him, and Arturo smiling at her. The singing was accompanied by a guitar, whilst others improvised by blowing on paper-covered combs. Sometimes they danced; but singing, either in chorus or solo, was the real object of these evenings.

In view of this almost universal passion for opera, it is not surprising that the citizens of Parma ended up by considering the Regio as their common property, in which they each had a personal interest. Hence the particular psychology of a Regio audience: a direct, violent, almost threatening participation in the performance which terrorized all the singers for a period of at least a hundred years. Frances Alda in her autobiography gives us an account of her performance at the Regio in Parma when, in *Lorelei*, Fapelli, who was playing Anna, missed a note. Immediately the whole audience started singing the song, and, adds the terrified Alda, sang it perfectly. She was so frightened that she

The Toscanini family, Milan, 1887

With his sister, Narcisa, 1876

Première of *The Girl of the Golden West*, Metropolitan, December 10, 1910, with Caruso and Destinn (p. 128)

With colleagues at Turin, 1912

wanted to run away. There were, in fact, examples of singers who not only left the theatre but the city itself. The case of poor Carini, Toscanini's 'cello teacher, was equally pitiful. Carini was playing at the Regio one evening. It was hot and his fingers were wet with sweat. He missed a note in his solo. Instead of furious cries of protest, because the Parma public was fond of and respected the old maestro, there was an immense and interminable silence. This silence, however, must have been more distressing to him than an outbreak of cat-calls, because he left the theatre heartbroken, swore never to play again, and resigned his teaching post.

A Parma audience was a raging, man-eating audience, which forgave nothing because nothing escaped it—no hesitation in execution or intonation—and which, as it adored singing and was ready to die for a perfect high C, was ready to tear to pieces the unfortunate singer who muffed it. It was an audience so fierce that, as in a game of ice hockey, the impresario had to have his reserves ready to replace an injured performer. So, when Toscanini shrieked and raged because of a mistake in phrasing, or cursed because of a wrong note, it was really an inhabitant of Parma, a member of the audience at the Regio, who was shouting. His invective and insults were the same as those which were hurled at the stage by an enraged audience. It is not without significance that at such times he often broke into Parmesan dialect.

In Parma, the typical member of the audience was in the habit of interrupting during the performance, and no one found it strange that in the middle of an aria, a voice from circle or boxes should offer paternal advice to singer or conductor. Volumes could be filled with Parma theatrical stories: the occasion, for instance, on which a diminutive tenor was making a valiant and unsuccessful effort to drag an elephantine prima-donna off the stage, when a voice was heard: "Hey, you'd better make two journeys!" Or the anecdote, which Toscanini was fond of telling, of the two warriors in *Norma* who both by chance had enormous noses; a voice from the house: "I can't hear you; turn your noses up a bit!" Another typical episode concerns Bonci, who came

D

from the chapel of Loreto to perform in *Falstaff*. At first the audience had not disliked him, though they found him a little short and squat and nicknamed him "Jack of Diamonds". But everybody expected great things from him when he came to the famous song in the third act. Bonci stepped forward and, as a preparatory gesture, raised his right arm. From the gallery came a quiet and cordial voice: "Down with that arm!" Bonci was frightened and immediately put his arm down. Not a laugh, not a comment from the audience. Bonci, reassured, proceeded with his song. The audience gave him a great reception, and his splendid career owes its beginning to that night. If the Regio audience approved of a singer, no auditions were necessary. Any impresario, anywhere in the world, was ready to give him a contract. This applied to Gayarre, Sammarco, Borgatti, Titta Ruffo, De Luca, Schipa, and even to Gigli, who was launched on his career by his victory at the singing competition held at Parma in 1914.

In all fairness, it should be emphasized that ferocity was by no means the only characteristic of a Parma audience. Their capacity for enthusiasm was even greater. A pure note, an elegant passage, a prolonged trill, a triumphant high note sent them into ecstasies. In no other city was the tradition of the virtuoso, idolatry for the performer, more alive. Parma produced Bottesini. It was Toscanini who said that, in his opinion, Segovia was the greatest virtuoso because he was able to enthrall an audience of three thousand with a delicate instrument like the guitar. What can be said then of Bottesini, who walked on with his double-bass, that ugly, catarrhal instrument with its bovine paunch and neck like a giraffe? Nevertheless, Bottesini was not only capable of performing the most pyrotechnical pieces on his double-bass, such as *Il trillo del diavolo*, but when he played sentimental pieces, no violin, 'cello, nor tenor in the world could produce such ethereal sounds, so insinuating and velvety.

This tradition of instrumental virtuosity is profoundly rooted in Parma. This fact not only explains the musical world of Parma, but also tells us a great deal about the men who came from there. The public of Parma had a far higher standard of musical educa-

tion than the public of most other cities. It went to the theatre
not only to hear the tenor, soprano, baritone, but also the first
violin, the oboe soloist, the cornet, and the trumpet. In Parma,
and perhaps only in Parma, the public is passionately interested in
every detail which concerns the orchestra. It not only knows the
principal players in the orchestra by name, but closely follows
their work and career. They all know, for example, that, in a
given opera, the first 'cello has a solo, and they are lying in wait
for him; all eyes are on him, they accompany him note by note
throughout the most difficult passages, and when he has safely
and surely arrived at the last note they break into applause. In
Toscanini's day Mori, whom they called "the most glorious", and
Edel, who was the finest trumpet player in all the duchies, were
both dead, but there was still De Stefani, the oboeist, and Cacciamani, the famous trumpeter. All these men were extraordinarily
popular. When they passed through the streets, mothers pointed
them out to their children: "Look, that is Cacciamani, that is
Beccali, that is Tovagliari." Beccali was a remarkable bassoon
player, and Tovagliari was an equally fine flautist.

An episode, which could only have happened in Parma, typifies
the almost religious attitude towards music. In 1921, at the most
acrimonious stage of the fight between Fascists and men of the
Left, representatives of various parties had proposed a truce.
Eventually a sort of pact was agreed upon whereby from that
time onwards the two factions recognized a reciprocal right to
hold public meetings, without the other side attempting any re-
prisals. A well-known eccentric of Parma, a certain Dr. Landini,
who at that time was a Fascist and turned against Fascism
immediately afterwards (for which he had to move into the mountains near Parma), took it into his head to find out whether the ad-
versaries were really adhering to the conditions of the pact. One
fine evening, with his hands in his pockets, he strolled across the
Ponte di Mezzo into Oltretorrente and went down Borgo S.
Maria whistling "Giovinezza", the Fascist song.

The pact had been concluded for the rest of Italy, but not for
Oltretorrente, which considered itself at that time a sort of red

Vatican, with extra-territorial rights. Before he had walked thirty yards he was pounced upon. Two swarthy faces were glaring at him: "Dirty Fascist, come with us." After a long walk through twisting streets, Landini was led into a little room almost bare of furniture, with a few men sitting around a table. They gave him a chair and started questioning him. What was he doing in Oltretorrente? He had come to see whether the pact was respected. "What pact?" asked their leader sardonically. "Why, the pact of truce between Fascists and Socialists," said Landini. Derisive laughter. The men began to argue as to how to dispose of Landini. One proposed to tie him up and throw him in the river Parma. Another said no, better finish him off with a knife, put him in a sack and cart him off to the country past the Barriera Mazzini. In the middle of the debate, which was carried on calmly and without haste, a little old man came in and took a good look at Landini. He took off his hat and scratched the back of his head doubtfully: "Surely this is Landini's son?"

"What? Landini's son? You're crazy!" Landini was the great bassoonist at the Regio who played the famous passage in *Elisir d'Amore*.

When the old man insisted that he had known him for years, his captors' faces grew long. Finally, their leader turned to Landini: "Get out of here at once, Fascist swine, and don't let us see your face again. And this time you can thank God that you are your father's son."

CHAPTER V

His First Laurels

When Arturo left Parma with his 'cello, he had been living with his Montani grandparents. Claudio Toscanini had departed, permanently, for Genoa some months before. He left his debts behind in Parma, and went off, optimistic as ever, to join a certain Signor Pelliccia. This man came from Cremona and proposed starting a drapery store, combined with a tailoring workshop. He was looking for a partner who was a good cutter and able to run the tailoring department. He was a dignified and persuasive gentleman and had no difficulty in convincing Claudio.

The Toscanini family never returned to Parma. Like all young and promising emigrants from that city, Arturo Toscanini went with a contract in his pocket. He was to be the first 'cellist for a season of Italian opera in Brazil. At this time the young communities of South America were going through a period of sudden and fabulous prosperity. They were clamouring for culture and anxious to attract any of its manifestations. Italian opera was a novelty in great demand. They paid well and the rate of exchange compared very favourably with the Italian—the Argentine peso was worth 40 Italian Lire, the Brazilian milreis 10—and there was a continual flow of theatre and opera companies crossing the sea for seasons at Rio, at São Paulo, Montevideo, and Buenos Aires.

The company of which Toscanini was a member had been engaged by an impresario, Claudio Rossi, on behalf of a Brazilian, Leopoldo Miguez, who considered himself the most distinguished Brazilian conductor. An Italian, Carlo Superti from Piacenza, was the substitute conductor. Toscanini was not the only Parmesan engaged by Miguez. There was a fellow student at the Conservatory, who had finished his studies at the same time, Ferruccio Catellani, who was later to make a great name for himself; there were also some male and female members of the chorus, as, in those days, there was a dearth of trained singers in South America, and an impresario had to bring everything from the big drum to the *répétiteur*.

The company left in March. The journey from Genoa to Brazil took at least twenty-five days. The steamers were small— from 2,000 to 5,000 tons—single screw. Electric light was still in the womb of the future. The lighting was by candle and paraffin lamps suspended from the ceiling and protected by iron grills like miners' lamps. There was no running water and only a daily ration of water for drinking and washing for each passenger. A wash-bowl and a small round barber's mirror were the only toilet accessories, even in the first-class cabins. These were aft; the second-class dormitories were under the bridge, the third-class were forward.

The bulk of the traffic to South America at that time was third-class or steerage. This was the heyday of emigration. The largest steamers could carry only 1,500 passengers, of whom not more than seventy at the outside would be travelling first-class. Arturo, needless to say, travelled steerage. For thirty days he suffered the same extreme discomforts as the peasant emigrants who were his fellow-passengers. He also went through the same process of disillusionment. America was beautiful, vast, and rich, but at first it did not live up to the exaggerated mental picture which the Italian emigrant carried with him.

Arturo's experiences were unfortunate. It was obvious from the very beginning that Miguez was incompetent. Nothing is more terrifying than the rapidity with which an orchestra finds this out. A conductor can pull wool over the eyes and ears of the superintendent, the impresario, the members of the committee, the critics, and even the audience, but he can never delude his orchestra. After the first sixty beats, all of them, from the first to the last violin, from the harpist to the tympanist, have condemned him once and for all, without having to say anything or look at each other. Such a situation involves a cold war between the podium and the players; frenzied gestures with the baton on the conductor's side, all sorts of acts of minor sabotage on the side of the players—whispering, talking, coughing, etc. The singers on the stage, prima-donnas, tenors, and baritones, who are any conductor's natural enemies, are delighted to side with the players. From that to complete chaos is but a step. Rehearsals are half an hour late. The usual amount of jealousy and bickering is intensified.

This was the state of affairs in the Miguez company at the end of the first week of the season at São Paulo. To make matters worse, Miguez and Superti could not agree. At first they argued and then there was open conflict. The company was on Superti's side. Not that poor Superti was a genius, but he was a good fellow, was moderately competent, and, above all, he was Italian.

The season dragged on in this way until the company was transferred to Rio. Here things rapidly came to a head. Miguez showed himself not only incompetent in dealing with music but also with money. When they reached Rio, the month's pay was owing. The atmosphere was gloomy, to say the least of it, that evening when they were due to open with *Faust*. Miguez was conducting, with even less co-ordination than usual. So much so that in the third act, when the orchestra appears on the scene, he completely lost control and the performance collapsed.

Miguez was a native of Rio, where he had many partisans. He wrote an open letter to the papers to announce that he was retiring from the company, which, he contended, had not fulfilled his hopes. It was thoroughly bad and unworthy of appearing on a stage so illustrious as that of the Teatro Imperiale of Rio de Janeiro. He had been forced to abandon his post because of the unjust and preconceived prejudice manifested towards him by the company, which, owing to misguided chauvinism, had not wanted to obey a Brazilian conductor. The statement finished by accusing Superti of instigating the insubordinate action of his compatriots.

This letter provoked a major scandal. What were Superti and his companions to do? The theatre had been sold out for the next performance, *Aida*. To cancel it meant destitution for the company, which was already owed a month's pay; it would also involve interminable complications because of the contracts already entered into with the management of the theatre, costumiers, etc.; it also involved the thorny problem of their return to Italy, which Miguez had not budgeted for. They decided, therefore, to proceed as if nothing had happened. So the good Superti stepped on to the rostrum, successfully concealing his nervousness by an outward appearance of great self-confidence, exactly on time.

But this was not his night. Before he could begin, the whole audience rose to its feet with the roar: "Down with the Italians! Up with Brazil!" It was the first and last time in his life that the unfortunate Miguez succeeded in leading with a superbly coordinated attack! Some of the gentlemen from the front rows of the stalls threw themselves on the luckless Superti, dragged him to one of the side-doors, and flung him out. (This was not the last incident of its kind in Superti's life. Six years later, at the Scala, he was substituting for Vanzo as conductor at an ill-starred performance of *Don Carlos*. Superti conducted with such incompetence that the indignant public demanded his expulsion from the auditorium.) Returning to the fateful night at Rio; the players were paralysed. Two or three of the more quick-witted of them had run on to the stage to consult with the others. There, terror-stricken and perplexed, high priests, warriors, and Ethiopian slaves cowered behind the curtain, which had been lowered, frantically searching for a solution. The audience were shouting and whistling and gave no sign of wanting to leave the theatre. The more courageous members of the orchestra were foɪ carrying on at all costs. But who would step on the rostrum? Who would be capable of pulling the performance together under these conditions and facing a rowdy and hostile audience?

Suddenly somebody suggested, "Toscanini."

"Toscanini? But Toscanini is a 'cellist." Nevertheless, the name was on everybody's lips. The man who shared a music-stand with Toscanini said that he was not there that evening. Not there! Was he ill? His companion had seen him an hour before the performance, and he had seemed in the best of spirits; someone suggested sending for him, and getting someone to conduct the overture in the meantime. Venturi, who was the leader of the chorus, was pushed forward and dragged to the rostrum like a lamb to the slaughter. At sight of him there was a roar of fury from the audience. The poor fellow jumped down and hid behind the double-basses.

Where was Toscanini?

For what was probably the first and last time in his life, Toscanini had played truant from the theatre. He had been spending the day with a girl and had brought her back to his hotel, fortunately only a few yards from the theatre. The messengers sent to fetch him pounded on the door. Toscanini's sleepy voice asked who it was. They told him to come to the theatre at once. Toscanini asked what for. "To conduct!" Toscanini told them to go to the devil. It was Toscanini's fair companion who opened the door to them. He was pounced upon and practically carried to the theatre. To his amazement the young man found himself on the stage surrounded by the whole company. A vehement argument ensued. They explained that he was their only hope, that unless the performance continued they would not have enough money to buy food the next day, and promised to help him as much as they could. Toscanini told them that they were mad. How could they expect him to conduct? . . . he had never conducted in his life. He had never even held a baton in his hand. He persisted in his refusal. It seemed unlikely that any argument would move him.

All of a sudden, his eyes focused on two faces, unexpected faces: two young members of the chorus, both from Parma. One of them, in particular, gazed at him imploringly. She had a simple, honest, peasant face—a face from home. She clasped her hands as if in prayer, then the poor woman broke into Parmesan dialect: "Come on, up with you, Toscané!" That settled it. It was the voice of Parma. He murmured: "Very well, if you want me to, I'll try."

Somebody put the baton into his hand. Somebody else started taking off his jacket and holding up a tail-coat for him to try on. Toscanini protested violently and said that he would wear his own jacket or none at all. Thus this young man of nineteen (his nineteenth birthday had been celebrated on the boat on the way over) began his career of lion-tamer in the lion's cage. Nobody, not even Toscanini, remembers exactly what happened subsequently. Either the audience had grown tired of demonstrating or they had come to their senses and were behaving in a rational instead of an emotional manner; or perhaps the unexpected sight of this beardless youth had shocked them into silence. The fact is that there was complete silence in the theatre. Toscanini mounted the rostrum, tapped on the music-stand, and gave the attack.

Toscanini remembered that he conducted the first scenes exactly as if he were conducting in a dream. He understood everything, saw everything: the hall in the palace of the king, Ramphis with his beard, and Rhadames with his paunch. But he felt as if, inside him, somebody or something else was moving his arms and his hands. After the first few beats, he ignored the score which lay open in front of him. It was his other self inside him who was moving his arms and his hands and who knew every note by heart, because, at the right point, he remembered to stretch the baton towards the violas, or raised the palm of his left hand to Rhadames, whose tempo was a little slow on the phrase: "*Il tuo bel cielo vorrei ridarti.*" It was the other self also who conducted the trio. Then he ushered in the accentuated triple time of the trumpets, which announced the arrival of the king. Here is the Messenger who drops on bended knee: "*Il sacro suolo dell' Egitto è invaso.*" "*Mio padre!*" wails Aida at that point. Heavens, what a cry of anguish! Toscanini wakes up. The other self is still conducting, but little by little Arturo feels that he is returning to consciousness, as if he were emerging from a thick fog. The bows flash, almost convulsively. Enter the chorus: "*Guerra, guerra.*" "*Io tremo,*" sighs Aida. "*Su del Nil al sacro lido—sian barriere i nostri petti.*" At that precise point of the chorus, Toscanini regains complete mastery of himself. The other self has disappeared. Now he has his feet firmly planted on the rostrum, he feels that he is in complete control of the orchestra.

He remembered that he made two mistakes that evening and, ever afterwards, whenever he conducted *Aida*, the two passages brought that evening back to his mind.

The audience became more and more enthusiastic as the performance proceeded, and he was greeted at the end of the opera with frantic and prolonged applause. The season was saved. The company remained at Rio till the end of the winter season, and the receipts continued highly satisfactory. And when they left for home in September, each member of the company took back with him a little hoard of savings, like every good emigrant.

This factual account of the first occasion on which Arturo Toscanini conducted a full orchestra in public may help to dispel some of the misconceptions, which have almost become a legend. It has been presented as a simple stroke of luck. Some of his admirers even seem to believe that some sort of supernatural agency intervened and that he was transported to the rostrum by magic. In fact it should be realized that this incident was the logical result of incessant and meticulous hard work. The orchestra chose him as their leader and conductor because they were conscious that he was the only one who knew the score by heart from first note to last: for, when the company was still at São Paulo, Arturo spent most of his free time helping to rehearse singers and instrumentalists, who realized that they were weak in some part of their roles.

Certain other historical facts should be noted, as they help to explain what happened at Rio. It will be remembered that Toscanini played the 'cello in the orchestra in the winter of 1885–6, during which the operas by Ponchielli, not previously performed at Parma—*Gioconda* and *Marion Delorme*—were on the programme. Ponchielli had been present in person. These two operas were a great success—poor Ponchielli's last triumph, as he was very ill and died shortly after returning to Milan.

Gioconda and *Marion Delorme* were interpreted that winter by an exceptionally brilliant cast; among the women there were Cattaneo, Mei, and among the men Figner and the baritone Menotti. On the same programme there were *Faust* and *Aida*. Now, who were the stars in the Rio performance? Figner and Mei, the same tenor and soprano as at Parma, whose qualities and inflexions Toscanini knew intimately. It was no simple stroke of luck: but luck was on his side.

When Toscanini left Rio, he took away with him more than a small sum of money. The citizens of Rio, long before the end of the season, had forgotten all about their hatred for the Italians, and now loved and admired them as much as they had formerly hated them. Innumerable dinners and receptions were given in honour of the company and, in particular, its conductor. On each occasion Arturo was presented with a valuable ring or tie-pin, cigar-case, impractically ornate conductor's baton, and so on. The boat docked at Genoa. His family lived there, in a house near the port, in the oldest and most picturesque part of the town, between Via San Lorenzo and Santa Maria di Castello. This is a typical quarter, traversed by narrow streets in which the houses are packed together like the leaves of an artichoke. The Toscanini house was one of the first of the artichoke leaves in the Via dei Notari.

Arturo emptied his presents out on the bed. Most of them were ugly, but they all seemed marvellous to his family, because they came from a fabulous world over the seas. His two sisters— Zina, who was now thirteen, and Ada, eleven—were delighted. Claudio Toscanini, who had almost begun to forget Garibaldi when he had heard the news of his son's triumph at Rio de Janeiro, embraced him tenderly. From the other side of the bed, Mama Paola, her hands clasped on her lap in the immemorial attitude of working-class mothers, gazed at him with the same frowning concentration which is characteristic of her son.

CHAPTER VI

Early Struggles

ALTHOUGH it started under the best of auspices, the Toscanini family's second attempt at settling in Genoa did not seem likely to be more successful than the first. The shop was in an excellent position. Claudio, skilled at his trade as ever, had attracted a number of clients to his tailoring department. But all too soon business began to fall off. The main reason, as usual, was Claudio Toscanini's inveterate habit of absenting himself from the premises. Previously he had confined himself to arguments and discussions about Garibaldi, but now he also felt an irresistible urge to boast about his son. Further, which was even more serious, Signor Pelliccia soon showed that he was far from being the great financier he had claimed to be. He was buying materials on credit and paying far too much for them. He was not even capable of keeping the books. In fact he, too, spent his time wandering all over the city, pursuing one wildcat scheme after another. The apprentices were left in charge of the shop, stole money, sold the materials, and put the proceeds in their pockets.

Soon after his return Arturo Toscanini realized that it would be up to him to support the family. His way of facing the problem was a typical example of the basic soundness of his character. He had been a conductor at Rio for a whole season. He had conducted sixteen operas. He had been an extraordinary success— a fact which, naturally, was known throughout the musical circles of Italy—and had aroused considerable interest. Nevertheless, Toscanini did not contemplate taking up a career as a conductor. He put his baton away in a drawer, philosophically, and proposed trying for a new engagement as a 'cello player. He might well have continued working as an instrumentalist for some time, if it had not been for a letter from the tenor, Figner, who had sung with the company in Rio with his friend Mei, reproaching him for hiding himself in Genoa and for not coming to try his luck in Milan.

Toscanini was very sceptical, but, when Figner insisted, he finally made up his mind to go to Milan. He took a room at the S. Michele Hotel, which was the annexe of the Hotel Al Leone, on the Corso at the corner of Via Durini. By a peculiar coincidence, it was in the Via Durini that he bought a house many years later. Figner was tireless in his efforts to help him, and introduced him to the obese and dynamic Signora Lucca, the soul of the famous musical publishing and managing enterprise which, at that time, shared with Ricordi an almost complete monopoly of the musical world. Signora Giovannina received the young man with great cordiality, but made no promises. She mentioned, casually, a single remote possibility. An opera, *Edmea*, by a young composer, Alfredo Catalani, was to be performed in Turin during the following October. It had already been performed at the Scala the previous winter, with Franco Faccio as conductor, and it had been a great success. Another conductor, who was popular at the time, Domenico Pomé, had been engaged to conduct in Turin. Pomé was busy at Treviso and had just written that he would not be free to go to Turin at the beginning of the season. Thus there was a possibility that Toscanini might be able to go to Turin to take the rehearsals of *Edmea* and perhaps conduct the first few performances; it was, naturally, understood that he would hand over to Pomé as soon as he had finished his season at Treviso.

Several days later, when Toscanini had already forgotten the matter, a letter arrived from Figner marked "Urgent". Figner wrote that he had been able to procure the score of *Edmea*, and suggested that Toscanini should run over it with him. They met in a small drawing-room in which there was a piano, and Toscanini started playing. After he had finished the second act, a gentleman, who was a stranger to Toscanini, came up and asked the maestro politely if he was reading the score for the first time.

"Good heavens, yes!" answered Toscanini. "Where could I have seen it before?"

"Then allow me," said the gentleman courteously, and brought forward his companion, whom Toscanini had not noticed. He was a thin man with a scholarly stoop, the face of a thinker, two burning and melancholy eyes, and long, fair hair brushed back from his forehead. It was Catalani, who had been sitting in a dark corner and had been following the whole audition. The stratagem had been successful. Catalani gave his consent, and Toscanini was sent by Signora Giovannina to Turin to prepare *Edmea*.

The season was to be held at the Carignano Theatre, and the impresario was Depanis, one of the high priests of the musical life of Turin at that time. He had been responsible for bringing Adelina Patti to Turin to sing in a spectacular performance of *Traviata* some years before. Catalani also proposed to be present in person. Toscanini had taken a great liking to this artist (Catalani was thirty years old), whose gentle voice, quiet gestures, and pathetic smile expressed the sadness which was characteristic of his music. They became firm friends. Toscanini, throughout the rehearsals, bombarded him with questions. Was the tempo of the *Filatrice* right? (The chorus of the *Filatrice* was so popular that Catalani himself made a transcription, much appreciated by the ladies who were studying the piano between 1900 and 1918.) The harps in the prelude to the third act, should the pitch be higher? Catalani's invariable answer was that he had nothing to say, because he considered that Toscanini knew the music as well as he did, as if they had collaborated in the writing of it.

Catalani was a typical product of that period of transition in Italy. His contemporaries, who read poetry or composed or painted in 1880–90, were very different from the generation which had preceded them. There was a violent revulsion against the conformity and hypocritical moral standards of the previous period. As a result, the literary world of Italy had, for a decade,

produced a generation of poets who eulogized suicidal and for-
bidden love and derided romanticism. It was a confused reflection of both the heroic and Wagnerian mythology and Baude-
lairian necromancy, with a definite predilection for the latter and
for the rhetorical canons of the *poète maudit*. Even Boito—the
Boito whom we have all known, old, loaded with honours, senator, president of academies, ornament of aristocratic salons—had
taken hashish in his youth.

Unfortunately this revolt lacked the only indispensable element which was essential for success: genius. They were all
attractive dilettantes, full of good intentions and ideals, but bad
writers. Catalani belonged to the second generation, whose protest had been transferred to a different plane. They were opposed
to the hypocrisy of the Philistines and to the prevailing medio-
crity, but were learning to express themselves with greater clarity
and force. Their idealism was no longer abstract but more personal and genuine. They were influenced by the imaginative
fantasies of the romantic movement which was sweeping over the
countries of the north, by the taste for legends, and the nostalgia
for the north itself, a twilit land of mists and moonlit castles.

For these young poets, love, or rather the search for romantic
love, was the object of life. They were always in love, and Catalani was a great lover in the romantic tradition. When Tranquillo
Cremona painted his famous picture *The Ivy*, which depicts a
man ecstatically clasping a young woman, who is straining her
fine body away from him, at the very moment when pride is about
to give way to the clamour of the senses, he chose Catalani as his
model. The woman who posed for the female figure was a niece
of the painter and secretly enamoured of the musician. Many
other painters asked him to pose for them and, when he was hard
up, he sometimes posed for a fee. He was always in need of
money, mainly because he was tubercular and went from doctor
to doctor, trying every imaginable cure at great expense. The
thought of death was constantly in the forefront of his mind, as it
is said to have been in the case of Mozart. He had a presentiment
of his early death, which may have been responsible for some of

Bruno Walter, Thomas Mann, Toscanini: Salzburg, 1936

Grubicy

With Enrico Polo, Turin, 1895

"His beloved Isolino . . ." (p. 197)

"August 25, 1938, in front of Wagner's villa . . ." (p.180). A rough pavilion, erected
in haste to replace the official one, which Toscanini had condemned for its
acoustics

the most beautiful passages in his music, that suggestion of tears, that frail charm, that pallor of a tarnished pearl. . . . His was a nostalgic spirit and his favourite instrument was the harp.

The libretto of *Edmea* was execrable. It was a rag-bag of all that is most conventional and most indigestible in a romantic libretto; castles, coats-of-arms, hunting-horns, fairies, minstrels, sly inn-keepers, unnatural fathers, demented heroines, broken troths, and sublime sacrifices. Edmea is a sort of Ophelia of the Elbe. When the brave Oberto departs she is forced by his father to marry Ulmo. She throws herself into the river and, when fished out by her husband, is found to have gone mad and wanders around, dressed like a fantastic water-fairy, until the end, when she falls into the arms of the inconsolable Oberto and recovers her reason; poor Ulmo poisons himself to allow them to marry, begging Edmea for the supreme gift of a kiss on the forehead: not at once—that would be asking too much—but after his death.

The fact that the opera was successfully performed not only at the Scala and in Turin but also in many other cities, both in Italy and abroad, was a miracle which could be explained only by the exceptional qualities of the music. Take for example the death of Ulmo, expressed by those lovely, groping, augmented fifths, soon to be used by Puccini in *Manon*. But the surprise, the real hit, was at the beginning of the opera, in the overture, in which Catalani wrote three pages of music which constitute a single irresistible melodic oration, carried out with such impetuosity, such magnificent outbursts of melody that no audience could help being swept off its feet. Indeed, it was in this overture that the young geniuses of Toscanini and of Catalani first really worked together. Everybody was astounded by the manner in which this slight, swarthy youngster of twenty vigorously attacked the harsh contrapuntal opening in D minor and carried it, without weakening, for sixty-four bars, raising it to the climax of its emotional appeal. The performance that evening was a revelation to the audience, who realized that a new operatic style had been born. *Edmea* had an excellent reception in Turin and

E

was a great personal triumph for Catalani. After the performance, when Catalani was surrounded by excited members of the audience who were congratulating him, Toscanini saw the unfortunate man's face contorted in a sudden spasm of pain. He grew pale, put a handkerchief to his mouth, and withdrew it stained with blood.

Shortly afterwards Pomé arrived to take over for the rest of the season. Toscanini stayed as his assistant conductor and rehearsed *The Flying Dutchman* for him. This was also to prove a great success. At that time Wagner was the subject of violent controversies all over Italy. This season at the Carignano was a Lucca season (the two main music publishers, Lucca and Ricordi, fought as keenly for theatres as teams compete for the football championship today). Hence a Wagner opera was considered essential, and this time *The Flying Dutchman* had been selected.

Toscanini orchestrated this opera, and Pomé conducted the first performance in Italy. There was nothing more for Arturo to do at the Carignano that season. That same December Bolzoni was conducting a series of concerts at the Vittorio Emanuele Theatre. Bolzoni came from Parma and was a well-known and successful conductor and composer. At the time when symphonic and chamber music were the cinderellas of music in Italy, he had the courage to compose nothing but concertos, quartets, quintets, and overtures, caring not at all whether they pleased the public or not, nor whether he made any money from them. He was another eccentric, with a good brain and a caustic wit.

Toscanini during his years of study at Parma had played on one occasion at the Regio in an orchestra conducted by Bolzoni, who had now moved to Turin and was director of the Lyceum of Music. Toscanini took it into his head that he would like to play under his old maestro, and he resumed his role of 'cellist in two of his concerts. One of the works played by Toscanini in these Bolzoni concerts was Beethoven's Second Symphony. A few years later, when he was dining in Bolzoni's house, which was in the Piazza Castello, his host, remembering those concerts, turned to Toscanini and said to him: "Now I can tell you, you wicked fellow. There were moments that evening when I could have throttled you." "Why, maestro?" asked Toscanini, laughing. "Because . . . while the others were playing you were leaning back, gazing up at the ceiling, and looking bored. You were one of a row of 'cellists and you had a series of separated entries. As I was conducting I looked at you and thought: 'How the devil can that fellow come in at precisely the right moment without looking at the score?' Each time I had my heart in my mouth, and each time, without lowering your eyes, out came your note at precisely the right instant. Word of honour, I could have thrown the score at your head."

Besides playing with Bolzoni, he gave a 'cello recital, as a soloist, at Asti, during the same Turin season.

He had an excellent press. Toscanini sent some cuttings to a close friend, Enrico Polo—the only occasion on which he is known to have done such a thing throughout his career. The reply from his friend, congratulating him, is still in existence. It is dated 1886: "All your old college friends ask me to tell you how delighted they are with your success. Bravo!"

In spite of Catalani's personal recommendations, expressed in the most glowing terms, Toscanini was not able to secure more than two seasonal engagements throughout the following year, 1887: one at Casale Monferrato, with *Africana* and *I Lombardi*, and the second at Verona, with *Gioconda*, *Carmen*, and *Aida*. This was the beginning of what might be called the peregrinating phase of Toscanini's career, which was to continue until 1894, when he was given his first permanent appointment at the Regio in Turin. It was a phase reminiscent of our own provincial touring companies, in a period which has now passed away. There were interminable journeys, one provincial piazza after another, the anxious waiting for the next engagement, the constant struggle to create something from almost nothing, the conflicts with cheap impresarios, making the best of indifferent singers and enthusiastic but inadequate orchestras. He was the everlasting pilgrim in small provincial hotels frequented by commercial travellers and filled, on market days, with farmers. There was the daily struggle

with the property-man who can never find what is wanted, with
the prima-donna who wants to sing three arias for her benefit
night; the petty political intrigues, the mayor who recommends
a friend for a job, the intellectual and influential lady who is
determined to give a dinner for the conductor, the officers of the
garrison who arrive late with a clatter of sword scabbards.

In between seasons there was a vacuum. There were months
of unemployment, which were never pleasant, even if they were
endured with fortitude. And there was a family to support.
Claudio Toscanini's short period of affluence in Genoa was a
thing of the past. In less than a year the business had gone bank-
rupt and Pelliccia had decamped, leaving innumerable unpaid
bills of exchange behind him. Claudio with his wife and daughters
followed Arturo to Milan. The family, practically destitute, had
settled down at No. 16 Via San Vito. The house still stands, in
spite of the bombing of the district.

The Toscaninis lived on the top floor. There was a tiny room
for Arturo and a slightly larger one for his parents and the girls.
There was no kitchen, and their meals were shared with their
landlords: a charming couple, very old, very kind, and completely
devoted to each other, Pietro and Luigina. The latter fell in love
with the two little girls, but, unfortunately, she spoke only the
Milanese dialect, and the children spoke only the Parma dialect!

Shortly afterwards, to their great regret, the Toscaninis had to
leave Pietro and Luigina and look for new lodgings because they
could not afford to pay for their meals. They eventually found
them, not far away, in the Via Cesare Correnti, which was then
called San Simone. Claudio Toscanini had secured employment
as a cutter in the workshop of an emporium, which was then one
of the landmarks of Milan, and the first of its kind in Italy—that
of the Fratelli Bocconi.

In February 1887 Toscanini played in the orchestra in *Otello*.
There had been a gap of sixteen years between *Aida* and *Otello*.
Verdi had been lying fallow. His reappearance with *Otello*,
libretto by Arrigo Boito, was, therefore, a musical event of extraordinary importance. There was keen competition among both

singers and instrumentalists to take part in the performance.
Toscanini offered his services and played as second 'cellist on that
memorable evening which was a renewed triumph for the great
patriarch of melodrama. Toscanini's motives, as usual, were enthusiasm for the music itself and a desire to learn and to perfect
himself. Faccio conducted, but Verdi attended the rehearsals. In
spite of his veneration for the maestro, young Toscanini had
not always agreed with his interpretation. A few years ago he
confessed to a friend: "Sometimes it occurs to me that perhaps,
when I, too, am old, I shall grow careless, involuntarily, like
Verdi at the rehearsals of *Otello*. For example, he was not at all
satisfied with certain passages of the double-basses. But he said
nothing."

In fact, Verdi in person criticized Toscanini's playing during
one of these rehearsals. The tall figure of the great man was seen
walking down the gangway towards the orchestra. Toscanini,
whose seat was nearer the auditorium than that of the other
'cellists, was watching him and wondering what he was coming
for, when the man who shared his music-stand nudged him and
said: "Look, everybody is getting up." Whereupon Toscanini
also rose to his feet. Verdi came up to him and said that he had
played the quartet too softly and asked him to play it more loudly
next time. Toscanini had too much respect for Verdi to point out
that he had followed the score, in which the passage in question
was marked pianissimo. The truth was that the leading 'cello,
Magrini, liked to show off his fine bowing, and thus played too
loud, and unbalanced the strings.

We have already mentioned the two other modest seasons,
which were his only engagements for the rest of 1887, for Casale
and Verona. His luck was not much better in 1888, except for the
fact that he made his début as a conductor in Milan. He was engaged for the spring season at the popular Teatro Dal Verme and
conducted *Forza del Destino*, *I Promessi Sposi* by Ponchielli, and
Francesca da Rimini by Cagnoni (this opera failed). His only
other engagements in that year were to conduct *Aida* at Macerata
and *Les Huguenots* at Novara. He took even more trouble than

usual over *Les Huguenots* because it was to be the inaugural performance at the new Teatro Coccia. His task became a difficult,
if not impossible one, because the tenor had fallen in love with the
prima-donna. Exhausted by passionate love-making off-stage
with the Queen of Navarre, the wretched man had already lost his
voice before the end of the rehearsals.

The year 1889 was also a meagre one for Toscanini: two
operas at Novara, *Aida* and *Forza del Destino*, and at the Vittorio
Emanuele in Turin, *Carmen* and *Mignon*. These latter two had
been combined in order to use the same mezzo-soprano, Lison
Frandin, who was famous for singing *Mignon* divinely. The next
year, 1890, was a complete blank up till October, except for a very
short season at Brescia, which may be of interest to music-lovers
because he conducted *Le Villi*. Among stingy impresarios Toscanini was already getting the reputation of needing too many rehearsals. From October 1890 till March 1891 he was engaged for
a season at Barcelona. He was then given an engagement to conduct *Cavalleria Rusticana*, at Senigallia, a small city on the
Adriatic.

These years were, indeed, lean years for Arturo Toscanini. It
may surprise and even shock the reader to be told that the salary
for a young conductor at the beginning of his career was never
more than 800–1,000 Lire per season (£90–£110). As the whole
burden of supporting the Toscanini family fell on him, it is not
surprising that he was forced to consider every possible means of
saving money. Thus, when he went to Brescia in 1890, he rented
a furnished room and took his mother with him to cook for him,
to avoid having to eat in a restaurant, however modest. To
supplement the family income they also took boarders in Milan.
It should be noted, however, that the boarders were very carefully chosen, and no one was accepted unless he came from Parma,
was a musician, and a friend of Arturo's. The word "boarder" is
used in the Italian sense, as the boarders lived elsewhere and only
took their meals at the Toscaninis'. The Toscaninis had moved
from the Via San Simone to the fifth floor of a house in the Corso
Torino. These five flights of stairs were a terrible ordeal for his

friend, Catalani, who used to pay frequent visits to Toscanini during the last years of his life. He arrived at the flat flushed, panting, covered with perspiration, and stretched himself out on two chairs while Mama Paola heated the coffee-pot. In those years Catalani had become successful, had composed *Lorelei*, and was about to commence his masterpiece, *La Wally*.

In spite of extreme poverty, life at the little flat in the Corso Torino had its compensations. The boarders from Parma were all young, bachelors and artists. They were always chattering and retailing the latest news, of the Scala and the Conservatory, an argument in the Galleria, Verdi's plan for a House of Rest for musicians, the rupture between Boito and the Duse. There were interminable arguments about the respective values of Wagner's and Verdi's music. It is perhaps characteristic of the fundamental sanity of Toscanini that he was in the habit of cutting short a heated argument between the protagonists of Wagner versus Verdi by saying: "You are arguing at cross-purposes. You should not say Wagner *or* Verdi but Wagner *and* Verdi!"

Even during this trying period of his life, Arturo was always cheerful and expansive and was always joking or playing practical jokes on his mother and his sisters.

At that time—we are speaking of the year 1890—Ada was fifteen and Zina thirteen. Toscanini enjoyed teasing them, and used to take them in the afternoon to have a glass of milk at the Swiss dairy, which was in a small park and was popular because the customers could see real Swiss cows being milked in the cow-stalls attached to the dairy. He was also fond of rambling in the country, and Ada remembers an excursion to Bergamo with her sister and a small army of musicians and friends, the Barberini and the Saffo Bellincioni among them. Arturo was in unusually good form, making Zina run down the sloping field with him so fast that they both ended up head-over-heels.

He particularly enjoyed teasing the buxom and high-spirited Ada, the more musical of the two sisters. Arturo had wanted her to study the harp at the Milan Conservatory. But Ada preferred the piano. Unfortunately, she was both lazy and incompetent.

She had persuaded an old maestro to give her a few lessons. These were given, for obvious reasons, when Arturo was out. Sometimes, however, on these occasions, hearing her strumming off-key used to cause him real agony.

It must not be thought that Arturo spent his life having a good time with his family. When he was unemployed he concentrated on his studies. There were times when he could not tear himself away from his music for whole days and nights. His mother relates that, when she went into his room in the morning to bring him his usual black coffee, she often found him asleep in bed with three or four scores scattered over the coverlet.

One of his friends still has in his possession a piano score of *Valkyrie* on which, as he had been unable to procure the full score, he had marked in great detail all the entries for orchestra. "The 2nd, 3rd flutes and 3rd bass clarinet usher in the movement of the triplet—the 1st bassoon enters on the 2nd beat—the 2nd on the 3rd," and so on. He was always playing; even when he was eating, his fingers were drumming on an invisible keyboard. He studied music and read books voraciously. At that time the Bologna school of writers were at the height of their reputation: Carducci (his favourite), Stecchetti, Panzacchi. He was a great admirer of Leopardi, and used to read him aloud to his mother.

It was not until 1892 that there was a decisive turn in Toscanini's career. In that year he had a stroke of luck: he was asked to conduct the first performance, at the Dal Verme in Milan on May 17, of Leoncavallo's *Pagliacci*. The composer, Ruggero Leoncavallo, was completely unknown. He was a funny little man with an enormous paunch, hair drooping over his forehead, and the long waxed moustaches which were the fashion because they were worn by the King, Umberto, and all the generals of the Italian army. Leoncavallo found the five flights up to Toscanini as distressing, because of his paunch, as Catalani had, because of his lungs. Leoncavallo was extremely versatile and had travelled all over the world, and had been everything from singing teacher to piano-player in cheap cafés. *Pagliacci* met with great success because it was the first "realistic" opera and defied the

convention of romantic librettos. Toscanini, with his extraordinary instinct for bringing out the best in any music, conducted
this new opera in a manner which gave full play to the exuberance
and sensual character of the work, and was largely responsible
for its triumphant reception. The rehearsing of *Pagliacci* was
particularly difficult, and Toscanini arrived home after the first
performance so exhausted that he threw himself fully dressed on
the bed and slept till the following midday.

There was a second important milestone in Toscanini's career
in the year 1892: the municipal authorities of Genoa wished to
celebrate the centenary of the discovery of America and the first
voyage of Columbus. They commissioned Alberto Franchetti,
who was then considered one of the most promising of the young
composers, to compose a grand opera around the figure of
Columbus, and they not only paid him and the librettist, but also
the expenses of the production at the Carlo Felice; a costly item,
as there were innumerable scenes, an enlarged orchestra, and
chorus. Luigi Mancinelli was engaged; with Mugnone, he was
considered the best operatic conductor of the day. All went well,
on the surface, throughout the rehearsals, but on the first night a
violent quarrel broke out between Franchetti and Mancinelli. All
efforts at patching up the differences failed. One or other had to
go. It could not be the composer, so it had to be the conductor.
A commission was dispatched to Milan to select a conductor to
take over from Mancinelli from the third performance onwards.
Nobody could be found willing to take over at such short notice,
except Toscanini, who pored over the score all night, travelled
to Genoa the next day, and arrived looking, when he stepped on
the rostrum that evening, as if he had just stepped out of bed after
a good night's sleep. *Columbus* is a clumsy, mastodontic opera
and quite unsuited for inclusion in the ordinary repertory.
Nevertheless, some of the music is good and deserves to be played
for its own sake, especially the so-called "Nocturne", when
Columbus, alone in the night on the deck of the *Santa Maria*,
anxiously searches the seas for a sign which will bid him go on
hoping.

Toscanini devoted the remainder of 1892 to Catalani. *Lorelei*, which had been performed in Turin for the first time in February 1880, had been on tour, and Toscanini revived it in February 1892. Catalani's latest opera, *La Wally*, had been successfully performed for the first time at the Scala in January 1892. This opera was to have an inaugural performance at Lucca, Catalani's native city, in September 1892. Catalani, naturally, wanted Toscanini to conduct for him.

The friendship between Toscanini and Catalani was one of the closest, if not the closest, in his life. They were utterly different, both physically and temperamentally, and thus may have complemented each other. Catalani was tall, thin, sickly, and melancholy; Toscanini was short, muscular, full of vitality and high spirits.

At that time Verdi's career was over, and with it a whole cycle of the Italian operatic tradition. With *Traviata*, Verdi had touched on the modern sentimental novel, but now new needs were felt: on the one hand, a more direct, realistic form of musical narrative, following Wagner's insistence on the supremacy of the drama; on the other, a lyricism that would be more flexible, more intimate, more elegant. This return to a freer expression in song, coupled with the new sense of scenic realism and its dramatic fusion with the score, was the kernel of the new movement in Italian opera.

Catalani stood on the threshold of this new movement. In *La Wally* one can find signs of the new melodic style, and of the new dramatic techniques. His special gift lay in his ability to gather together, in a new free form, and without lapsing into the stale melodramatic conventions, a grand combined movement, in which the aria and the choral comment are fused in a glorious whole. In this respect he was unique and unbeatable. Two examples: the funeral of Anna in *Lorelei*, when the deep and melting tones of the song are broken by short, interrupted, and contrapuntal phrases like the silent lamentation of tears. Or the dance in *Wally*, that thrilling and provocative dialogue which runs its contrapuntal course along the sinuous line of the triple rhythm, as serpentine as temptation; that voluptuous hesitation and no less impatient assault; the repelling hand and the languid glance; the tremulous lips, moistly awaiting the kisses withheld for so long; no other young Italian composer would have been capable of combining in a simple burst of melody the expression of such a complex of changing and contradictory emotions.

Toscanini still remains convinced that Catalani was a great and genuine musician, a real creative artist.

Catalani's death was a heavy blow to Toscanini. We know something about the details. Towards the end of August 1893 Catalani felt tired and ill and decided to take a short holiday in Switzerland, on the Gotthard tunnel in one of the many villages between Faido and Airolo. Toscanini took him to the station and saw him off. A few days later a friend casually mentioned the fact that he had heard that Catalani was seriously ill. Subsequently Toscanini found out that Catalani had returned almost immediately to Milan and was nearly at death's door.

Toscanini hurried to Catalani's house and learned that he had had a violent haemorrhage in the train and had been brought back the same day. His librettist for *La Wally*, Illica, was at his bedside. During the next ten days Toscanini rarely left his friend, whose condition became steadily worse, and eventually telegraphed to Zurich to Catalani's mistress, who arrived the next day. She stayed with him two days, but Catalani wanted Toscanini to stay with him. He wanted Toscanini to give him his medicines. He wanted to talk with Toscanini about music. He was jealous of Puccini, who also came from Lucca. *Manon* had appeared for the first time that year, at Pisa. Toscanini had conducted it.

"Do you really like it?" said Catalani. "Believe me, Arturo, it is not sincere. That man is not sincere." Toscanini comforted him: "Come, come, you are the composer of *Wally*. Why should you worry about anybody else's music?" The evening before his death, Toscanini asked the doctor if there were any danger for that night. The doctor replied that there was none, that he would last for several days. He died that night.

The loss of his best friend coincided with a minor crisis in

Toscanini's own career. He had to make a decision, a difficult decision for a musician. Was composing compatible with his other activities? He wrote music with facility, every kind of music. But he was convinced, and always believed, that he was not capable of writing great music. According to Toscanini's standards, which have always been exacting and inflexible, any music which is not a creation of genius is useless music.

The point was reached when Toscanini felt that his compositions were useless, if not entirely sterile. His decision on this subject may have been influenced by a visit to Bologna in 1888, to hear *Tristan and Isolde* conducted by Martucci. He travelled with the baritone Sparapani, a curious and versatile character. He had started his career as a painter, then studied music and finished up as a baritone, but his real passion was composing. In 1886 an opera of his, *Don Cesare di Bazan*, was performed at the Manzoni in Milan. Sparapani was disappointed by Toscanini's lukewarm attitude towards his great work. They had innumerable arguments, which may have helped Toscanini to clarify his ideas on the subject of his own compositions.

The ideological disagreement was brought to a head that night in Bologna. After the second act of *Tristan and Isolde*, Sparapani went out into the foyer. Toscanini ran up to him—or rather charged him like a bull, head low and eyes flashing fire. "Now, what do you think of your wretched *Cesare di Bazan* or that famous '*Son gelosa*' of mine? Rubbish, musical worms in comparison with this divine music, this hymn of infinite love! It is disgusting to go on writing music, making fly-specks on paper, paper which could be put to better use for wrapping sausages."

From that moment onwards Toscanini never wrote another line of music.

Was Arturo justified? His early works could be divided into three groups. One of them during his student period in Parma, which we have already described. The other is a group of eight romances composed by Toscanini while he was still in college, of which one copy is still in existence, dedicated in his own handwriting to the distinguished singer, Antonio Superchi. The

latter was the baritone for whom Verdi wrote *Ernani*, who was
then already an old man and had retired to live in Parma. The
third group was that of his published romances. They were all in
tune with the taste of that period. They were all, technically,
extremely competent.

Probably his best work was the romance called *Autunno*. It
was composed around a short poem by Felice Cavallotti—deputy,
poet, and journalist, impassioned orator with a partiality for
Toscani cigars; a paunchy and bombastic *bonhomme*, who died
tragically in a duel.

On the basis of this slight poem, Toscanini constructed an intensely intimate fragment of music, which is a foretaste of the
rhythmic and tonal innovations of Debussy and the new French
school. This piece would be well worth discussing in some detail
because it already bears some of the earmarks of the style of his
conducting; the extreme abundance, graduation, and subtlety of
the colouring, so much so that there are as many as five different
colour indications within three beats. A final peculiarity should
be noted: an incurable predilection for the minor key. Of twelve
pieces, at least ten are in the minor: three in F minor, two in D
minor, and two in A flat minor.

The day that Toscanini decided to stop composing, he also
started a tireless search for all copies of his works, whether in
manuscript or in print, to withdraw them from circulation. His
ideal would have been to collect them all and to make a bonfire of
them.

CHAPTER VII

Recognition

———

THE year in which Toscanini can be said to have reached maturity is 1895. From that year onwards his name is bound up with the sweeping change, which could almost be called a revolution, in opera and in musical interpretation, which was to be accomplished during his lifetime, and largely by him.

The most active stage of this revolution lasted three years, 1895–8, in Turin. Turin, in those days, was an aristocratic city in the literal sense of the term. A rich and cultured aristocracy still flourished, even in the absence of a Court. There was also an intelligent and progressive middle-class. Furthermore, Turin was almost on the borders of France, and was therefore the first of the Italian cities to feel the impact of French fashions, literature, and ideas. It was for this reason that the Piedmontese industrialists were the first to grasp the importance of the automobile and that Turin has since become the Italian Detroit. Because of its aristocracy and its industry, Turin was the city with the best clothes, the most lively and enterprising students; the city in which the best people spoke French, the city of delicious chocolate, *grissini* (long cylindrical rusks), smart dressmaking-shops, and *chanteuses*.

Although Turin then had only 350,000 inhabitants, there were twelve theatres which were always open. In one of them, the Scribe, French companies played light opera throughout the year. The musical life of the city was equally lively and flourishing. There were continuous seasons of opera in at least three theatres: the Regio, the Vittorio Emanuele, and the Carignano. There

were concerts and performances at the club of the artists, celebrated throughout Italy (the brothers Giacosa, Giuseppe being a
successful comedian and Piero, a medical man who was an artist
as well as a scientist; the brothers Calandra, of whom Edoardo
was a novelist and poet, and Davide a sculptor and the moral head
of the young school of Turinese sculptors, which included Bistolfi, Canonica, Rubino; Camerana, a singular combination of
magistrate and *poète maudit*). There was even a club for double
quintets which gave regular performances.

The mainspring of Turinese musical life was Giuseppe Depanis, son of the celebrated impresario of the Regio. Depanis
was a lawyer but did not practise his profession. He earned a
modest income as administrator of a brick-and-tile factory. He
was a small, ugly man, but he was a genius and his passion was
music. He suffered from a stammer, but when he spoke about
music, even in public, he became eloquent. He was the most fervent Wagnerian in Italy and contributed largely to the recognition
of Wagner's works. His book on *The Ring* is still in existence.
He was the musical critic for the *Gazzetta Piemontese* (which was
the precursor of the *Stampa*), a paper which had two editors, one
after the other, who were both enthusiastic music-lovers, Felice
Romani (who had been Bellini's librettist) and Ippolito Valletta.

Depanis, who had originally been elected, quite by chance, a
municipal councillor, retained this post for almost twenty years,
until he was dismissed by the Fascists; he was at one time assessor
to the Finance Committee. In that capacity, and because of his
knowledge of music, all theatrical and musical problems were referred to him. It was natural that, with his earnest and studious
approach and unusual gift for synthesis, he should devise a comprehensive plan for dealing with these problems. It was in this
way that he met Toscanini. They had already met, indirectly, because of their common friendship with Catalani, with whom Depanis had corresponded over a long period.

His experiences during his years of apprenticeship as a conductor had opened Toscanini's eyes to the faulty attitude, on the part
of both the audiences and of the theatre managements, towards

opera in particular. It was not only the repertory that was ossified, but also the impresarios; the singers took incredible liberties with their parts; and the great publishing houses exercised an unwarrantable tyranny over the opera houses and their choice of operas.

It was time to break the vicious circle, time to restore style and dignity to the operatic world, to restore the authority of the producer, the designer, and the conductor; and to induce audiences to behave in a disciplined and deferential manner towards opera as an art. Otherwise there could be no true aesthetic participation, as there can be no prayer without intimate silence.

On all these points Toscanini and Depanis were in complete agreement. It was due to the inflexible determination of these two men that a reorientation of culture and musical interpretation became possible throughout Italy. The formation of a municipal orchestra, the reform of the Turin Lyceum of Music, Toscanini's three seasons at the Regio, and the cycle of symphonic concerts in 1898 were also offshoots of this partnership. At that time there were no permanent orchestras in Italian theatres. Orchestras were recruited, haphazardly, by impresarios whose main preoccupation was to save money. A few good players, who had to be paid well, rubbed shoulders with a larger number of poorly paid, bad players. It was in Turin that the idea of a permanent orchestra was born, permanent in the modern sense that every instrumentalist is engaged on a long-term contract. The first of these orchestras was the Turin municipal orchestra mentioned above.

The reader will remember how Enrico Polo wrote to Toscanini, on behalf of his college friends, after the first performance of *Edmea*. Polo finished his studies and took his diploma two years after Toscanini, the year of the first performance of *Otello*, for which Polo also succeeded in securing an engagement as instrumentalist. For a brief period the two friends were together again. For some years Polo remained in Milan, permanently engaged at the Scala, and was one of the group of friends from Parma who boarded with the Toscaninis. Considerable prestige is attached to a permanent engagement at the Scala, but the salary of a young

violinist in the orchestra leaves much to be desired. Polo therefore accepted a number of engagements abroad. This enabled
him, with the help of a Maecenas from Parma, Count Sanvitale, to
spend two and a half years in Berlin and perfect himself at the
celebrated "Hochschule" of Joachim.

In the summer of 1895 Polo had come to Savigliano, in Piedmont, as the guest of the mayor, who was an enthusiastic violinist.
One day his host showed him a Turin newspaper containing the
announcement of a competition for the post of violin teacher at
the reorganized Lyceum of Music, combined with that of first
violinist in the new municipal orchestra.

"Why don't you compete?" his host asked.

On the appointed day Polo went to his hotel in Turin, the
Albergo del Pozzo, and, on his way in, ran into Arturo Toscanini, who was coming out. "Arturo!" "Enrico!" The two
friends threw their arms around each other. "What are you doing
here?" said Arturo. "I'm here for a competition." "I'm here for
a competition, too." Arturo was one of the judges, Enrico was a
competitor. They spent the day together, dined together, and
over coffee Arturo confessed that he was in love, really in love
this time, and also told Enrico that his *innamorata* had a sister
who was so breathtakingly pretty that Polo would certainly fall
in love with her as soon as he saw her. Polo sniffed, supercilious
bachelor that he was. The object of Arturo's affections was Carla
De Martini, who later became his wife. Her sister Ida was studying to be a singer.

Toscanini was not only in Turin to judge competitions, but
also for a three-year engagement as conductor of the opera seasons at the Regio, and the main attraction on his programme that
year was *The Twilight of the Gods*. Toscanini could not find a
singer for the third Rhinemaiden. Ida De Martini was recom-
mended to him by a singing teacher and Toscanini consented to
give her an audition, to which Ida came accompanied by her
mother and sister. It was in this way that Toscanini met his future
wife. The Martini family came to Turin for the rehearsals, and
thus Polo met Ida.

F

This period at Turin, 1895–8, was undoubtedly the decisive period in Toscanini's career. For the first time he was enabled to apply his unrivalled capacity for *constructive* interpretation. All his seasons in Turin were constructive. To Toscanini, conducting did not mean going from theatre to theatre, making the usual routine and ritual gestures. It was an organic conception, in which every part had to be functionally pre-arranged in order to achieve a supreme and inimitable expression of drama and music. His ideal was that of an integral performance. Fortunately for the future of opera throughout the world, Toscanini did not restrict the application of this fecund principle to Wagnerian opera, but also extended it to all types of opera, and especially to the great Italian school of the nineteenth century.

The arrangement of his programme for the three seasons was particularly original, and constituted his first innovation. These programmes can be divided roughly into three groups: the first, the most important, was the group of Wagnerian operas, *The Twilight of the Gods* in 1896, *Tristan and Isolde* in 1897, *Valkyrie* in 1898. The second group consisted of the usual repertory operas, such as *Mephistopheles* and *Norma*. There was also a *Re di Lahore* and *Falstaff*. The latter was performed on December 27, five days after *The Twilight of the Gods*. This relationship was by no means casual, as Toscanini throughout his life believed passionately in coupling the works of Wagner and Verdi. The third group consisted of new operas. At this time there was a veritable burgeoning of new operas, as can be deduced from the fact that eighty new operas were performed in 1896. In this third group there were seven new operas: *Savitri* by Canti, *La Bohème* by Puccini, *Emma Liona* by Lozzi, *Andrea Chénier* by Giordano (although this had had one performance in Milan the year before), *Forza d'Amore* by Buzzi Peccia, *Hero and Leander* by Mancinelli, and *La Camargo* by De Leva.

During this period Toscanini had already developed his subsequent conducting technique, as well as the many idiosyncrasies which are so characteristic of him; above all, his meticulous accuracy and the utter inflexibility of his respect for every detail of the score. He had already begun the fight, which he waged assiduously and mercilessly throughout his life, against mistakes, against the slightest negligence of tempo, staccato, and legato. At his orchestral rehearsal of *The Twilight of the Gods*, Toscanini immediately launched into the so-called Funeral March, to assess the quality of his orchestra. The drum had hardly beaten the second C when he rapped his baton against the music-stand. "You have forgotten the accent," said Toscanini to the tympanist, who looked at his part and said: "But I cannot see an accent." "Very well," answered Toscanini, "then put it there, because Wagner wrote it that way."

Any Toscanini fan could tell you thousands of anecdotes of this kind, but this was probably the first. This ultra-meticulousness is applied to everything—scenery, costumes, lights. One of the few survivors of that period, the lawyer Omodei, remembers having seen Toscanini leave the orchestra during a rehearsal and stalk on the stage to examine the boots of the members of the chorus. Conductors had never been known to take an interest in such things. And the detailed originality of the *mise-en-scène* at the Regio astonished public and critics alike.

Toscanini did not confine his attention to the stage. Previously, conductors, even famous ones, had been the obedient servants of the public. Did the public want an encore? Conductors gave them an encore. Did the public want the tenor to prolong a high note for five minutes? The conductor folded his arms and waited for the tenor to finish. Toscanini was the first to revolt against this tyranny. Thus commenced his fight with the audiences which lasted for at least twenty years.

One of his first innovations was to dim the lights in the auditorium during the performance. The reader, even if he has not read Stendhal's amusing notes on Italian theatrical customs, may know that attending the performance of an opera even as late as the middle of the nineteenth century was almost more of a social function than an artistic one. You came to see your friends as much as to hear the music. Toscanini therefore needed the full weight of Depanis's support for his decision to put out the lights.

On this occasion, the performance of one of Wagner's operas, the audience was so astounded that it did not protest. In fact, there were no difficulties during the first year of this innovation. At the beginning of the following season, however, during a performance of *Tristan and Isolde*, there was a chorus of protest as soon as the lights were dimmed. A violent battle ensued, not only between Toscanini and the audience, but between two sections of the audience itself: Wagner-lovers on the one hand, who wanted the lights dimmed, and anti-Wagnerites, who wanted the lights bright. Both sides were shouting at the top of their voices: "Lights, lights!" "Keep them out!" Toscanini stopped the orchestra. There came a voice from the stalls, in Turinese dialect: "Go on playing, Mr. Trumpet-player!" On that particular evening the blackout party was victorious. The conflict, however, turned into an organized vendetta, and the next performance was pure pandemonium. The impresario implored Toscanini to consent to a compromise, and the performance was conducted in a half-light, neither dim nor bright. Toscanini, as a gesture of protest, conducted the whole of *Tristan and Isolde* with his wrist on his knee, hardly moving his baton. This infuriated the elegant occupant of a stage box, who leaned over and shouted at Toscanini: "Mind your manners, sir!" Toscanini rapped back at him: "You mind yours, please!"

Another of his conflicts with the audience concerned the question of encores. Toscanini had always been violently against this practice, but had done nothing about it until this Turin period. It was in *The Twilight of the Gods* that he first refused to give an encore for the Funeral March. From that time onwards he conducted all his operas straight through from start to finish without the usual interruptions for an encore. He sometimes made an exception to this rule for first performances.

On this subject there is an amusing story about what happened at the first performance of Enrico De Leva's *La Camargo*. The ill-fated De Leva, who had a certain reputation as composer of futile but elegant songs, took it into his head to compose an opera around the celebrated ballerina, and had an execrable libretto written for it. The music was also feeble, so much so that, at the first performance, the audience started booing. There was, however, an intermezzo in the form of a minuet, between the first and second acts, which was graceful and pleasing. Part of the audience demanded an encore. Toscanini started playing it. The hostile section of the audience started booing and there was pandemonium. Toscanini, with his usual obstinacy, having once granted the favour of an encore, was determined to finish it; the curtain was immediately raised for the second act on an empty stage. Toscanini attacked the minuet again. Thus he, who loathed encores, imposed an encore on an audience who no longer wanted it! A stubborn man.

His dislike of applause, his refusal to take a curtain call, his reluctance to appear in person on the stage were already well marked at this time. These idiosyncrasies formed a part of his character and might be said to be inborn. There was an occasion in Parma when he was still a student, and played at a school concert at the Regio. When he had finished his piece, his family and their friends burst into applause. Young Toscanini dropped his 'cello and took to his heels. In his own words: "I can't help it; it overwhelms me."

Of all the new operas which Toscanini conducted during this period in Turin, the most successful was *La Bohème*. It was largely responsible for Puccini's increasing popularity with the Italian public. The success of *La Bohème* also acted as an incentive for the younger school of composers: Mascagni, Giordano, Leoncavallo, and Cilea. That performance at the Regio was a memorable one. Half of the royal family of Italy and critics from all over Italy were present. Puccini himself was there with his rubicund face and the partly benevolent, partly sly expression of a peasant from Lucca. The Princess Letizia, who at that time passed for a sort of Piedmontese Madame Sans-Gêne, called him to her box, and he stayed there throughout the third act, thoroughly intimidated, with his hands between his knees. The evening was also notable because it marked the beginning of a long, though tempestuous, friendship between Toscanini and Puccini.

To complete the story of this year, it is necessary to mention Toscanini's concerts. In the first year (1896) he had already had the idea of ending the season at the Regio with an orchestral concert. Piontelli welcomed the suggestion with enthusiasm. Piontelli was a typical impresario of the period; half artist, half businessman, hot-blooded, bombastic and a *bon vivant* of the first water; extremely competent at his job but not too scrupulous about money. With his exceptional flair he recognized Toscanini as a great artist, and, as a rule, their relationship was remarkably free from misunderstandings or conflicts. This was not the case, however, when Toscanini was rehearsing his orchestra for the first concert. Toscanini was not satisfied, and demanded a further orchestral rehearsal. Piontelli claimed that it was unnecessary. There was a long argument, ending with Toscanini asking: "So you refuse me another rehearsal?"

"I consider it quite superfluous!" answered Piontelli. "Well, you can conduct the concert yourself," and Toscanini stalked out of the theatre. The following evening, when the concert was almost due to begin, there was no sign of Toscanini. Piontelli was in despair and, with Polo and Depanis, jumped into a carriage and drove to his hotel, the same Albergo del Pozzo in the Via Bogini. There they found Toscanini quietly reading in bed. In spite of their combined and impassioned pleading, he refused to get up until Piontelli agreed to a further rehearsal that evening and to postpone the concert to the following evening.

On the first programme there was, as well as the Seventh Symphony of Schubert, an astounding novelty for that period, the *Tragic Overture* of Brahms, included in the programme at the suggestion of Polo who had heard it in Germany. Brahms was still alive, and this was the first time it had been played in Italy.

Turin was one of the first cities to start the tradition of great annual Exhibitions. In 1884 Turin had invited orchestras from all over Italy to compete in a series of concerts. The orchestra from Parma had been conducted by Campanini, and a music-student called Arturo Toscanini had come along as a spectator.

In 1898 the Exhibition was a particularly large and successful

one. Enormous crowds flowed incessantly through the grounds
and various buildings, gaping at the mechanical marvels exhibited,
including the latest internal-combustion engine, railway loco-
motive, and steam loom.

On the occasion of this greatest of Exhibitions, the organizers
were anxious to arrange for a musical manifestation which would
beat all records: the municipal orchestra was to perform two
cycles of concerts throughout the period of four months, twice
weekly in the great hall of the Exhibition. At the last moment it
was found impossible to organize an adequate rotation of conductors, as they all had engagements for seasons in provincial
cities or abroad. Depanis came forward with the suggestion that
a single man, Toscanini, should conduct all these concerts: prepare, orchestrate, and conduct more than forty concerts in four
months!

There were more than two hundred works on the programme,
which covered every kind of music, from symphony to operatic
overture, from concerto for violin and orchestra to sonata for
pianoforte solo, from cantata with chorus to quartet; a vast ensemble which was more like a concert-goer's encyclopedia. We
must not forget that Verdi was still a contemporary. Brahms had
died the year before. Still alive were Tchaikovsky, Dvorak,
Grieg, Rimsky-Korsakov, Massenet, Humperdinck, Goldmark,
Raff, and Sinding; pieces from whose works figured in the various
programmes. Of contemporary Italians, representatives were
Martucci, Sgambati, Bolzoni, and Sinigaglia. Besides Verdi and
Rossini (the first number on the programme of the first concert
was the Overture to *Forza del Destino* and the last item was the
William Tell Suite), Catalani, Ponchielli, Franchetti, and Manci-
nelli supplied operatic pieces.

But the novelty *par excellence*, the great event of the cycle, was
the *Pezzi Sacri* of Verdi ("*Stabat Mater*", "*Laudi alla Vergine*",
"*Te Deum*"), which had been played for the first time on April 8
of that year at the Paris Opera House. Toscanini, accompanied
by Depanis, visited Verdi at Genoa to clear up some points as
to the deciphering of certain passages. Verdi had heard of

Toscanini because Boito, who had been present at the performance of *Falstaff* in 1896, had sent him a letter praising the interpretation, and welcomed him with great cordiality. The *Pezzi Sacri* were played on three occasions: May 26, 28, and 30.

On June 21, 1897, Toscanini and Carla De Martini were married. She was the daughter of a man who had a foreign-exchange business and who died before Toscanini and Carla met. He had not been very successful and had left his widow only moderately provided for. Besides her younger sister, Ida, Carla had a brother who became a barrister and practised at Como, where he died in tragic circumstances. Ida was fair and had blue eyes, contrasting with Carla, who had dark brown hair and was short and plump. She had large, brown, velvety eyes and a flawless complexion; she had a cheerful temperament, and was vivacious, and had her fair share of the frank and physical realism inherent in the Lombard character. She had never studied music, but had an intuitive understanding of it and had a good ear.

It was a case of love at first sight—serious love, destined for marriage, unfashionable for a man of his age in that decade of elegant adulteries. There had been two previous abortive attempts at marriage, one with a respectable young lady of Bologna, whose philistine parents spurned him because he was a musician; the second with a not so respectable lady who exploited him ruthlessly, and was the only person known to us, throughout Toscanini's life, who was able to make him neglect his work.

Shortly afterwards, Polo fell in love with Ida, who reciprocated his feelings. Ida's mother was against the match. She could not stand another musician in the family! Nevertheless, with the connivance of Carla, the marriage eventually took place.

The wedding of Carla and Arturo cut across all the customs of the period—much to the distress of the relatives—and was like many modern weddings: no relations, no procession, and no banquet. To escape both families, Toscanini staged the wedding at Conegliano Veneto, 190 miles from Milan, where his friend and impresario, Piontelli, had a sumptuous villa. He was greeted

at the station by a gaping crowd and a municipal band. He therefore hurried through the ceremony and left immediately with his
wife—there is a family story that he was so enraged that he refused to eat for two days.

His wife was soon to realize what it meant to be the wife of a
dedicated musician. Two months before the wedding, Piontelli
had engaged him for a short season in Venice at the Rossini, the
main attraction of which was Puccini's *Bohème*. It proved to be a
hectic season because a rival impresario, Barilati, had taken the
Fenice and advertised another new *Bohème* composed by the
author of *Pagliacci*, Leoncavallo. There were polemics between
the House of Ricordi and the House of Sonzogno, each accusing
the other of unethical conduct. Thus, under the clear skies of a
Venetian spring, the city of canals, decked with banners and
crowded with visitors for the inauguration of the Exhibition of
International Art, was the site of a duel to the death of the two
Bohèmes. Leoncavallo's *Bohème* was not lacking in good music,
but the libretto was trivial and patchy (Leoncavallo whose
friends, paraphrasing Voltaire, claimed that he was neither lion
nor horse but donkey, was foolish enough to believe that he was
a poet). Toscanini's presentation of Puccini's *Bohème* was, as
usual, full of spirit and feeling. Puccini won.

In August, when the young couple had just returned from their
honeymoon, there was the battle of Bergamo. Celebrating the
centenary of Donizetti's birth, the Bergamots had organized a
programme around a gala season in the public theatre of the city.
The first performance was to be *La Favorita*, conducted by Toscanini, who arrived to find an extremely bad company, the reverse of what he had been promised. In spite of all his efforts, the
first opera, on the inaugural evening of August 23, was so poor
that he refused to conduct the second, *Lucia*; when the Bergamots arrived at the theatre they found posters informing them
that instead of Toscanini, who was indisposed, the conductor
was to be Eraclio Gerbella. The Bergamots were so enraged by
the absence of Toscanini and the poor quality of the performance
that they hurled at the stage everything they could lay their hands

on, including benches, which endangered the lives not only of
Lucia but of the whole breed of Lammermoors. The turmoil was
such that the garrison troops had to be called in to clear the
theatre.

The ill-fated season was cut short, and the centenary committee, obviously composed of nit-wits, attempted to regain lost
ground by a series of concerts, which were embellished by names
such as Joachim and Melba. Toscanini was also to conduct the
first concert.

Many of the music-lovers of Bergamo were disgusted with
Toscanini for not having conducted *Lucia*, and they soon lashed
themselves into such a state of indignation that they were ready
to accuse him of deliberate insult to Bergamo and to Donizetti.
To understand the passions engaged, it is necessary to know Bergamo, know the delicate colouring and the silence of the Citta
Alta: those narrow streets without alleys, lined by one great bare
doorway after another leading to patrician palaces and where,
even today, during many hours of the day, the streets are completely empty except for cats, lay-sisters muffled in their black
shawls, and an occasional priest. On the evening of the concert,
Toscanini had hardly set foot on the rostrum when shouts
thundered from the audience: "Down with Toscanini! We want
him out of Donizetti's theatre!" He turned and pointed his baton
at the shouting crowd in the pit and roared: "Buffoons!" And, as
usual, started walking towards the door. Mayor, committee, the
leading players in the orchestra, and the patronesses went after
him and pulled him back. In the end, he allowed himself to be
persuaded. In the meantime, the audience, ashamed of its bad
manners, applauded him vigorously. But Toscanini was in such
a state of irritation that he conducted with reluctance and without
any of his usual verve.

CHAPTER VIII

Opera

THE year of his marriage also marked the beginning of another life-long relationship for Toscanini: with the Scala Opera House in Milan.

In view of the cardinal importance of the Scala to Toscanini's career, we propose to give a few historical details. Up till 1815 the Opera House eked out a precarious existence solely on the proceeds of gambling. Its revenues were derived entirely from gambling-booths, set up in the bars. In 1815, when Milan became, once more, Austrian, the Scala was one of the first institutions to suffer from the puritanical rigours of Austrian law; gambling was immediately prohibited. The theatre was closed for two seasons, until the new Emperor, Francis II, granted a subsidy of 200,000 Lire a year. And so, until 1859, in which year Austrian rule came to an end, the Scala was maintained by the Emperor. The first kingdom of Italy was governed by Depretis, Sella, and similarly austere and niggardly men of the Right, who travelled second-class themselves to save a few Lire. So the Scala was again without a protector. Finally, the municipal authorities of Milan reluctantly agreed to finance the Opera House, and little by little parted with increasing sums, up to 240,000 Lire a year —a not inconsiderable sum for that period.

The solution was a paradoxical one, because the municipality received very little in return for its money, as the box-holders were the main beneficiaries. It should be explained that, when the theatre had been built, under Marie-Thérèse, the private citizens who had clubbed together to finance the building had allotted most of the shares to themselves; in fact, the land on which the theatre was built was the property in perpetuity of the owners of four main rows of boxes. The municipality in Milan, successor to the royal house of Austria, inherited the least profitable part: the portico, the vestibule, the corridors, the stalls, the stage and so on. The municipality profited by the receipts from the stalls, the fifth row of boxes and the galleries, but it was expressly specified that in return for these seats the municipality should bear the expenses of the performances. Thus, in actual fact, all the municipality gained was a large deficit.

At a certain juncture, the box-holders agreed to contribute a small annual sum; in 1900 it was calculated that each box, with a capacity of at least four people, contributed 20 Lire per performance, or exactly the price of a single stall. Meanwhile, the box-holders could re-sell their seats for whatever price they could get!

The rise of the Socialist movement in Italy made the situation even more complicated. The municipality was forced to provide social services which had been entirely lacking (previously there had been no sanitary or public health services, nor public assistance). All this cost money, and the municipality's income had not increased. The Socialist majority on the Municipal Council was not slow to point out the burden and injustice of spending 240,000 Lire a year on an Opera House to which the ordinary public had no access, but only a restricted class of the nobility, the gentry, and rising middle-class of shop-keepers. To save the situation, the mayor, Vigoni, proposed a compromise, reducing the contribution from 240,000 Lire to 180,000 Lire a year; and he cunningly reinforced his proposal by producing a letter from Verdi. But the mayor's motion was defeated, and the money was diverted to providing free meals for schoolchildren from needy families.

This decision, so disastrous for the Scala, was made in July 1898, and all the musical circles of Italy were in an uproar when it was learnt that the Scala would not open its doors for the 1898-9 season. Hundreds of suggestions and proposals were submitted and abandoned. There was a decisive meeting of eminent citizens

at the *Patriottica* club, which had its premises immediately opposite the Opera House. A pro-Scala committee was elected with
the object of opening a public subscription, of persuading the
box-holders to increase their contribution, and of inducing the
municipality to reconsider its decision and to grant at least a
small subsidy.

Finally, on December 26, 1898, the Scala reopened. It was a
gala night. Nowadays, when theatre-going dress is so informal,
it is perhaps difficult to recall the brilliance of a gala night at that
time. It was a period of stability dominated by the middle-aged
and the old. Young men were never seen at the Scala, which was
the microcosm of a society based on a semi-feudal aristocratic
tradition. The seating was a reflexion of the social hierarchy of
the moment. The second row of boxes was recognized as being
the best and was reserved for the old aristocratic families. The
first and third rows of boxes and the stalls were occupied by the
successful and therefore wealthy members of the *bourgeoisie*, the
pick of the industrialists and business men, and the stage-boxes
were filled by officers of the garrison and members of fashionable
clubs. The whole audience glittered, flashed, jingled, and rustled
with gold, jewels, silks, and sparkling eyes.

The new Scala was administered by a private company, the
"Limited Company for the Exploitation of the Scala Theatre",
with a capital of 300,000 Lire, which, as the negotiations with the
municipality and the shareholders had not been completed,
assumed complete responsibility for running the theatre for a
period of three years.

The company was dominated by two salient personalities:
Boito, and the president, Duke Guido Visconti di Modrone. The
latter was the undisputed head of Milanese society, by birth,
wealth, elegance, and ability. He had inherited a large fortune,
which he was steadily increasing. He was one of the first of the
great Milanese textile industrialists. He was an engaging mixture
of grand seigneur and modern business man, with simple and
modest manners. He was a splendid-looking, tall man, with a
long, immaculately-waving, white beard.

The Duke was the business man, and Boito the musical expert. He was at that time a power in the musical world: he had written the librettos for *Otello* and *Falstaff* and was known to be Verdi's friend and confidant. He was also the composer of *Mephistopheles*, one of the most popular of contemporary operas. Boito's reputation had been enormously enhanced by the fact that he had not taken advantage of the success of *Mephistopheles* by immediately following it up with another opera. He had, in fact, previously announced a successor, which was to be called *Nero*. Everybody was convinced that it was going to be his masterpiece. But the months and years slipped by, and *Nero* remained shut up in his head, and in the elegant salons of Milan all the countesses stared at that noble skull, wondering if they could see signs of its creative burden.

There was a third member of what was now called the directorial trio, Giulio Gatti-Casazza, who had been appointed the first "general manager" of the Scala, a precedent of importance for the future organization of opera in Italy. He was a man of no artistic gifts, solid and dull. But he had common sense, tact, opportunism, authority, and a certain flair.

Of the three, the Duke was completely ignorant of music, and Boito was the most competent, but sedulously avoided responsibility. Gatti-Casazza was a good organizer, the first of that type in Italy's opera houses. The trio might well have amounted to no more than a competent management, had there not fallen among them a stimulating and provocative reactor—Toscanini.

Boito's main function in relation to Verdi, who was too old to travel, was to go around and supervise the productions of the great old man's operas. In this capacity he had visited Turin in 1896 to see how Toscanini produced *Falstaff*. He was much impressed by the manner in which the young conductor had tackled an exceptionally difficult opera, and had written to Verdi to this effect. He had returned to Turin in 1898 for the *Pezzi Sacri*. Hence, when the problem rose of choosing a conductor for the Scala, Boito put forward Toscanini's name. It was also Boito who worked out the details of Toscanini's contract, and the final letter, engaging him, was signed jointly by the Duke and Boito.

Toscanini was careful when he came to the Scala to provide against any possible misunderstanding. Clauses in his contract specified that his independence and authority were guaranteed, and gave him powers wider than any other Italian conductor had ever enjoyed. He had the right not only to choose singers and instrumentalists, but also to settle the number of rehearsals, and to have some control over the scenery and stage sets, etc.

His authority was put to the test from the very beginning. It had been decided that *Norma*, by Bellini, was to be one of the operas performed. There was some difficulty in finding a suitable prima-donna. Toscanini finally chose Ines De Frate. The production was put in hand; auditions, rehearsals, fittings, scenery, posters were all complete by the middle of January. The date for the dress rehearsal was fixed. The stalls were filled for the occasion with privileged auditors. There were murmurs of approval when the curtain rose on the grove of the Druids. After the chorus, there was the great aria: "*Casta diva*". Everything seemed to be going well, as the scene between Adalgisa and Norma was reached and the ensuing vocal trio in which the three protagonists are suddenly confronted and pour out their passions in a cataract of sound. When the act was over, Toscanini stood motionless with his baton pointing downwards, pressed against his right leg; his left hand was nervously twisting his moustaches—one of his most characteristic gestures.

Duke Guido rose to his feet and approached him, circumspectly: "Maestro, is there something wrong?"

"Yes, the whole performance!"

"What, do you mean the production is wrong?"

"Not only that, nothing is right."

"Well, what is to be done?"

"I am sorry; there is only one thing to do—abandon the whole idea of *Norma*."

The usual interminable arguments followed, but Toscanini remained obdurate. The trouble, he explained, was radical: the prima-donna was unsuitable. De Frate was good enough in lyrical parts: but she had neither the personality nor the power to render Norma. Ricordi, the publisher, proposed a compromise: perform *Norma* and have it conducted by a substitute. Toscanini categorically turned down this suggestion, and *Norma* was struck off the programme. At the end of the season the members of the Council of Administration were still smarting under what they considered Toscanini's unwarrantable use of his dictatorial powers, and they proceeded to take action. They decided that the only way to put Toscanini in his place was to modify the contract. The other parties to the contract—the mayor Vigoni, Count Annoni, the president of the delegation of box-holders, and Duke Visconti di Modrone—proposed to modify, in front of a notary public, articles IX, XIII, XVI, XIX, XXIII of the contract. A further modification provided that "powers conceded to the conductor should be made subject to the consent of the Council of Administration of the Limited Company for the Exploitation of the Scala Theatre". Unfortunately, the Directors had not realized that they had to deal with that impossible kind of employee, a revolutionary. Revolutionaries pay no attention to notaries public; there are only two ways to deal with them: either let them do their worst, or burn them. Duke Guido, Count Annoni, and Mayor Vigoni were good men who would not have hurt a fly: so they let Toscanini go his own way, and the notarial act was never executed.

One of Toscanini's revolutionary innovations at the Scala was to continue to give effect to his notion that Wagner and Verdi, or rather Wagnerian and Italian opera, stood on the same level of musical and aesthetic importance. This seemed extraordinary in those days, when it was generally accepted that they stood at opposite poles and that the Wagnerian music-drama "of the future" was gradually superseding the Italian lyric opera.

So, during the 1898–9 season, Toscanini presented *The Mastersingers* and *Falstaff*; in 1899–1900, *Siegfried* and *Lohengrin* with *Otello*; in 1901–2, *Valkyrie* with *Messa da requiem* and *Trovatore*; in 1902–3 *Luisa Miller*, *Ballo in Maschera* and the third

act of *Parsifal.* (In the 1900–1 season Wagner alone was represented, by *Tristan.*)

Toscanini's second reform was closely connected with his first.
At that time Italian opera was rapidly losing ground not only in
Italy but all over the world; the intelligentsia had lost interest in it
and was flocking to Bayreuth. Toscanini realized the reason for
the decadence of practically all Italian opera, with the exception
of Verdi—and even he was too infrequently and inadequately
performed. First of all, the old Italian repertoire had to be critic-
ally revised; but what was more serious, the interpretation,
becoming more and more distorted and corrupt, had completely
altered the values of the operatic language and frame. The
virtuoso, tenor, soprano or baritone, held complete sway and
overthrew all balance. In consequence, the masterpieces of the
great composers, Rossini, Bellini and Donizetti, were being
completely ignored at the expense of the French and Italian
"moderns": Bizet, Meyerbeer, Gounod, Thomas, Massenet,
Saint-Saëns, or Puccini, Mascagni, Leoncavallo, Giordano,
Franchetti, Mancinelli. A good example of this neglect was that
when Toscanini produced, at the Scala during the 1901 season,
that delicious opera *L'Elisir d'amore,* it had not been performed
there for twenty-two years!

In those four seasons he revived the *Elisir, William Tell,
Linda, Trovatore, Ballo in Maschera,* and *Luisa Miller.* There
was a real battle over *Trovatore,* which had not appeared at the
Scala for over twenty years. When the rumour spread that Toscanini proposed to disinter that old mummy, it was greeted with
derisive laughter. He, the progressive Toscanini, the champion
of the Wagnerites, who had made such a success of *Tristan?*
Toscanini was determined to eradicate the prejudice against
Trovatore once and for all. The opera is a difficult one and is by
far the most austere of the great trilogy, which it forms with
Rigoletto and *Traviata.* But it is perhaps the most characteristic of
all Verdi's works. It can almost be called quadridimensional, as
the emotions of the characters are not closely linked to cause and
effect, but are simultaneous and superimposed. Towards the end,

G

Manrico's death, the identification of the Count, and the wild triumph of Azucena, take only sixteen bars: murder, exposure, and catastrophe in sixteen bars!

Verdi had poured into *Trovatore* all his violent plebeian credulity and his instinct for sublime trivialities. Hence, to produce it at the Scala in 1902 was a gesture of great audacity. All Toscanini's friends and supporters were convinced that he was making a mistake. In fact, it was a revelation and a triumph. This was a typical example of the manner in which Toscanini rejuvenated Italian opera.

At first, the unrivalled character of these performances was falsely attributed to the idea that Toscanini had somehow modified the original score, using some trick of musical cookery to bring it up to date. It is essential to emphasize again that the contrary is true. Toscanini's technique was always based on an exact and meticulous interpretation of the score. To this he brought his own incomparable rhythmic instinct: the composer's metronomic and tempo instructions were followed faithfully, but on these Toscanini built his own organic and elastic texture of living, breathing, rhythmic balance. This is what he meant by that "giving each note its own room". At first this scrupulous insistence on the rule of tempo was far from welcome in Italian opera houses. It offended all the singers who had come to regard the famous arias as their personal property; all the bellowing tenors; it offended the audiences who had become conditioned to that style of presentation, and the whole network of vested interests—agents, impresarios, teachers—who believed that their percentage commissions rose in exact ratio to the length of time that their pet singers could hold their high notes. And all this network was subordinate to a yet more powerful one, equally outraged—that of the music publishers.

It was inevitable from the beginning that the reformer Toscanini should encounter his excommunicator, Giulio Ricordi, who for twenty years was virtually dictator of the operatic world. He was an able and astute business man. As head of the House of Ricordi, he controlled the bulk of the Italian operatic heritage from Bellini to Ponchielli; through this control, from his dim and inaccessible office, he held a knife at the throat of every impresario in the world; and thence he had increased yet further the extraordinary power of Ricordi's. It became a sort of control point, through which anybody who wished to put on a season of opera had to pass. He had "backroom" power over programmes, casts, and conductors; but he did not allow it to be used solely for commercial advantage. His interior motive force was a passionate faith in the House of Ricordi, but it was complemented by an equal passion for music: by his profound and sincere adoration of Verdi, for example, or for Puccini.

He had, however, blind spots, and one of these was his inability to appreciate Wagner. This incomprehension may have been a rationalization of the emotion aroused in him and the House of Ricordi in 1870, when his then rival, Giovannina Lucca, brought Wagner to Italy for the first time, an event that threw Ricordi's into a formidable panic. When the two houses, Lucca and Ricordi, were amalgamated in 1887, the whole Lucca repertory, including Wagner, passed over to the House of Ricordi. Even then, when Wagner had become one of his own composers, he continued his tactics of opposition and sabotage. This was probably because he was only allowed to control the Italian rights in Wagner, not the world rights, as he did with other composers; and the Wagner family being as commercially rigid as it was, the probability is that he made little enough out of that.

It was not long before Toscanini found himself up against the formidable Signor Ricordi. A clash was inevitable. Ricordi's dislike of Toscanini was partly the latter's fault. Ricordi's hobby was composing—pompous and mediocre pieces. He composed under the pseudonym of J. Burgmein, and had once sent a composition for orchestra to Toscanini, hoping to have it performed during the Turin celebrations in 1898. It was an open secret who the real composer was; but Toscanini rejected the piece, and did not even reply, as his bad habit was. This could not be forgiven by the publisher, *faux bonhomme* as he essentially was.

The first open conflict was over the performance of *Falstaff*.

Ricordi criticized the performance and even went so far as to say that it was like a "mastodontic mechanical piano"! Boito, however, was able to reassure Verdi by letter that "this was a splendid *Falstaff*". From then onwards Ricordi waged a systematic campaign against Toscanini. When talking to his sycophants he referred to Toscanini as "our superman". As he also controlled the *Gazzetta Musicale* of Milan, he was able to ensure a continuous flow of articles criticizing Toscanini's interpretations, always unfavourably. He always attacked the same points: rigidity of execution, an outward and mathematical accuracy, the lack of that poetry essential to the Italian style.

Trovatore provided a magnificent opportunity for Ricordi to vent his spleen. Toscanini had decided to present it in the season following the death of Verdi, together with the *Requiem*. Ricordi, who controlled the performing rights, began by declaring that he would not allow *Trovatore* to be played at the Scala if Toscanini was conducting. Toscanini was, justifiably, indignant. If it had not been for the intervention of mutual friends and, in particular, of Boito, who dissuaded Ricordi, there would have been an open scandal. After the triumph of the first performance, Ricordi's opposition fizzled out, but the two were by no means reconciled until much later. At this period Giulio Ricordi's son, Tito, was beginning to take an active part in his father's business. Arguing with Toscanini one day, he said: "You two are an impossible pair of characters." To which Toscanini retorted: "Yes, but at least I keep to my own affairs, whereas your father makes a practice of interfering with everybody else's!" Eventually, when Ricordi began to see that Toscanini's interpretations, so far from ruining Italian opera, were helping greatly to establish the fame and fortune of his own new composers—especially Puccini—he became more friendly towards the conductor, and even, from time to time, began to praise him in the *Gazzetta Musicale*.

When somebody was once nostalgically recalling the "good old days" at the Scala, Toscanini answered, shaking his head: "Alas, all the happy memories of my life have been so short!" However, his first seasons at the Scala must have been among the least short of the happiest periods of his life. His musical career was established on a sound basis, in the greatest opera house in the world, at an age when his contemporaries were still nowhere; and he was happily married. In March, 1898, a son was born to him. He had thought of returning to Turin, but his engagement at the Scala invalidated this plan, and he remained with his family in Milan. At first they lived in the De Martini house in Via Speronari, and then in Via S. Vincenzino. They finally settled in via Principe Umberto. A few years later, in 1903, Enrico Polo, who had married Ida De Martini, moved to Milan to accept the chair of Professor of Violin at the Conservatoire, thus bringing the two families and the two sisters together again.

In the meantime a second child had been born, a girl. Toscanini had called the little boy Walter, in memory of his friend Catalani—Walter is the principal character in the *Lorelei*. He gave his daughter the name of another well-known figure in the works of Catalani, Wally. It was a striking example of his tenacious, almost sentimental, attachment to old friendships.

In 1901 Giuseppe Verdi died and Toscanini sincerely mourned him. Toscanini had seen Verdi on various occasions, but apart from a fleeting glimpse of him at Busseto when he was at college, his first meeting with him was in 1894, when he was conducting at the Genoa Politeama, with *Tannhäuser* and *Falstaff*. Piontelli took the company to pay their respects to the maestro, who was living at Genoa. Toscanini was overwhelmed at the prospect of meeting the august master, so that, on the very threshold, he ran away and had to be dragged into the house by his less sensitive companions. Toscanini's silence melted in the sunshine of Verdi's affable and cordial reception, and he plucked up enough courage to submit a slight difference of opinion between himself and Pini Corsi, on the style of rendering Ford's phrase: "*Quella crudel beltà—sempre è vissuta in grande fede di castità*"; Pini Corsi took it at a rapid and rhythmic tempo, and Toscanini felt that it should be slower and more accentuated. Toscanini's version was approved by Verdi as the correct one, in spite of Corsi's claims that Verdi himself had taught him *his* way. Verdi said, smiling, that when he had supervised a performance of *Don Carlos* in Paris in 1877, returning two months later he could not recognize a single one of his own instructions. The third meeting in 1898 with Depanis has already been described. During the first years at the Scala, Toscanini met Verdi several times, when the latter stayed at the Hotel Milano. Their last meeting was on January 21 or 22, 1901, when Toscanini was shocked to see Verdi looking so old and tired. He died on the 27th.

On February 1, Toscanini conducted a memorial concert at the Scala which was most impressive; on February 26, when the bodies of Verdi and Giuseppina Strepponi were transferred to the Casa di Riposo, founded by Verdi for old musicians, and where his tomb still is, Toscanini conducted a chorus of 900 voices: "*Va pensiero sull'ali dorate*".

In these years Toscanini made several journeys abroad. The first was, in 1899, a pilgrimage to Bayreuth, mainly to hear *Parsifal*, the performance of which was restricted to that theatre for many years by Wagner's express wish. In letters to his friends he made certain criticisms of the execution, but the opera made a tremendous impression on him. Gatti-Casazza accompanied him, and they found other Italian pilgrims at Bayreuth: the tenor Borgatti, who was to sing Siegfried at the Scala the following year; Perosi, Giordano and Campanini: the latter disliked *Parsifal* intensely, and found it incomprehensible. Through out his visit Toscanini argued and bickered with him.

In 1902 he went to Berlin, then to Eisenach to visit Bach's house. Previously he had been to Hamburg, where he had been invited by Raoul Gunsbourg, director of the Monte Carlo Theatre, to see his scenic adaptation of *The Damnation of Faust* by Berlioz, which Toscanini intended to produce the following season at the Scala. Gunsbourg, who, thanks to the proceeds of the Monte Carlo Casino, was able to afford magnificent productions, was arrogant and presumptuous and took unheard-of liberties with librettos and scores. In *The Damnation of Faust* which he seriously called "*mon édition*", he had cut, transposed and modified in such a shameless and purposeless manner that

Toscanini was infuriated. He buttonholed Gunsbourg after the performance and told him frankly that he considered his version an offence to Berlioz. Back in Milan, Toscanini asked Sonzogno to procure the original score and produced the opera in its authentic entirety.

The Toscanini family took their holidays with the Polos. In 1898 they had been to Ceresole Reale in the Piedmontese Alps. This was the beginning of Toscanini's passion for mountain-climbing, an activity to which he returned each year until 1925, when he spent several holidays on the lakes. In 1902, after a short stay in the Dolomites at Tai di Cadore, the family moved to Salò, on the Lake of Garda; in 1905 to Pré-St.-Didier in the Piedmontese Alps. Toscanini's climbing companion that year was a young man of nineteen, son of his wife's cousin. The latter recalls their crossing of Mont-Blanc, when they had with them the two famous Balmaz brothers as guides and stayed on the mountain for two days.

During the succeeding years the Toscaninis gradually abandoned the mountains for the sea, largely for the sake of the children. Levanto and Viareggio were two of their favourite resorts. Nevertheless, Toscaninis' love of mountains remained with him and he associated them with the highest manifestations of poetry and music. In his own words: "As I stand on my rostrum about to conduct Beethoven, I feel as if I were at the feet of an immense mountain, preparing to climb it."

CHAPTER IX

Back to the Scala

In 1901 the three-year trial period of the Scala came to an end. As the municipality had made a further reduction in its contribution, bringing it down to 60,000 Lire per annum, Duke Guido Visconti had organized a new company of a somewhat different nature to run the Scala for the following season. He had grown tired of putting his hand in his own pocket (for the 1898–9 season alone he had made a personal contribution of 78,000 Lire—about £8,500), so he called on some of the big names in the industrial aristocracy, which was flourishing at that time. He formed a new council, which was largely composed of cotton magnates, such as Turati and Ponti, and also included the Erbas, the founders of the pharmaceutical firm which bears their name. The reorganized Scala management had successfully concluded the 1901–2 season and was starting the second season when Duke Guido died on November 15, 1902.

His four sons—Uberto, Jean, Giuseppe, and Guido—stepped forward as one man to take over their father's responsibility in the Scala, and all joined the Council. The Visconti stood firmly behind the Scala, but it should be emphasized that Toscanini had now become by far the greatest asset of the company.

His reputation had been earned by hard work and exceptional qualities, and was in no way due to lack of competition. There were a number of first-class conductors in Italy at this time; among whom Giuseppe Martucci was perhaps the most eminent. There was also Mancinelli, a valiant musician, who had composed symphonies which deserve to endure (Toscanini has often

played his *Scene Veneziane* and the *Fuga degli amanti a Chioggia*
at the N.B.C. in recent years); Mancinelli had made his name as a
conductor in South America, had conducted in London for many
years, and also at the Metropolitan from 1907 to 1911. There was
Leopoldo Mugnone, one of the old school of exuberant and fiery
conductors. He was Neapolitan, violently eccentric, and would
never talk anything but the Neapolitan dialect, even when he was
conducting. There were Mascheroni and Vanzo, Vigna and Vitale.
They were all excellent musicians: but could not compare with
Toscanini, because they lacked his unifying concept of style, his
uncanny capacity for synthesis. None of them became a legend as
Toscanini did. Toscanini was the first conductor to give the
Italian musical public the feeling that they could rely, in all his
performances of every different kind of music, on an absolutely
unwavering standard of excellence in performance.

His "legend", however, did not of course spring mainly, or
even chiefly, from his talent. As is the way of fame in the world,
it fastened on all sorts of irrelevant anecdotes and features of the
kind that appeal to public curiosity. The first aspect of his personality that became really famous was his incredible musical
memory.

A photographic musical memory is not a unique phenomenon:
in 1887 there was the famous case of Pezzoni, a horn-player at the
Scala, who transcribed from memory the whole score of *Otello* to
enable it to be "pirated" at Buenos Aires, in spite of Ricordi's
withholding permission. However, before Toscanini there was
only one conductor, von Bulow, who had made a practice of conducting without the score; and though this habit represented the
least remarkable aspect of Toscanini's prodigious memory, it was
the thing that caught the popular imagination. Toscanini always
conducted from memory, and from his earliest days never found
any difficulty in doing so.

Many anecdotes are told to prove the infallibility of his memory, such as: Toscanini stopping an orchestra in the middle of a
rehearsal and saying: "Gentlemen, *da capo*; eleven beats before
number forty-four," or: Toscanini at the first dress rehearsal of

Columbus, is approached by Frigerio, the stage-manager, who, in a great state of agitation, reports that he has been testing the bells and that a certain note is missing. Toscanini, after an instant of reflection: "Don't worry, Frigerio, that particular note is not played in *Columbus*." (This anecdote was repeated later about a bassoon player. Ventura rushes up to Toscanini and tells him that the key of his bass F sharp is broken. This time the reply is: "But there's no bass F sharp in your part tonight!") Or: Toscanini stops in the middle of a terrific crescendo and points his baton at one of the middle-desk violinists, Mazza from Parma, and says in dialect: "Tighten your third string a bit." And poor Mazza says: "Damn it, you can't get away with anything." There was also the occasion when he rebuked a player for not playing a note sharp. The player shows him his part in which the note is not written in as a sharp. Toscanini sends for the score and demonstrates that the note is, in fact, scored as a sharp.

There are also many anecdotes about his irritability and outspokenness—a quality which always appeals to the public, as it seems to bespeak those rare qualities, frankness and courage. Taubman recalls the occasion when a committee of instrumentalists was appointed by the orchestra to protest against an epithet, even more offensive than usual, which Toscanini had flung at them, and they addressed their protest to the director, Gatti-Casazza. "But," asked Gatti-Casazza at one point, "you must tell me what he actually said?" The committee were palpably embarrassed. One of them plucked up enough courage to murmur: "He called us castrated eunuchs!" "Oh, gentlemen," answered Gatti-Casazza, smiling indulgently, "if you could only hear what he calls me."

We have already spoken of his hatred of applause and his reluctance to come forward and take curtain calls. After a time his audiences accepted these idiosyncrasies, even expected them and loved him for them, though of course the cynics hated his "innovations"; Toscanini was one of the first to have the doors of the auditorium closed at the beginning of an act, so that late-comers had to wait until the end before entering. This was not at all to the taste of the men about town, compelled to rush excellent dinners in order to be at the Scala on time. Equally resentful were fair occupants of the stalls, obliged to leave the feathered hats in the cloakroom.

Toscanini's relationship with the four sons of Duke Guido was not quite so satisfactory as it had been with their father, who had been a fanatical supporter of Toscanini, had not minded his defects and had known how to handle him. The four sons formed an attractive enough group, with their fine elegance, their aquiline Visconti noses, their large eyes and distinguished moustaches. Uberto and Jean, the two eldest, had both been cavalry officers in crack regiments, and were cosmopolitan and large-minded business men. Giuseppe was perhaps the most original and versatile; he had married an Erba and started a scent business of his own; he painted, wrote, and was always *au courant* with the latest tastes and tendencies. He adored the theatre, and used to act in plays which he put on in his own house. Guido, the youngest of the four, was the only one who had any knowledge of music, having studied at Milan, and at Bologna with Martucci, and become something of a composer and conductor.

Uberto inherited the chief post as President of the Scala; and his idea was that it should become a centre of that fashionable world which he himself admired, the aristocratic *mondaine* world of elegance and wealth, and social prestige. Holding this aim, it was inevitable that he should come into conflict with Toscanini, who always maintains that he is a "man of the people". He has always kept, even after he had become a wealthy man, a tenacious streak of popular psychology, an innate diffidence and hostility towards "society", and particularly towards the type of aristocrat who clings to tradition and title.[1] Duke Uberto, with his cavalry moustache and his enamelled smile, his aristocratic height and his slightly patronizing air, was exactly the type to get on Toscanini's nerves; and the maestro, with his touchiness, his fanaticism, his somewhat plebeian speech, and his intolerance of

[1] Later, opposing the marriage of his daughter Wally to Castelbares, his final argument was always: "Besides, the man's a count!"

upper-class convention, was equally certain to irritate the Duke. There were continual skirmishes between them, until Toscanini left the Scala in 1903.

This story has never been properly told. It is well known how, on the evening of March 11, 1903, during a performance of *Ballo in Maschera*, Toscanini, annoyed by the insistence of the audience in demanding an encore from Zenatello, suddenly, with one of his characteristic gestures, stepped down from the rostrum and disappeared. It is also known that he left Genoa the following day for Buenos Aires. Actually, the incident was merely the culminating point of a long series of misunderstandings and conflicts.

Toscanini's original contract with the Scala covered the period 1898–1901. When this period was over, Toscanini expected Duke Guido to discuss the details of a further contract with him. But the Duke carefully avoided mentioning the subject. It seemed to be taken for granted that he would conduct throughout the following season, and he was asked to choose the operas for the programme. Toscanini did so, and went off for a season he had been engaged for at Buenos Aires. When he came back, everything continued as before, including his salary. At the end of the winter season 1901–2 the same thing happened: embraces, fulsome compliments, presentation of a commemorative medallion, but no mention of a contract. Toscanini by this time was embittered but said nothing.

At the end of 1902 preparations were being made for the coming season. Toscanini supervised them as usual. Still no mention of a contract. This time Toscanini boiled over; he went to Gatti-Casazza and spoke to him, roughly as follows: "These gentlemen of the Council seem to consider me as a sort of conductor in perpetuity at the Scala. It is most flattering for me to feel that I have become a permanent part of this noble theatre, like the statues and chandeliers; unfortunately, I have a family, a growing family. My salary in 1898 was 12,000 Lire. My contract lapsed two years ago; I go on conducting as before, but no one seems to have the remotest intention of mentioning an increase in my salary. During this period I have seen fabulous increases in salaries granted to

others. Emma Carelli, for instance, who owes her career entirely
to me, has been raised from 12,000 Lire to 36,000 per annum. Do
you consider that fair? It upsets me to have to take the initiative
in this matter; I think that you will admit that I have been more
than patient. In your capacity as director, you will mention the
matter to these gentlemen and ask them to consider my case."
(12,000 Lire was approximately equivalent to £1,300.)

Gatti-Casazza asked him to name a figure. "As they have
raised the Carelli from 12,000 Lire to 36,000, would it be indis-
creet if I asked to be raised to 20,000?" A few days later Gatti-
Casazza told Toscanini that he had spoken to the Duke, but nothing happened. Days, weeks, a month passed by and still not a
word. Then the Duke died. Soon afterwards Uberto summoned
Toscanini and had a long talk with him. They talked about
everything under the sun except the contract. Finally, Toscanini
one evening ran into the third Visconti son, Giuseppe, who was
familiarly called Zizi. Zizi smiled, slapped him on the shoulder
and said: "Well, maestro, that little matter, you know; let's make
it 18,000. . . ." Toscanini turned his back on him.

Toscanini accepted the engagement for the summer season at
the Opera House of Buenos Aires, and he was due to embark at
Genoa on May 12. He asked to be excused from conducting the
last performance of *Ballo in Maschera* on the evening of the 11th.
But everybody insisted on his continuing to conduct. *Ballo in
Maschera*, with Zenatello, had been one of the most successful
operas of the season, and had been a special personal triumph for
the tenor. The applause for him was so frequent and prolonged
that Toscanini began to believe it was part of a manifestation
directed against himself. On this last evening—the famous evening of May 11—the public started applauding immoderately after
the barcarolle in the first act. A little later in the act the tenor
sings the aria "*E scherzo od è follia*", one of the most charming and
capricious pages in Verdi's music. This was followed by such frantic applause for Zenatello, and with such prolonged cries for encore,
that Toscanini, irritated by these continual interruptions and dis-
tractions from the course of the opera, refused to give an encore.

The audience booed and protested so furiously that Toscanini left
the theatre there and then, and went straight home. His wife,
astonished to see him back so soon, asked him: "Is it finished
already?" "Yes, for me it is finished!"

This time Toscanini stayed away from the Scala for three years.
He was being paid 10,000 Lire—in gold—per month for the season of three months in Buenos Aires (1902), which meant that he
received in one month practically the same sum that the Scala paid
him for the whole five months of its season. And so, for the first
time, he was able to save some money. Toscanini said he put
aside 10,000 Lire; but his statements about money have never
been reliable; it never interested him. His wife said that the sum
was much larger.

In the following year, 1904, he returned for a further season at
Buenos Aires. The intervening periods were spent in Italy. In
that same year he also conducted an important season at the
Comunale in Bologna, culminating in *Siegfried* with Borgatti. He
conducted a few concerts in Rome, and while he did not return to
Milan, he did give a performance at Lugo! This was a little city
in the Romagna, with not more than 10,000 inhabitants. Why
did Toscanini, who was now recognized as one of the leading
conductors in the world, go to Lugo? Toscanini was friendly
with a modest double-bass player, a certain Murari, a native of
Lugo. Murari said to him one day: "Why don't you come and do
Aida at Lugo?"

"Why not?" answered Toscanini. The theatre was minute,
with a mediocre orchestra, to say the least of it. Nevertheless,
the performance of *Aida* was magnificent, because Toscanini
had brought with him a group of first-class singers, who had
accepted a modest engagement at Lugo, simply to sing under
the maestro.

The following winter, just after the New Year, the Toscanini
family moved to Rome for some months. They took an apartment in Via Sicilia. Toscanini wanted to prepare a series of
concerts at the Accademia di Santa Cecilia, and took the opportunity of taking his family to visit churches, museums, ruins, and

art treasures of the capital, with his usual conscientiousness. He lived a quiet and retired life in Rome and fought shy of the official musical life which was dominated by Count San Martino, whom he disliked, preferring the company in musical circles of his friends, Ippolito Valletta and Nicola D'Atri, who were both prominent critics. It was really a period of study, and one in which to make a closer acquaintance with his children, especially Giorgino, the youngest, who was by way of being his favourite. He also made one visit of exploration to Sicily.

During that time he was reading and analysing a vast amount of the music of contemporary composers. It was then that his first knowledge and admiration of Debussy began; in a letter to a friend he mentions his particular liking for *Pelléas et Mélisande*. He also seems to have been impressed by the *Sinfonia Domestica* of Strauss, which he considered a formidable composition from the technical point of view, but of debatable artistic value. He defines Strauss as a "secessionist full of ability", which explains why, to the horror of the musical conservatives, he became one of the first conductors in Italy to introduce Strauss to a wide public. He also wrote to his old friend Polo to say that he had "devoured" Mahler's Fourth Symphony, but his curiosity and excitement had faded away into regretful hilarity by the end of the work. His final opinion of the Mahler was a poor one: "So good-bye to any idea of doing it at Turin"—for he was also in the process of preparing a programme of concerts with Depanis for Turin. "Where is one to turn?" he asked; and said he would anxiously wait for Tchaikovsky's Fifth Symphony, another in D by Dvořák, and Elgar's Variations.

Thus Depanis reappears on the scene. The news that Toscanini had left the Scala raised hopes that he would come back to Turin. Depanis finally succeeded in arranging for Toscanini to conduct the carnival season of 1906 at the Regio. On the evening of December 26, 1905, after an absence of seven years, Toscanini stepped on to his old rostrum and conducted *Siegfried*. The season included *Madam Butterfly*, *The Damnation of Faust*, *Lorelei*, and *Siberia*. Depanis organized a tour to follow immediately after the end of the opera season. This started in Turin with three concerts, in which Toscanini for the first time played Debussy's *Nuages* and *Prélude à l'Après-midi d'un Faune*. Then they went to Milan (Teatro Lirico), Parma, Bologna, Trieste, Venice, Brescia, Como, and back to the Lirico in Milan.

This was the first of Toscanini's grand orchestral tours. It is perhaps appropriate at this point to recall that Toscanini in these years had been rebuilding the concert repertory as assiduously as he had that of opera: carefully blending the best of the old with the best of the new. His activity in the concert world during this time, in which we have mainly followed his operatic career, had been intense. In his earlier programmes—the Scala season of 1900, for instance—there are still to be found many pieces selected from opera, display pieces chosen for their virtuoso effect; for instance, the prelude to the last act of Ponchielli's *Marion Delorme*, which is respectable as well as spectacular, but rather trite when set alongside Wagner or Beethoven. There are also single movements from quartets, played with the strings doubled up; the *Saltarello* from Grieg, or the *Andante* from Tchaikovsky Op. 11. He even presented in a symphonic programme, which included the Third Symphony of Brahms and *Leonora* No. 3, a vocal selection, the duet from the second act of *Tristan* sung by Arkel and Grani.

Later these heterogeneous elements disappear from his concert programmes. They become simpler and more selective, with a solid nucleus of symphonies—chiefly Beethoven, Haydn, Mozart, and increasingly Brahms—with Wagner as dramatic relief. Occasional excursions were made into the field of the best modern composition. It was the origin of a style of programme-building which he kept all his life and which is suggested in a letter of 1905: "I am hesitating in the choice of the symphony for my first concert, between Beethoven's Third or Sixth, or the E flat of Mozart. These would lighten a programme of which the first half will be the Overture to *The Bartered Bride*, *The Swan of Tuonela*, *Tyl Eulenspiegel*, and the *Siegfried Idyll*. I should be sorry not to do either *Eroica* or the *Pastoral*."

A notable date in his career was April 18, 1902, when he conducted Beethoven's Ninth Symphony for the first time in Milan.

After a further season in Buenos Aires, where his favourite son, Giorgino, died of diphtheria—a terrible blow to him who, already on the train leaving Milan, had felt a sudden impulse to leave the child behind—Toscanini returned to the Scala in 1906. In the same year his father, Claudio, died at the age of seventy-three.

The Scala was in need of Toscanini far more than Toscanini needed the Scala. After Toscanini's departure, Visconti di Modrone and Gatti-Casazza had engaged Cleofonte Campanini, who was a great admirer of Toscanini. A strange fatality, however, seemed to dog the footsteps of the conductors who were asked to succeed Toscanini. The orchestra had not taken to Campanini. There was increasing dissension, culminating in the whole orchestra walking out on Campanini during a rehearsal of *Fra Diavolo*, after which he resigned, and left Milan and Italy. Further, the management had become disorganized. There was a disastrous loss of efficiency, department no longer co-operated with department, nepotism and favouritism were rampant. Discipline was relaxed to a dangerous extent. The Scala became more like an elegant club than a theatre. Duke Uberto and his top-hatted friends lounged and gave gay parties in the management's office, which was then on the *entresol*, just above the present box-office.

It cannot be denied that Duke Uberto was an interesting figure; although he was furiously attacked as a conceited trickster, he in fact controlled the operatic scene in Milan for fifteen years. He may have been imprudent with money, but he certainly had that essential gift of the impresario, a talent for showmanship. Old Duke Guido, with his modesty and his old-fashioned correctness, never achieved the popularity that attended the handsome, but somewhat bounderish, figure of his son. Uberto was a member of the new generation, a generation which knew the value of publicity.

Now, the theatre, a natural shrine for beauty, not seldom

H

accompanied by promiscuity, has always had an obvious attraction for gentlemen of fashion. In those days at the Scala, the ballet, and particularly its female stars, was without doubt the chief interest of the immaculate and wealthy friends of Duke Uberto. It was the consequence of this influential interest—a custom dictated by the whims of Cupid, rather than by theatrical art—that performances of opera would invariably be followed by a full-length ballet. It seems astonishing to us that after a full *Mastersingers*, for instance, there should be staged a long ballet, but in 1899 that opera was in fact always succeeded by the ballet *Carillon*; and, of course, opera composers were always expected to provide a chance for the management to show off its ballerinas. Even Verdi had to do it, in *Aida* and *Otello*.

Toscanini therefore returned to the Scala with mingled feelings of relief and apprehension. Although he had earned a great deal of money and his reputation stood higher than ever, he still felt more at home at the Scala than anywhere else. He had, however, always felt an intense dislike of ballet, and this innate feeling had been reinforced in the intervening years. There were many battles in which Toscanini attempted, not always successfully, to have the ballet scenes cut out of his favourite operas. He was adamant in refusing to couple what he called "serious opera" with ballet. As far back as 1887 at the Scala, when the impresario Piontelli had insisted on coupling a ballet, *Michele Strogoff*, with the first performance of *Otello*, Toscanini, 'cellist in the orchestra, had felt this to be such an insult to the venerable Verdi that he persuaded all the younger members of the orchestra to play out of tune when they came to the ballet. They were all duly fined, and so was he.

In those days, to oppose the ballet was to raise a hornet's nest, and no other conductor or impresario would have dared to attempt it. Dancers were considered to be an indispensable part of the social framework, and every faithful subscriber to the Scala had his favourite star, to whom he sent flowers on gala evenings. Nevertheless, Toscanini fought on, and in the season of 1900–1 he finally succeeded in getting the ballet excluded on Wagner evenings, in spite of the lamenting protests of Duke Guido, Gatti-Casazza, the accountant Cazzaniga, and of course, all the ballerinas' furious "fans".

It was therefore with horror that Toscanini returned, after his three years' absence, to find that the ballet had assumed an even greater importance than before at the Scala. Ballerinas and ballerinas' mothers and protectors strolled about the theatre as if they owned it. They even walked about the stalls and stage during rehearsals; and it was this that gave rise to the first stormy scene between Toscanini and Duke Uberto and his followers.

An idea of the atmosphere in the theatre at this period can be gained from the occasion when Toscanini arrived, with his usual punctuality, to find chorus ready, tenor ready, but no prima-donna. He waited for a few minutes, then ran to her dressing-room and burst in without knocking. There he duly found her, reclining on her couch, with Duke Uberto in close attendance. Without a glance at the Duke, Toscanini ordered, "Signora, the orchestra and your colleagues are waiting; kindly come at once."

As might be expected, however, the greatest trouble blew up over an occasion in which some dancers were involved. One evening, during the performance, Toscanini heard loud whispers and giggles coming from the wings. When the act was over he had inquiries made as to who had been talking and laughing during the performance. It appeared that it was a group of ballet-girls, and Toscanini insisted on having them heavily fined. Two days later it occurred to him to find out whether the fine had been collected; and he was told that the Duke had personally intervened, had cancelled the fines, and had also gone to the length of altering the regulations, to the effect that, in future, ballerinas would be exempt from paying fines. The same evening Toscanini put up an order signed in his own handwriting, forbidding the entry of Duke Uberto into the theatre during rehearsals. An employee, a conductor, was throwing out the President of the Scala! All Milan was in an uproar!

In spite of these alarums and excursions, the 1907 and 1908 seasons were memorable ones, both for reforms and for performances.

Toscanini's first reform was to make the refusal of encores official. On the opening night of the season notices were put up in the foyer to say that the management had decided, for reasons of order and artistic continuity, to instruct the conductor not to grant any encores. So the long controversy was finally settled.

His next reform was to alter the position of the orchestra. Verdi, as far back as 1871, had been the first to complain about the orchestra's instruments blocking the view of the audience, with the double-basses "forming a sort of hedge". Wagner, as we know, wanted the orchestra to be entirely invisible. The management, at Toscanini's insistence, appointed a committee, with an engineer, Cesare Albertini, at its head, and sent representatives to Germany to investigate the question of lowering the orchestra. The committee, on which Toscanini, Boito and Puccini also sat, decided to have the position of the orchestra lowered. Boito's was the only dissenting voice, and so as a compromise the excavation was limited to three feet. The innovation was tried out for the first time at a performance of *Lohengrin* and was greeted with universal approval, except by Giulio Ricordi, for whom it was an excellent opportunity for writing another sneering article about Toscanini, accusing him of apeing Bayreuth.

Another innovation was the substitution of a curtain which opened sideways instead of the old-fashioned drop which was lowered from above. On this occasion also Boito was violently opposed to the idea. In support of his argument he invoked a scenic effect used in *Mephistopheles*, in the finale. He pointed out that when the curtain was lowered, at a certain point it concealed the whole of the chorus at the back of the stage and brought into relief, in the foreground, the figures of Elena and Mephistopheles. He claimed that a curtain lowered from the side towards the centre would ruin this effect. Toscanini ironically asked about the old drop-curtain coming down to conceal the principal figures, first their heads and then their trunks, and so on to their feet.

Some of the more memorable operas conducted by Toscanini in this period were *Gioconda*, which had not been performed at the Scala for eighteen years, and *Aida*, in which Zenatello sang

Rhadames, and which even wrung praise from Ricordi. The culminating event at the end of the first season, however, was the introduction of three new foreign operas: *Pelléas et Mélisande*, *Louise* and *Salome*.

There is a curious story about the production of *Salome*. When Richard Strauss, the great new success of that glorious first decade of the twentieth century, announced that he had completed his second opera, *Salome*, immense curiosity was aroused all over the world. Toscanini was determined to be the first to produce it in Italy, at the Scala, and approached the publisher, Fürstner, only to be told that Turin had stolen a march on him and that the *première* had been reserved for the Regio. Toscanini would not acknowledge defeat, and travelled immediately to Berlin with his wife and Enrico Polo, who spoke fluent German, to intercede with Strauss in person.

Strauss was living at Potsdam. They made an appointment for the next morning. They arrived at the house and Polo rang the bell. At the sound of the bell, Toscanini changed colour and the same chaplinesque scene occurred as the one on Verdi's doorstep twelve years before. Toscanini turned tail and ran away. His wife ran after him. The maid opened the door and showed Polo into Strauss's room. When told that Toscanini was too shy to come in and see him, Strauss said, "Too shy to see *me*? Oh, my God! Well, we will go and see *him*." They found Toscanini further down the street, arguing with his wife. Polo later supposed that the maestro had been overcome with sudden embarrassment at being unable to speak German.

Strauss confessed that he, personally, would have wished nothing better than to have the first performance of *Salome* in Italy conducted by the illustrious Toscanini, but he did not see how he could get round the Turin contract, which had been signed and the deposit paid. Toscanini suggested a compromise with two simultaneous first performances to be produced, one at Milan and one at Turin. Strauss did not think that Turin would agree to this.

The following evening Toscanini, Strauss, Polo and Fürstner

met for dinner. At first there seemed to be no solution to the problem, but after long discussion Strauss turned to Toscanini with a smile and said: "Perhaps we can find a way. . . . Suppose the Scala were disposed to pay a big sum of money, then, what do you say, Fürstner?" Toscanini leapt to his feet, pale with indignation, and cried, "Then your sacred respect for your word is all a question of money. . . . No, no, if that's the way it is, I am not interested!" And he stalked out of the room.

The next day he left Berlin, but was still revolving the problem in his mind. He finally arrived at a typical Toscaninian compromise. The Scala made another contract with Fürstner stipulating that the Scala should have the exclusive rights for the second performance. *Salome* was performed in Turin on December 23. Toscanini announced the dress rehearsal of his *Salome* for December 22, and invited so many guests to this dress rehearsal that the theatre was filled, and the performance became a virtual première. There is no law against a management having an invited audience for a dress rehearsal! And so Toscanini had the last laugh.

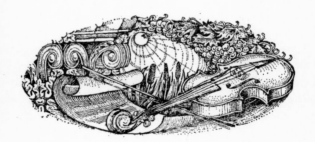

CHAPTER X

The Battle of Broadway

During the 1907–8 season the amazing news spread about that Toscanini and Gatti-Casazza were going to America. Two years before, in 1906, Heinrich Conried, director-general of the Metropolitan, had offered Toscanini a contract, which the latter had refused. This was largely due to Toscanini's disinclination to put himself in Conried's hands. Conried was a likeable and picturesque character, but presumptuous and dictatorial. In 1907, however, his health deteriorated, and it became obvious that he was no longer fit to work. During the summer the president of the Committee, Otto N. Kahn, was in Paris and made inquiries with a view to appointing a successor. Count San Martino suggested Gatti-Casazza.

Gatti-Casazza's behaviour throughout the duration of the negotiations was a model of prudence and good sense. He was fully aware of the fact that he was incapable of running a theatre of major importance by himself; the Metropolitan less than any other, as he was completely ignorant of the English language. He proceeded therefore to imitate the crab, who is wise enough to realize that his belly is his weak point and procures an actinia for protection. The actinia was at hand: Toscanini, who was not happy at the Scala. The Metropolitan had already made an attempt to sign him up. If he were to succeed in persuading the Metropolitan to renew the offer, and Toscanini to accept it, he would be in an impregnable position. This, in fact, is what he succeeded in doing. As he confessed later, in his autobiography, when he started his negotiations with Kahn in the following July, he made his own agreement absolutely conditional upon the offer to Toscanini being renewed; he had, of course, in the meantime made sure of Toscanini's consent.

In January 1908 the secretary of the Metropolitan, Cottenet, came to Milan and the two contracts were signed together—for three years, with a mutual option for renewal year by year.

This decision of Toscanini's and Gatti-Casazza's, which was officially announced in February, was severely criticized in Italian musical circles. This was largely due to the fact that the Italians, in general, thought of America as a land of machines, businessmen, cowboys and gangsters, quite incapable of appreciating any artistic manifestation, in marked contrast to the refinement and culture of their own country. Toscanini's decision was regarded as an avaricious betrayal, and Ricordi attacked him for his "acute dollaritis".

His last season at the Scala was to be a sad one, with one misunderstanding after another, which accentuated the ill-feeling of the audiences, due to their vexation at his approaching departure. To begin with, there was the performance of *Louise*, which Toscanini had insisted on including in the programme and which fell flat. Then there was the even more lamentable disaster over *Pelléas et Mélisande*, which was greeted with violent hostility, so much so that most of the audience left the theatre immediately after the performance without clapping, while only a small group of fanatical fans stayed to applaud. Toscanini, contrary to his usual custom, immediately joined the artistes on the stage, and himself applauded the opera and the composer.

This was followed by a deplorable, long-drawn-out and embittered quarrel centred on an unsuccessful composer called Gaetano Coronaro, who had been professor of composition at the Milan Conservatory of Music. He came from Vicenza and was an excellent teacher but a mediocre composer. Toscanini had rejected several of his compositions, as he did not think them worthy of serious attention. When Coronaro died, one of the Visconti sons, Guido, who had been a pupil of Coronaro's, tried to persuade Toscanini to conduct one of his works, as a friendly gesture to his old teacher, at one of the annual concerts which he was in the habit of conducting for the Society for Symphonic Concerts. When Toscanini refused, insisting that music not good enough to be played in a man's life was no better after his death, Guido Visconti di Modrone called a meeting of the Council and persuaded them to approve a motion that Ettore Panizza should conduct the last two concerts of the season instead of Toscanini. Panizza, who was a young man, first accepted, then became scared and did his best to refuse the honour, but Visconti insisted. Toscanini went to the length of suing the Society for Symphonic Concerts. The case went to court, and ended in a compromise. Feelings remained bitter on both sides. Toscanini must have felt that his best course was to spend some time on the far side of the Atlantic.

The New York of 1908 was very different from the New York of today. The principal sky-scrapers did not yet exist. There were only a few lines on the subway, the first of which had been inaugurated in 1904. There was no elevated railway, no Queensborough or Manhattan Bridge, no Madison Square Garden, no Rockefeller Center, and no Rock'n Roll. . . .

Toscanini stayed at the Astor, right in the centre of New York, on Broadway at 45th Street, not far from the Metropolitan. At this period the Metropolitan Opera House could almost be called a German stronghold. It is a well-known fact that the Germans played a predominant part in the musical education of America; there had been a consistent flow, throughout several generations, of musical pioneers, singers, instrumentalists, conductors, and organizers, from Germany. It was perhaps no coincidence that two of these pilgrims came from Hamburg, the most musical city in Germany and the birthplace of some of the first liners that made their way to the New World: Schlesinger, who was one of the foremost experts on Beethoven, and Timm. There was also Anton Reiff from Mainz, who became vice-president early in the history of the Metropolitan and who was the first of a long line of German vice-presidents. There was Scharfenberg, a pupil of

Hummel. Of the more eminent conductors, there was Eisfeld, and the genial Karl Bergmann, who in 1866, a few months after the first performance of *Tristan and Isolde* at Munich, gave a selection from the opera in New York.

The man who was primarily responsible for establishing the German musical hierarchy in New York was Anton Seidl, a Hungarian by birth, brought up in Germany; he came to America with credentials from no less a person than Wagner himself. He conducted for the Philharmonic Orchestra, but, as soon as the Metropolitan opened its doors in 1885, he was engaged as the first conductor. As Wagner was then at the height of his immediately posthumous fame, and Seidl was his prophet, the Wagnerian repertory was early established at the Metropolitan. In 1886 Seidl conducted *Tristan and Isolde* at the Metropolitan— before it was ever performed in Paris, and two years before its first presentation in Italy.

In the same years Leopold Damrosch, who had arrived from Germany in 1871 to direct one of the large German choral societies of New York, founded what became the reigning dynasty of German music in America. He created the Oratorio Society and the New York Symphony, which for many years was the great competitor to the Philharmonic Orchestra. He was a man of extraordinary musical ability, as were his two sons: Walter, who conducted at the Metropolitan and presented a memorable season of Wagnerian opera in German there in 1895, and Frank. It was Leopold Damrosch who was responsible for bringing Tchaikovsky to New York in 1891 for the inaugural festival of Carnegie Hall—in those days the whole range of new European music, from Italian to Russian, came to the U.S.A. (Tchaikovsky left many of his scores to Leopold Damrosch, and they finally found their way into the library of the N.B.C.) The whole organization of the musical life of New York was in fact in the hands of Germans, and the public had learnt to prefer German composers, German music and opera. As late as 1911, when Pulitzer died and left $900,000 to the Philharmonic, the will expressly provided that a part of this legacy was to be devoted to the performance and playing of three specified composers: Beethoven, Wagner, and Liszt. And of course it should not be forgotten that those were the days of Germany's greatest power and influence throughout the world, when sixty-five million Germans (save a few hot-heads) worshipped Kaiser Wilhelm II as if he had been sent by God to give them sovereignty of the world.

Therefore, when Toscanini and Gatti-Casazza hastened to make their first visit to the Metropolitan, they were rather like two Italian Daniels walking into the lions' den. Conried was no longer there, but André Dippel was still acting as general administrative director. All Toscanini's predecessors had been German: Mottl had not been able to get on in the Metropolitan; but there were still Hertz and Gustav Mahler, with his great reputation as a composer and his scrupulous artistic taste. Germans were everywhere. Löffler designed the sets and scenery, there was a German ballet-master, a German administrator, even the head of the claque was a German, Scholl! And the organization was administered on the rigid bureaucratic German model, with directors, vice-directors, secretaries, vice-secretaries, assistants, inspectors. As Toscanini has since recounted, when a German director wanted a chair moved on the stage, everything stopped. He called a conscientious gentleman, who immediately referred it to another conscientious gentleman, and this one to a third, and so on. When Toscanini wanted something moved, "Without stopping conducting, I would make a sign to Romei, and one minute later the chair would disappear, or the table, or the wall, or even the vast Mme. Destinn herself."

Toscanini soon discovered that there was a state of growing chaos behind the decorous façade. Every individual in the organization was primarily concerned with his own position and his own interests. The place was a hotbed of intrigue, and everybody interfered with the organization and put in a word for somebody else; the influential shareholders interfered, and so did the box-holders of the famous "diamond horseshoe", which was the exclusive preserve, theoretically, of the old Knickerbocker families. The stars used to send their agents to dictate their whims about rehearsals, castings or any other matter they pleased.

There was a complete lack of discipline; flagrantly among the singers, who took unheard-of liberties, and who were Toscanini's first target. He adopted his usual technique, and took responsibility for the whole vast organization on to his own shoulders. He had protected himself to a certain extent at the time of signing his contract, which specified that he was to conduct the Wagner operas, and specifically mentioned *Tristan and Isolde*, *The Mastersingers*, and *The Twilight of the Gods*. This fact must be mentioned in connection with his conflict with Mahler. Conried, in 1907, when he had failed to secure Toscanini, had signed up Mahler, who had become prominent through his magnificent work at the Vienna Opera. He took up his post at the Metropolitan in December 1907, and one of his first productions had been his favourite opera, *Tristan and Isolde*. When Mahler heard that Toscanini had asked to conduct *Tristan*, he wrote to Dippel requesting that he, Mahler, should be given an exclusive right of conducting *Tristan and Isolde* at the Metropolitan. Mahler's widow, in her biography of her husband, claims to have seen all the telegrams exchanged between Dippel and Toscanini on this matter, telegrams in which the maestro, she says, was lacking both in respect towards and understanding of his colleague. Toscanini denied this. He said that if he asked to be allowed to conduct *Tristan*, it was only because of the insistence of Gatti-Casazza, who considered it essential; if he had really believed (and this was Dippel's fault) that Mahler was seriously upset by the idea, he would have conducted another opera. There was never any warmth of affection between Mahler and Toscanini, who were temperamental and musical opposites.

Mahler left the Metropolitan in 1909 to go over to the Philharmonic, and his departure was the first breach in the German wall. It was not that Mahler in person represented a threat to Toscanini's position. Mahler was incapable of conducting an intrigue, as is clearly proved by his failure whenever he attempted to take up the cudgels on behalf of his own prestige. This was the case in Vienna, where he was defeated by a ballet-master, and at the Philharmonic, where he was completely outmanœuvred by a violinist, a certain Jonas, whom he had appointed inspector of the orchestra and who was responsible for alienating Mrs. Sheldon and all the members of her committee of matrons. But at that time his reputation was at its zenith, and the fact that a man of his prestige had to give way to the Italians proved that a real change in policy was taking place at the Metropolitan. The second was the departure of Dippel, who had lorded it over Gatti-Casazza, and who was transferred by the Council to the Metropolitan in Chicago in 1910. These events, and a willingness to adopt radical changes in Metropolitan policy, were largely due to the effect of the Hammerstein business upon Kahn and the two executives, William K. Vanderbilt and F. Gray Grisvold, who, with him, were responsible for policy. Hammerstein, who was a cigar magnate, had a passion for opera and had founded the Manhattan Opera Company, taken a theatre, and produced an excellent repertory of the best modern French and Italian opera. The success of this new venture was so great, and so much to the taste of the public, that it made Kahn and his colleagues realize that they needed new blood and would be wise to follow the advice of Toscanini.

As usual, with the monotonous inevitability which characterized him, Toscanini, installed at the Metropolitan, was promptly concerned with one thing only: quality. Back-stage manœuvres have no value in the theatre; it is only the quality of the performance which counts. Toscanini, from the very beginning, spared no effort to arrive at his objective. As it was then constituted, the Metropolitan was a gigantic machine. On certain occasions as many as twelve or even fourteen performances were given in six days. The principal male singers, who were the darlings of the public, were under constant pressure. Caruso actually managed to sing on forty evenings in a single season (at $4,000 per evening); De Luca pushed this figure up to forty-four. It was this intensive and crushing burden of labour which had brought about the bureaucratization of the theatre, not only to facilitate the distribution of labour but also as a form of individual precaution, to prevent individuals being worked to death. For this reason all the other conductors appointed assistants and aids, to whom they entrusted the preparation of various parts of the performance, contenting themselves with combining them in the final phase.

To everybody's consternation, Toscanini showed from the very first day that he was firmly determined to work himself to death. He took everything on his own shoulders. He began with endless probing, a restless hunt for the slightest imperfection, tireless supervision of every detail, irritating ubiquity—which meant that he was always on the spot, at all hours of the day. He was adamant about rehearsals; if he said that there were to be so many rehearsals, he meant what he said and would not let the number be reduced by a single one; this was the exact opposite of what had been happening at the Metropolitan: management and conductors had always come to an agreement, in the end, in order to spare expense.

The list of singers at the Metropolitan at this time was formidable. For Italian opera there were Caruso, Bonci, Scotti, Amato, Campanari; and the women, Sembrich, Farrar, Gadski, Eames, Destinn, Frances Alda, and Louise Homer. For German opera there were Burrian, Knote, Burgstaller, Goritz, van Rooy, Blass, and Waterous. These singers had got into the habit of doing exactly what they liked, for they considered themselves to be the centre of attraction. They interfered with everything, including the casting, and even the choice of the operas. Toscanini immediately made it clear that while he was in charge, everybody would have to mind his own business. For some time there was constant friction and perpetual quarrels between stage and podium. This is shown by the manifesto signed by a group of singers at the Metropolitan in favour of Dippel, at the time of his dismissal. The most important members of the cast of the theatre addressed a letter to the Council deploring, not only Dippel's transfer to Chicago, but also the fact that he was not given a three-years' contract like Toscanini and Gatti-Casazza. This letter was signed not only by Farrar, Sembrich, Eames, and Scotti, but even by

Caruso, who was the most courteous, well-balanced, and intelligent of colleagues and who, later, was to become one of Toscanini's most devoted collaborators.

There were also differences, perhaps even greater ones, with the orchestra. Toscanini had to bring his treatment to bear on the players as soon as they started rehearsing *The Twilight of the Gods*—which he had not chosen by chance, one can be sure. Most of the instrumentalists were Germans; they had been accustomed to German conductors and "Wagnerian" interpretations. The whole conception of Wagnerian music might be called "titanic", and the word could be applied with even greater force to German post-Wagnerian music, such as that of Strauss and his followers, von den Stucken, von Hausegger, Burmeister. Mahler's First Symphony was actually called *The Titan*. It was inevitable that the traditional interpretation should also be oriented along these lines. Hence, the German conductors concentrated exclusively on bringing out the sonorous masses of sound; amplifying the verticalism to the maximum on the one hand, and, on the other, fusing and doing away with the episode in the identity of an overflowing whole; one way of expressing the Wagnerian "*Weltanschauung*", a process of perpetually dissolving the unit in the infinite, the infinite in the identical.

Toscanini's interpretation of Wagner was based on an entirely different kind of appreciation. He was aware of the grandiose structure, the cyclic architecture of the music, but to him this was only the framework for the marvellous multiplicity of melodic patterns; it was the richness of the detail which appealed to him: Siegfried's forest might seem gigantic from a distance, but every branch, every leaf, was full of murmuring voices. In this orchestral forest Toscanini brought out the indescribable beauty of the sounds: soft, velvety, a texture of magical tones and harmonies. The warp of orchestral richness and the woof of flowing melody was not, for Toscanini, incidental to Wagner's creation, but rather the full substance of Wagnerian expression, through which the Wagnerian world became articulate and came to life. This was an entirely new interpretation of Wagner, analytical, sensitive, vibrant, but constituting a magnificent and logical whole. It required all Toscanini's indomitable will-power and passion to weld the orchestra into the matchless *ensemble* it eventually became.

In the seven years which Toscanini spent at the Metropolitan he conducted eighty-five different operas (including different "revivals" of the same opera). (This is not to speak of non-operatic pieces, such as the Verdi *Requiem*, complemented by the Prologue to *Mephistopheles*, played during his first 1908 season, and Beethoven's Ninth Symphony, played in 1913.) The fact that only thirteen of these eighty-five operas were German is the best indication of the revolution in Metropolitan policy which Toscanini was able to bring about. Of the remainder, fifty-nine were Italian, ten French, and three Russian. Of the fifty-nine Italian operas, forty were by contemporary composers—an extraordinary proportion for the Metropolitan, and even for the Scala.

He was, as usual, faithful to Verdi, with a decided preference for his later operas. Ponchielli was represented by *Gioconda*, which was such a triumph that it was repeated for three successive seasons. Of the contemporary composers, Puccini was given the lion's share: *Butterfly*, *Tosca*, *Manon*, *Bohème*, hardly a programme without one of them, *Tosca* for five seasons, *Madam Butterfly* for seven consecutive seasons! *The Girl of the Golden West* was given its world *première* at the Metropolitan, as was *Madame Sans-Gêne* by Giordano. Toscanini's old friend, Catalani, was not forgotten and at last had a posthumous success with *Wally*. Franchetti's *Germania*, Mascagni's *Cavalleria Rusticana*, the *Amore Medico* and *Le Donne Curiose* by Wolf-Ferrari, who was just becoming well known, and the *Amore dei Tre Re* by Montemezzi, were all given. The latter opera, a flat failure in Italy, had an extraordinary success at the Metropolitan and found continuing favour in America.

From 1900 to 1914 was the period of efflorescence of the new Italian opera, which started in 1890 with *Wally*, *Cavalleria Rusticana*, and *Bohème*. It could not actually be called a "school", as it

At Milan, with his daughter Wanda Horowitz

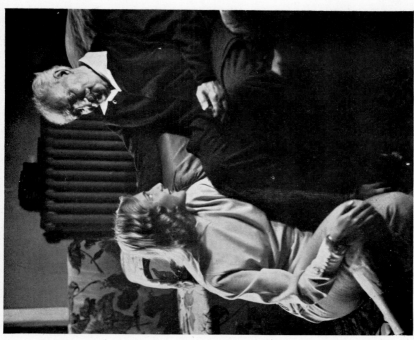

With his granddaughter Emanuela, 1956

With his granddaughter Sonia, 1942

possessed no specific aesthetic principles nor its own system of harmony, nor any definite dramaturgy. It was an empirical and composite generation of musicians, insatiable borrowers from other composers; above all, they adopted the Verdian realism (*Otello*), and perhaps borrowed even more from the French school of realism, which was more amiable and accommodating, and thus more congenial to these men, who had grown up in the easy-going atmosphere of the world of the Umbertos; first of all from the immortal *Carmen*, then from Gounod and from Thomas. It borrowed little or nothing from Wagner, except certain features of orchestral sonorousness and timbre, and those prudent thematic limitations which were also to be found in Bizet's work.

It was the Italian drawing-room ballad which had an immense, though not obvious, influence on these young operatic composers; it was the period when such ballads sung by Denza, or by the celebrated Tosti, sent drawing-room audiences into raptures all over the world. We must be careful not to underestimate the value of this contribution. The writers of these ballads, who passed into oblivion later on, had the merit of infusing inspiration and life into the popular Italian song. It is of no importance that they watered them down and "bourgeoisified" them, because there is no doubt that with them the popular Italian songs, especially the Neapolitan and Tuscan songs, became enhanced with a style and some degree of culture; on the other hand, ballads and serenades of Piedigrotta are responsible for the cadences and inflections of the drawing-room ballads.

In this way an essence of popular singing was transferred, naturally, to melodrama or opera, which was ready to absorb it. It was Eugenio Gara who, in his book on Caruso, showing how much the singing technique of Caruso had in common with the spirit of *bourgeois* realism, stressed the hidden affiliation between the style of the Neapolitan street tenor and the Italian opera of that period. The influence of this lyrical fashion is reflected in the very structure of the new melodrama, which only appeared to abandon the "set piece", and affected to have the dramatic continuity of action which any composer after Wagner would

I

be ashamed not to adopt; while in fact action is neglected, and the emphasis is on one thing only: the ballad, the great solo set piece. It was Giordano who once enunciated the absurd precept, half seriously, half in fun: "Find a good song, and then make an opera around it." Even the old operas had their ballads; the aria and the cavatina can, from a formal point of view, be considered ballads and nothing else. But if we take a "ballad" from Verdi, for example, we will find it animated by a very different spirit. In Verdi the soliloquy is always, exclusively, a function of the drama. Like the monody of the ancient Greek tragedy, it is not a parenthesis in the action, but actually a part of the action; it is a kind of scene represented inside the characters, in which they debate their problems, adjust the internal situation or their passions before proceeding to the next action. It is, therefore, always inseparable from the characters, almost incomprehensible without them.

The ballad, on the other hand, has now become an intermediary accessory. In the theatre it is put into the mouth of a specific character: but in fact it stands by itself, an aria for the sake of having an aria.

In any case, what is certain is that this contact with the living fountains of popular song caused the young composers of the period to break out into a warm and copious vein of song. The vein was caressing, sentimental, exclusively amorous, somewhat emphatic in apostrophe, a trifle lachrymose in its abandon, but sincere, spontaneous, cordial, and from time to time resulting in really beautiful melodies. The chords it prefers to touch are those of affection and nostalgia. In fact, the musicians who used it most successfully (Catalani, Puccini, Cilea) are fundamentally elegiac, "Bellinians"; it is not by accident that Bellini himself is the nineteenth-century composer who was closest to the popular song, from which he derived some of his finest inflections. It was easy and "catchy" music, which impinged at once on the ear, and therefore became popular. In those years during which it flourished—from the beginning of the century to the war of 1914—new operas were announced by coloured posters, just as films are advertised today. The day after the first performance, the ballads were being sung everywhere, in abbreviated or selected forms, whistled by boys, strummed by street orchestras. It was the swan song of melodrama. Ever since, it has plunged into the difficult and tortuous path of prosodic and tonal research, retreating farther and farther from the popular vein.

It is true that these composers had other faults. Their exceptional capacity for producing fascinating melodies was not complemented by any degree of synthetic imagination. They lacked coherence. Their plots were usually copied from others. They were always feverishly searching for a subject into which they could fit their melodies. A case in point was that of Pacchierotti, who had put to music a libretto of Fontana. Owing to some misunderstanding, this libretto proved to have already been sold and put to music by someone else. As he did not want to waste the score, which had been finished and completely orchestrated, Pacchierotti approached another librettist. The latter wrote an entirely different text and adapted it to the music so expertly that the composer did not need to change a single note. The final result was execrable. The composers flitted from popular drama like *Cavalleria* to historical drama like *Chénier* or *Columbus*, from an eighteenth-century environment like *Manon* or *Adriana* to an exotic environment like *Iris* or *Madam Butterfly*, from the folklore of *Wally* and *Amico Fritz* to the fable of *Oceana* or *Turandot*. Even for Puccini, who knew what he wanted far better than the rest of them, the search for librettos was a recurring calvary, as a perusal of his letters demonstrates. It is this paucity of invention that was chiefly responsible for the total submersion of most of the output of those years.

Toscanini did more than any other conductor to make the reputations of these musicians of his own time. It was he who had conducted the first performance of *I Pagliacci*, Franchetti's *Columbus*, Mascagni's *Iris*, Cilea's *Gloria*, and Mancinelli's *Hero and Leander*. He sponsored them, he dedicated himself entirely to their success, hiding any inner doubts he felt about their quality. Perfectionist that he has always been he cannot have failed to notice their inner weakness, the absence of a real moral and dramatic complex. But they were his colleagues, the composers of his own generation, and he faithfully did his duty to them, spreading the knowledge of their works outside Italy, and getting the best of them performed on the international stage. That seems to me to be the central purpose of this stage of his career—the seven years at the Metropolitan, and the season at the Châtelet in Paris: where he even had the temerity to present Puccini's *Manon* for the first time to a French audience, and risk the comparison with Massenet's *Manon*.

Another important feature of these years was Toscanini's meeting with Caruso. Caruso might have been created especially at that moment to be the voice for the new type of Italian opera, particularly for Puccini. Spontaneous, airy, natural as rippling velvet; and just at this time developing an extraordinary quality in the lower register, reflecting the melancholy sweetness of the baritone; it was the perfect instrument for expressing what was human and true in Puccinian melody. He sang Rudolph, Des Grieux, Cavaradossi, and in the vibration of those tender and persuasive notes—notes redolent of the sun, rocks, the sea— there was something more: the distant echo of a lost world, the forgotten plaint of an ancient people. And when soaring, soaring, that voice reached its summit, that celestial B which seemed like a star in the sky, what audience could resist him?

CHAPTER XI

The Drum Major

THE outbreak of war in 1914 was a shattering blow to the musical world, even in America, which seemed at that time so remote from Europe. Curiously enough, Toscanini had started his own war against the German Empire seven years earlier, at the Metropolitan. In the same way, much later—in 1935, 1936, and 1937, when illustrious democratic statesmen were still kow-towing to the dictators, and English and American reporters were photographing the villa of Claretta and Goering with all his medals—we shall find Toscanini at Salzburg and Tel Aviv, waging war on his own account against Hitler and Mussolini. That is the way he was made.

At the outbreak of war, Toscanini was on holiday with his family at Viareggio. Even in this holiday resort, the conflict of opinion which was convulsing Italy was as lively as elsewhere.

From the first cannon shot there was a serious split in Italian public opinion. On the surface, judging from certain important factors in Italian life, it was to be expected that Italy should be Germanophil. The Church was Austrophil, because of its historical connections with the Hapsburg monarchy. The Court was Germanophil and was largely responsible for the Triple Alliance. The commercial world was Germanophil, not only because of the miraculous industrial achievements of the Germans, which had fired the imaginations of their Italian counterparts, but also because the banking and commercial interests in the two countries had become increasingly close and intertwined. Further, by a curious coincidence, the parties of the left were strongly influenced by German thought, because Germany, the birthplace of Marx and Engels, had the highest mass standard of culture and wages, with its gigantic trades unions, which were a model for the Socialists in other countries.

All these factors should, logically, have inclined the Italians to sympathize with Germany. On the other hand, they had always found it difficult to get along with the French. There had been a rift for many years, for a number of seemingly contradictory reasons; the French seizure of Tunis had caused much resentment and bitterness, as had the hostile attitude of France during the war in Libya. There had been a long series of insults and humiliations, which had occasionally alienated even faithful democrats. Still, immediately France was invaded, most of Italian opinion rallied to her side, and needless to say Toscanini was unequivocally with it. Every evening he waited eagerly for news of the Battle of the Marne. The pro-German party was equally vocal, and unfortunately Puccini was one of them. His house was at Torre del Lago, but he frequently came to Viareggio to visit his daughter-in-law, Fosca Leonardi, in Via Colombo. The Puccini and Toscanini families practically lived together: besides the parents, there were the three Toscanini children (Wanda was the third), Puccini's son Antonio, and the three Leonardi children.

Puccini, in ordinary life, was a man of the greatest charm. He was a simple man, always cheerful, kind, and naturally courteous. He was full of zest and curiosity and had a fund of common sense, as well as a highly developed sense of humour. His hobby was sport and practical science, and he was interested in the technique of everything, from the latest type of motor down to the most modern rubber boots. He was equally fond of good food— and hence he gained much popularity at Viareggio! On the other hand there was a strong element of the solid burgher in his character, and he prided himself on being a good money-getter. It was probably this element in his character which attracted him to the Germanophil party. Further, there was an element of *pique*, because his *Manon* had been severely criticized in Paris; Lalo, for example, had written that "it was not music"! In Germany his operas were universally admired and were constantly performed.

Toscanini and Puccini had always been close friends. There was, however, a basic divergence of character between them. Puccini was fundamentally material, jovial, and easy-going; Toscanini fundamentally saturnine and perfectionist. It was inevitable that they should disagree on the question of the war, for they disagreed over almost all questions of men and things. At one stage it seemed as though nothing could prevent a permanent estrangement. Puccini, depressed by the news from his publisher, Ricordi, of falling receipts, exclaimed that, as far as he was concerned, the Germans could not capture Paris too soon. When this came to Toscanini's ears, he shut himself up in his house, preferring not to go out because—he said—if he had met Puccini he would have slapped his face. He would only emerge to take an evening walk on his terrace; when his friends would talk to him from the street, begging him to forgive Puccini: which he eventually did.

At the beginning of the winter of 1915, Toscanini left Italy to return to the Metropolitan. He carried the sadness and anger of the war with him, however, and the inevitable daily pinpricks at the Metropolitan irritated him more than ever.

For some time there had been increasing differences of opinion between Toscanini and Gatti-Casazza, who, once firmly installed, started playing "house politics" in order to consolidate his position. He was careful not to say or do anything which might possibly offend Kahn, the president, or the other members of the Council. As part of his policy, Gatti-Casazza started a campaign of petty economies, which infuriated Toscanini. A typical instance occurred in Chicago on the first occasion that Toscanini took the Metropolitan Company to that city. The opera was *Aida*. In the second act, when the band comes on to the stage with the triumphal march, Toscanini found the performance unsatisfactory, and quite different from when he had rehearsed it in New York. After the performance, Toscanini questioned the band-leader, who explained that Gatti-Casazza, for the sake of economy, had refused to send the band from New York, and had instructed the leader to find players as best he could in Chicago. The result, of course, was a violent row, and an ultimatum to get the proper band before the next performance. Gatti-Casazza on his side found Toscanini increasingly difficult to deal with, and quite impossible to convince that the theatre had to pay its way, and that therefore all the best, and most expensive, singers in the world could not be engaged for every performance.

When Toscanini left the Metropolitan he was no longer on friendly terms with Gatti-Casazza. In fact, they did not see each other again for many years. A long time later, Giovanola, finding himself beside Gatti-Casazza at a dinner, said to him, speaking of Toscanini: "I understand he is a very nervous man." Gatti-Casazza almost bounded from his chair and retorted: "Him a man? He is an hysterical female!" They were eventually reconciled through Gatti-Casazza's second wife, Rosina Galli. At that time Toscanini was conducting the Philharmonic. Rosina Galli at the end of a concert went round to congratulate Toscanini, and told him that Gatti-Casazza was ill in bed. Why did he not go to see the invalid, she asked, and cheer him up? So Toscanini went to visit his old friend.

It can be seen that there were many causes to produce the state of mind that impelled Toscanini to his decision to leave the Metropolitan. He had a long discussion with Kahn, who would not believe that even Toscanini would be independent enough to give up such a lucrative and important post—he had been receiving $42,000 a season. Toscanini was, as usual, adamant, and left the Met. without a backward glance. It has often been said that he hated the Metropolitan. The story is told of a conversation he once had with Fiorello LaGuardia, in which the talk turned to theatres and fires, and Toscanini said with a laugh, "Well, if anybody sets fire to the Metropolitan, call me and I will come and stoke the fire!"

It should be explained that Toscanini had kept as much in touch with Italy as possible throughout his Metropolitan period.

In 1909 he had conducted in Milan the first popular concert organized by the professors and students of the Milan Conservatory. In 1910, in Rome, he had performed the *Messa da Requiem* at the Costanzi. In 1912, in a cycle of concerts at the Teatro del Popolo, he had conducted one concert entirely dedicated to Beethoven, and one to Wagner. In 1913, which was the centenary of the birth of Verdi, the Scala had organized a great Verdi season and Toscanini came back to conduct the *Requiem* and *Falstaff*. In the same season Mugnone conducted *Nabucco*. Just before this he organized a short commemorative season in the little theatre of Verdi's home town, Busseto, and threw himself into the arranging of it with characteristic enthusiasm. From Milan he brought Albertini, who had carried out the changes at the Scala in 1907, to alter the stage and lower the orchestra. He brought Alessandro Borioli from Turin to handle the management. Even the audience was specially selected, and all Toscanini's friends, musicians and critics from Milan, Turin, Bologna, and Rome, sat beside farmers and peasants from the surrounding country, many of them old friends of Verdi himself.

This small theatre seated only 600 people. Toscanini played *Falstaff* and *Traviata* with an orchestra of forty professors of music, and *Falstaff* was particularly successful. Toscanini was so pleased with it that he repeated it at Busseto in 1926, and never forgot it. Many years later he remarked to some friends: "Before I die, I want to conduct *Falstaff* once more at Busseto."

In 1911 Toscanini had bought a house in Milan in Via Durini, a fine seventeenth-century mansion, with a spacious courtyard. In 1915, when Toscanini returned to Milan, it was, he thought, for good, and for the first time the family would be able to settle down at home. Unfortunately, it was war-time. Toscanini's son, Walter, had joined up as a volunteer; the maestro had never done any military service himself, but he was determined to do something, and he decided that the best service he could render was to raise money. He therefore proceeded to conduct charity concerts all over Italy; one of the first was for unemployed musicians, whom he assembled to give a grand popular concert at the Arena, with war songs, the chorus of *Attila*, and some Beethoven. The concert, which attracted 40,000 people, ended with a spectacular chorus of the whole audience, lit by improvised torches made out of newspaper.

His greatest success in that year was the season of opera which he organized from September 18 to November 28, 1915, at the Teatro Dal Verme, which brought in the fabulous sum, for those times, of 369,000 Lire. Toscanini engaged all the best singers of the period, from Storchio to Stracciari, from Farneti to Caruso. The latter was unusually depressed, because of the attacks of the *Matin*, which had accused him of being pro-German, and he wanted to leave after the first evening because the audience, he thought, had not applauded him with their usual enthusiasm and had shown their awareness that, in the prologue to *Pagliacci*, he had been out of tune.

The enthusiasm was indescribable. I remember that *Traviata* as if it were yesterday. There will never be another Violetta to sing with such unutterable perfection, moving, laughing, loving, suffering, as the slight and gentle Rosina Storchio; poor, dear woman; her enormous, seductive eyes, her delightful coquetry, her gay tenderness, her fresh spontaneity: a skylark.

His next contribution to the war was more direct. He had already conducted several concerts for the soldiers in the war-zone, but on August 13, 1916, he actually sounded the attack and acted as what might be called the drum-major. He did not usually get on well with generals, who, he said, reminded him of singers; but he was friendly with General Antonio Cascino, commander of the 8th Division, who was to take the famous Monte Santo, one of the most hotly contested hills of the war. Toscanini promised that as soon as the General had occupied the summit, he would come up and conduct hymns for his soldiers. He kept his promise. The mountain was still under gun-fire when Toscanini arrived in civilian clothes, with a cyclist's cap on his head, and took up the baton. (General Cascino was later killed, on that very hill.) Toscanini was also at the front at the time of the grand offensive in 1917, when the Austro-German Army poured over the Isonzo and occupied half of the Veneto, up to the Piave. At this time an orchestra had been formed in the 2nd Army, which held the front of the middle Isonzo, and Toscanini had been asked to train and conduct it. During the offensive the High Command completely forgot about the orchestra, and Toscanini went on with rehearsals while everybody else was in retreat. Toscanini considered himself under military orders and refused to move without a regular order to fall back. He let the players go only when Austrian shells actually began to fall on the village where they were rehearsing. Toscanini went back to Milan, an exhausted man, and when he arrived after an endless night of train and sorrow, for the first and only time his family saw him crumple, untidy and unshaven.

Throughout the war Toscanini continued to include Wagner, Beethoven, and the other German composers in his programme, in spite of the inevitable stupid protests. This caused another of his celebrated collisions with the audience, in 1916 in Rome, when he included in the programme the *Siegfried Idyll* and the funeral march from *The Twilight of the Gods*. Leaflets which had been especially written for the purpose were showered down on him by the chauvinists, who wanted all German music banned for the duration of the war. Toscanini stopped the music, and made one of his fulminating exits.

The anxious and terrible years of the war were not without compensations for Toscanini. His friendship with the painter, Vittore Grubicy, was one of them. Painting had always fascinated him. He often said: "I do not know which I like best, painting or music." In Turin he had been friendly with many artists, and in particular with Bistolfi, and used to visit him for many years in his house near Moncalieri. It was Bistolfi who sculptured the bas-reliefs for the tomb of his son, Giorgino. It was also Bistolfi who advised the Concert Society to pay Toscanini for a concert by giving him a picture by Fontanesi, *Il Navalestro di S. Mauro sul Po*, which is one of the jewels of his private gallery.

Vittore Grubicy more than anybody else was his guide in the field of painting. In a world which is famous for its eccentric characters, Grubicy was perhaps the most eccentric of all painters.

He had originally been a critic and picture-dealer, but had never tried his hand at painting. On a business visit to Holland he had gone to see his friend, the painter Mauve. The painter's wife told him that her husband was having a nervous breakdown, and had gone to a little village in the country, and would see nobody. When Grubicy came to the village, the painter was so furiously indignant, that Grubicy, to calm him, said that he had only come to paint his portrait. Mauve did not believe him, but said that he would leave him for two days with his own box of colours and then come back to see whether he was lying or not. To his own surprise, Grubicy was able to paint an extremely good picture. Grubicy was a *pointilliste*. His name is still unappreciated, if not unknown, but he was, in his way, a great painter of an entirely original and sensitively developed style. Most of his paintings were delicate landscapes painted on very small canvases.

One of his idiosyncrasies was to paint over the same canvas innumerable times, year after year. Another was a great disinclination ever to sell his pictures. On the rare occasions when he consented to sell one he always, later, made frantic attempts to buy it back. Toscanini had to use a cunning ruse to acquire his first Grubicy painting, a landscape under snow, exhibited in Florence. Toscanini fell in love with the picture and wrote to a mutual friend, the painter Benvenuto Benvenuti, to ask his advice. The latter eventually thought up the stratagem of writing to Grubicy that a famous female coloured singer, for whom he invented a fabulous name, a star in Egypt and America, had fallen in love with his picture and wanted to buy it. Even Grubicy was attracted by this unusual proposition. The trouble began when Grubicy, regretting the sale as usual, wrote to Benvenuti and proposed to buy the picture back. Benvenuti and Toscanini were reduced to sending an imploring telegram in French from the imaginary singer and sending her so-called secretary, a young acquaintance well instructed in his role, to fetch the picture. The joke was found out later, when Grubicy discovered the hidden picture at Toscanini's house.

Toscanini's appreciation of Grubicy's painting was deep and

sincere. It was also closely connected with his musical sensibility, as emerges from the following extracts from a letter written to Grubicy in 1913: "I spend many hours of the day in the most delightful corner of my house, delightful, thanks to you, for it contains so much of the best part of you. It is my favourite way of detaching myself from the material reality of life, seated in front of your exquisite song 'October Mist', to live in the thought, in the ecstasy of the thought, which animates it. What wonderful music it arouses in my imagination. Faint, elusive music, but so warmly harmonious! I hear it, not with my ears, but with my soul. How blessed are you, dear Vittore, to have been able to express your supreme spirit in such song!" The extraordinary affinity between these two men, is shown by a note written by Grubicy in 1910: "To me, the colours and shapes of a scene represent musical values, now simple melodic waves, now harmonic chords, rich in polyphony, but with every note distinguishable." The curious, and ironic, thing about this relationship was that Grubicy was completely deaf; while Toscanini had the finest ear in the world.

Grubicy was immensely impressive, not only because of his sensitive face and his beard; he was also tall, proud, and erect. He always wore a top-hat and an old-fashioned, black top-coat. He had to carry an ear-trumpet, but such was his dignity that he might have been carrying a sceptre. Toscanini was devoted to him, and had a key to Grubicy's front door so as to be able to visit him at any time. They would spend hours together while Grubicy painted, or in arguments about music and painting. They used to go to the cinema together, too, for Grubicy was very fond of it. This was before the days of talking pictures, when every cinema had a pianist, generally execrable, particularly in the afternoon, to play during the projection. Toscanini, to please his friend, shut his ears to the torture of the piano and, as he is extremely short-sighted, could distinguish nothing on the screen, while Grubicy enjoyed the film and heard nothing.

When Grubicy died in 1920, Toscanini was as inconsolable as he had been at the death of Catalani. He always tried to keep track of his pictures, and collected many of them himself.

CHAPTER XII

The Scala Again

THE period immediately after the end of the war was an un-
settled one in Italy and in Europe; and it also seemed to bring a
break in Toscanini's career. His activities were unusually limited
and lacked continuity. He was offered various posts, but unexpected difficulties always seemed to arise and the engagements
fell through; an offer to conduct for a season in London, and one
in Warsaw, failed at the last moment. He even went to Vienna
for a contract, but nothing came of it. It was a crucial period for
him from a financial point of view, for throughout the war years
he had not earned a penny, and the money which he had saved in
America was used up. He seemed to be suffering from a reaction
after the emotional strain of the war, and to be unable to make up
his mind to the next step.

Merely a symptom of this general dislocation was his strange
political adventure in 1919, when he allowed his name to be included in Benito Mussolini's list of candidates. In view of his
violently and consistently anti-Fascist attitude in later years, his
friends find difficulty in explaining this incident. The facts are
that Toscanini was much upset by the excesses of the left wing of
the Socialist Party, which included insults to the flag and physical
violence to officers of the regular army. The second and more important reason was that Mussolini's programme, as published in
the *Popolo d'Italia* in 1919, included the following items: (1) The
decimation of the fortunes of the wealthy; (2) confiscation of
war profits; (3) heavy increases in death duties, the proceeds of
which were to be devoted to soldiers crippled in the war, war in-

valids, ex-soldiers, and their families; (4) confiscation of ecclesi-
astical property, to be handed over to public assistance organiza-
tions; (5) a radical reform of the army. There were also constitu-
tional proposals tending towards the abolition of the monarchy:
it was in fact an entirely republican programme. Toscanini has
always been consistently anti-monarchical.

This whole affair was a fiasco. Toscanini was more than reluctant to appear at meetings, and ended by sitting self-consciously
silent and embarrassed in the corner farthest away from Mussolini. In the end, the Fascist list gained no seats, and Toscanini
himself gained hardly any votes. With considerable relief, he
gladly paid up his 30,000 Lire deposit and washed his hands of the
whole affair.

The Scala was also going through a bad period. Duke Uberto,
at the end of the war, refused to take any further responsibility
for it; a co-operative venture of players and singers tried to put
on a season, but it failed; and the Scala was again closed down.
Fortunately, it did not have to close its doors for long, thanks
to Emilio Caldara, who was at that time the Socialist mayor of
Milan, an excellent character who left behind him the memory of a
true father of the city.

Caldara approached Toscanini with the idea that the Scala
should become a great, autonomous institution, rather like a
university, a hospital, or a library. The two men agreed that the
first step was to free the Scala from the control of the box-holders.
They were able to accomplish this owing to the fact that the Scala
had been closed and earning no money during the war, and so the
box-holders had received nothing but bills for their share of up-
keep expenses. Even the most tenacious of them were therefore
not sorry to hand over, and thus Toscanini and Caldara were able
to organize what was called "The Autonomous Institution of the
Scala Theatre", *Ente Autonomo del Teatro alla Scala*, which took
over complete responsibility for the whole theatre, including
the boxes. The Articles included a compromise clause giving
the box-holders preferential treatment for the first nine years of
the organization's existence. The city corporation also handed

over its rights in the theatre, and promised a subsidy for nine years.

The president of the new council of management was Caldara, supported by Enrico Mascheroni, brother of the conductor, Edoardo Mascheroni, who was supposed to function as Caldara's musical brain. Strangely enough, though Mascheroni was a bigoted conservative, he and Caldara worked well together. The council confined itself to the administration and technical organi-ization and left the musical organization entirely to Toscanini.

Of the old orchestra of the Scala, after three years' suspension, little was left. Most of the members had dispersed and found work elsewhere, so the orchestra had to be reconstituted. Like a good general preparing for war, Toscanini proceeded to enrol his new members. Among the concerts conducted by him during these years (he gave eight in Rome between January and May), he had been asked to conduct six in Padua in June, on the occasion of the International Fair which was to open there. Padua, which had an excellent Conservatory under the direction of a consum-mate musician, Francesco Pollini, was a first-class forcing-house for players, especially 'cellists, trained in the school of the formid-able Cuccoli. Toscanini proceeded, so to speak, to scoop off the cream of the Padua orchestra and carried off a number of good players, such as Crepax, De Conto, Oblach, and Scabia.

As soon as he returned to Milan, he set to work. It was, after the Turin orchestra, the second he had created in his own image and likeness. To create a new orchestra from scratch is one of the most fascinating tasks for a musician. It is not a question of mak-ing a list: so many violinists, so many 'cellists, so many trumpets, and so on, and then attaching a name to every item on the list, according to ability, established either by experience or an examination. An orchestra is not merely a simple assortment of players; it is more like a living organism, an organism of sounds: what the Germans call, pedantically but graphically, a *Klang-körper*, or sonorous body.

It became known as the Toscanini Orchestra, and in America as the Toscanini Scala Orchestra, and was to remain for many years,

With De Sabata: "the two great conductors had a long chat together in the empty auditorium" (p. 180)

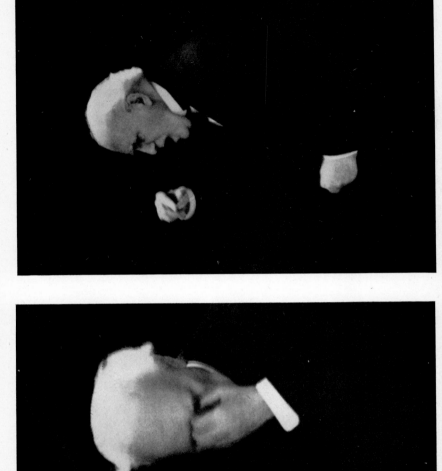

Farewell N.B.C. Concert, April 4, 1954: "The last act of a human drama" (p. 214)

with slight changes, one of the finest orchestras in existence. Musical historians like Weissmann and Della Corte have praised its perfect balance and the incredible quality of the single groups, arrived at by selecting the players not only according to their technical ability, but by their temperaments and the quality of their instruments. Even in ranking individual players in the various groups, Toscanini succeeded in overcoming all personal considerations of seniority or career and made them accept the belief that there were no "firsts" or "seconds" but that all, irrespective of the music-stand they happened to be allotted to, had the same task and the same importance.

After enrolling and completing his new orchestra, Toscanini decided to give it a long period of training and organized a colossal tour, starting at Como on October 29, with the Italian part of the tour finishing at Naples on November 29; during those thirty-two days he gave thirty concerts. The American part of the tour then started in New York on December 25, travelled through the whole of Canada and the United States (each carriage of the special train had a large Italian flag painted on it), and finished at Providence seventy-seven days later, after having given sixty-eight concerts. The second Italian tour started in Naples on April 20, 1921, and finished in Milan on June 16. During this, he gave only thirty-six concerts in fifty-eight days, because he had to break his tour by going to Milan for a fortnight to arrange about the forthcoming Scala season. Nevertheless, this illustrates Toscanini's superhuman energy, more like a human Diesel engine than a man; to be able to infuse with his own enthusiasm, for two hundred and twenty-eight days, ninety-eight men with their weaknesses, nostalgias, physical disabilities, and idiosyncrasies; not to speak of overcoming the material difficulties of organization, rooms not reserved in hotels, trains being late, etc., and get them all to give a superb concert in a different place every evening. For instance, Toscanini arrived at Quebec eight hours after his orchestra; and in Montreal his first violin, Ranzato, slipped on the ice and broke his wrist. All those who took part in this tour are unanimous in paying tribute to the maestro's wife,

K

Signora Carla, who accompanied them throughout the greater part of the tour and, according to the needs of the moment, played the part of governess, scout for reserving rooms, and adviser, trained nurse and mother to the younger members of the orchestra.

There were always some who could never be satisfied and who often poisoned Toscanini's existence. Whenever food and lodging were provided by the management, nothing was right; when, on the other hand, they were given a daily sum for maintenance, they economized by going to the poorest class of hotel. There was, in particular, a horn-player, Liverani, who was such a trial to Toscanini that, when he left the orchestra of his own accord at Naples to compete for a chair at the Conservatory, Toscanini said to him: "Rather than have a troublesome fellow like you, another time I will do without a horn."

On the whole, the tour was an extraordinary success. Half way through it, the orchestra played with the precision of a watch, to such an extent that on one occasion at Cleveland, when the maestro was so late for a rehearsal that the orchestra was convinced he was not coming, Ranzato gave the attack so that they would not wholly waste their time. The piece was Strauss's *Don Juan*. It was begun and, as the oboe was about to play, Toscanini arrived, stood at the back of the auditorium, and listened with a smile on his face. Later, someone spotted him and called out to the orchestra, which stopped playing. Then Toscanini came forward and said jovially, as he mounted the rostrum: "Very good; excellent! Now I see that I can go back to Italy with a tranquil conscience."

A whole chapter could be written about Toscanini's relationship with his orchestra, and books could be filled with the stories that have been told on the subject. Most of them are about his legendary irritability at rehearsals, his outbursts, rages, and scathing invective. It would not be justifiable to think that he always behaved in a similar fashion. If, after a first attempt at persuasion, no result was arrived at, if one group continued to miss the attack, if an instrument persisted in mistaking a note, his reaction would be either a violent flare-up or utter depression. I doubt whether anybody else could look as piteous as Toscanini, when he shook his head, let his arms droop by his side, clasped his hands behind his back with his baton allowed to hang limply, and murmured: "Shame, shame!" As the orchestra maintained a hushed silence, his shoulders were bowed and were shrugged disconsolately from time to time as if to say, "This is the end." His voice was agonizing on these occasions, like a lost soul, a noble being humiliated and tortured by malicious and pitiless enemies. On one occasion at the N.B.C. during a rehearsal of *Falstaff*, irritated beyond measure by the incompetence of the flutes, seemingly amazed by the fact that they were not aware of how they were torturing him, he lamented with the accents of crucifixion: "Don't you understand? . . . It is like to give me . . ." and as he could not think of the word in English, gave himself a loud slap and added with a groan, "a slap." Or he would exclaim, sardonically emphasizing the words, "Bad players . . . bad instruments."

In most instances his players, who knew and loved him, took all this in their stride—but not altogether lying down, as on the occasion when Toscanini shouted in an access of rage: "It is too much; I am sick and tired of putting up with you!" To which a player answered quietly, "And what about us? We've put up with you for twenty years."

Sometimes, however, he went too far, and several legal actions were taken against him. The worst incident arose from a rehearsal in Turin. Exasperated because a violinist had wrongly played a sharp twice running, Toscanini leapt off his rostrum and seized the player's arm. The latter, as he snatched his arm away, hit his elbow against the music-stand and scratched the corner of his eye with the tip of his bow. It drew blood, the man went off, and Toscanini stopped the rehearsal. He was not, however, aware that the player had been wounded, and he was astonished when the next day his friend, Avvocato Omodei, who had been to see the oculist, told Toscanini that the man had had a miraculous escape. Toscanini at first refused to believe it; but when Omodei explained to him that if the bow had pointed a fraction of a millimetre lower the violinist would have lost his eye, which would have been a real tragedy, as he was already blind in the other eye, Toscanini was so upset that he wept. (This was probably the source of the fictitious story that Toscanini once put out a player's eye with his baton.)

The violinist went to court immediately, but the case was complicated by the fact that the wound took twenty days to heal. According to Italian law the time allowed for the hearing of a simple case was ten days. Fortunately, therefore, definite proof that the wound had taken more than ten days to heal was lacking, and the case was disposed of in a lower court on payment of an indemnity, on the basis of a report by Treves, who had recourse to Article 48 (absence of free will and consciousness of one's own acts), invoking the principle of the irresponsibility of the conductor; for genius must be considered irresponsible.

The second law-suit was later, during the period of the *Ente Autonomo*. One of his violinists, Licari, was an excellent player but got increasingly on Toscanini's nerves because, at the moment of attack, he would always hitch up his trousers, adjust the handkerchief on his shoulder, stretch first one arm and then the other to free his cuffs, and altogether make himself thoroughly comfortable, before placing the violin under his chin and eventually attacking his first note, generally rather late. Toscanini began to boil with rage as he watched him, and one day, having stopped playing to make some remark to the oboes, he turned to Licari with the words: "You always come in at the last moment. I want the violins ready two beats before the attack. I have no use for sluggards!"

Licari turned to his companion to ask if he knew whom Toscanini was addressing. Toscanini heard and retorted: "I am talking to you; you are a sluggard! You cannot play the violin; next year you will not be in this orchestra!"

"I could not care less," answered Licari derisively. This infuriated Toscanini and he burst out: "You are a very poor player. . . . You are an incompetent teacher and your pupils will be nothing but incompetents." Licari got up and left the hall, and

Toscanini shouted after him: "At last that horrible fellow is gone; he's been driving me mad for the past five years!"

The next day Licari took his case to court. On the morning of the hearing the court was crowded with journalists and a seething mob of friends and enemies. The judge, Quaini, had, however, settled the case in chambers and had drawn up a document which both parties were willing to sign. This stated that the maestro possessed absolute rights of artistic censure. As Licari bent over the table to sign, Toscanini muttered: "Imbecile!" Muggiani, his lawyer, cried: "For heaven's sake be quiet; you will ruin everything." To which Toscanini replied: "I only meant that if I had been in his place I would never have signed!"

Although it did not end up in court, the most violent conflict between him and the orchestra took place at the Scala, also during the period of the "Ente", because of an incident during the rehearsals of the *Diavolo sul Campanile* by Lualdi. Gui was taking the rehearsals. The composer, for the finale of the opera, had attempted a grotesque concerted movement in which singers, chorus, orchestra, and bells vied with each other to see who could make the loudest noise. The result was such a confused cacophony that one day, during piano rehearsals on the stage, Gui took hold of Colombo, who was standing near him, by the hand and made him hit the keys at random, saying: "Hammer as you like; it makes no difference." At the final rehearsal, when it came to the unfortunate finale, the members of the orchestra lost their heads. Gui protested energetically, one of the players retorted heatedly. Gui was disgusted, left the rehearsal, and went to find Toscanini to lodge a complaint.

Toscanini burst like a rocket into the players' retiring room as they were putting their instruments away and discussing the incident. Toscanini flew into an ungovernable rage. There was a heavy table in the middle of the room. Toscanini grasped it, like a wild beast shaking the bars of its cage, with such violence that he injured his hand. He used equally violent language. He called them cowards; he said that they had insulted Gui, which was tantamount to an insult to himself, but that they were cowards and did not dare to speak in that manner to him. He cursed them in unmeasured terms. Caimmi, first double-bass, professor at the Conservatory, was the only one who spoke up: "Maestro, you have no right to use such language to us; we always do our duty." Some of the players were so frightened that they ran and hid in the lavatories. In the end they succeeded in leading him away.

The players, who were amused at first, agreed later that it was impossible for them to put up with such insults without loss of elementary dignity. They declared that they would not play again until Toscanini had apologized. That same evening Nastrucci, together with the director of the Scala, Scandiani, the secretary Colombo, and Tripiciano, who was secretary to the players, went to Toscanini's house and found him at the dining-table. Nastrucci acted as their spokesman. Toscanini was in a filthy mood. Nastrucci attempted to soften him by talking to him in Parmesan dialect: "Maestro, do eat; I see from your plate that you have eaten nothing; we can discuss the matter afterwards."

Toscanini replied sourly: "It is you who always provoke me to making scenes."

Eventually the discussion became more amicable, and in the end Toscanini was persuaded to make a formal withdrawal of everything he had said.

To attach too much importance to these quarrels, misunderstandings, and outbursts of temper, would be to do Toscanini a great injustice. The people who worked with him day by day, through all these years, shared his enthusiasms and were proud as well as fond of Toscanini. He on his part gave them a large share of his affection, and considered all of them as his personal friends. Throughout his life, with rare exceptions, his friends were not the well-known and successful, but the ordinary run of working musicians with whom he came into contact, including the employees in all departments of the theatre, his players, chorus leaders, and members of the chorus. One of Toscanini's idiosyncrasies was never to write letters, but in the early days of the Scala he never moved away from Milan for a day without sending a note or a postcard to his substitute, Sormani. During his Metropolitan period his two closest companions were the *répétiteur*, Marchesi, and the chorus-master, Romei. The former was a man of great character and erudition and an expert on composition, and the latter, whom Toscanini had brought with him from the Scala, was a man of military and authoritative bearing, an excellent musician with a phenomenal memory. He spent much of his spare time with these two. They took their meals together in a small restaurant on 68th Street, the proprietor of which came from Parma.

One of his other lifelong friends was another fine chorus-master, Setti. In fact, for obvious reasons, nearly all his friends were good musicians. We have already mentioned his long and faithful friendship with Enrico Polo, which was paralleled by his friendship with Nastrucci, first violinist at the Scala. His father had been a violin teacher at Busseto, Verdi's home-town; he was a rosy, plump fellow, always cheerful and always joking.

Toscanini's taste for companions of humble origin never varied, and he brought to people and their faces the same extraordinary accuracy of memory that he had for music. When he came back on visits to Italy from America, even in recent years, his first thoughts were always for his old companions. In 1951 he ignored invitations from the Prefect, the mayor and members of the aristocracy, and had himself driven all the way to a remote village in Tuscany, because he had heard that an old friend, Betti, a violinist, whom he had not seen for ten years, was seriously ill and bed-ridden. He had brought him a magnificent radio from America.

His players appreciated this side of his character and knew that they could count on his help both inside and outside the theatre. They knew, it is true, that he was strict, impatient, aggressive, and sometimes unfair. On occasion they may have disapproved of him, hated him, and cursed him. But, on the other hand, they knew that in their work they could always count on him; that he was always ready to support them; that, at the crucial moment in which everything is suspended on a thread of sound, he gave his soul, his nerves, and would have given his blood to ensure their giving a

good performance. They realized that he was extremely exacting
—that, for example, even if fifty instruments were playing simultaneously a vertiginous progression of bischromes, he was determined that all the notes should be played rigorously one after the
other, and even in the loudest fortissimo he would not tolerate an
approximation, the slightest hint of confusion. But they also
knew, with absolute certainty, that he would give each of them,
without exception, the tempo necessary for executing that note.
They knew that every tempo, once fixed by him, would remain
exactly the same, even after the lapse of several months. They
knew that at the crucial moment for the player, when playing
solo, he would be there to help them through the difficult passages
and to facilitate their work in every way.

Toscanini had a very soft spot for one of his clarinet players,
an old man called Capredoni, who was simple, serene, and eccentric and who lived alone in a garret with his clarinet and a chicken.
Capredoni, when worried by difficult passages, used to send the
maestro, in his dressing-room before the performance, a note:
"Maestro, I depend on your help at the finale of the first act," or,
"Please assist me in the repeat no. 54. Devotedly yours, Capredoni." His players learnt to have absolute faith in him and knew
that he made them play better than any other conductor. This
was put into words by one of the players, shortly after Toscanini
had left the Scala for the first time. He was walking away from
the Scala with one of Toscanini's successors, who was complaining
bitterly about the poor playing at the rehearsal. Whereupon the
player replied: "You may succeed in making us play badly during
rehearsal, but you will never succeed in making us play badly at a
performance, because we cannot forget what we have learnt from
Toscanini."

CHAPTER XIII

The Scala is Mine

DURING this period, when somebody, wishing to flatter him, assured Toscanini that the Scala was the finest theatre in the world, Toscanini smiled and quoted Verdi, who used to say that at least ten theatres had claimed to be the best in the world during his lifetime—"I should be curious to know which is the *second* best. . . ."

Whatever its international rank, it cannot be denied that during this period the Scala won world pre-eminence in the sphere of opera. It shone with the magic of that most difficult and complex manifestation of art, balancing between technical virtuosity and artistic inspiration, a sort of cross between poetry and the flying trapeze.

Toscanini was the moving power of this true operatic resurrection. The times were propitious. The post-war audiences, avid for music and colour, sat in elegant clothes in a newly decorated auditorium, with new scenery and new lighting, looked and listened rapturously to a performance which was invariably perfect. This recurred, not for nights, or a winter or a year, but for eight long years. During that whole period the Scala was the centre of an exclusive, almost worshipping, interest in opera. The performances were inspired by Toscanini's enthusiasm to such an extent that each opera gave, to performers and spectators alike, the impression of continual revelation and discovery.

The cult of opera in Milan was not confined to the rich, but extended to all classes of the population. Every night the tram-drivers used to make a special stop in the middle of Corso

Sempione, some distance from the regular stopping place, and wait until Signorina Anita Colombo, secretary of the Scala, had gone into her house and closed the door.

Even Toscanini was possibly never quite so single-mindedly creative in his work as he was at this time in the Scala. Music was always an absolute religion to him: but never did he seem more utterly, almost mystically, dedicated. For the very first time in his life, at fifty-four years old, he was the master of a great theatre. The Scala was finally his, completely, without any possibility of interference. His was the ardour and exaltation of the new owner of a priceless treasure. He seemed to live almost without food or sleep, and for months on end his continuous output of energy and work was incredible. His collaborators would ask: "But when does he sleep?"—like the unhappy Lert, who, on his first day at the Scala, was kept at the theatre for a lighting rehearsal until three in the morning; he had just arrived home and got into bed, when he was aroused by a telephone call from the maestro, who asked him to be at the Scala next morning punctually at eight! Toscanini practically lived at the Scala, and, if he went home to the Via Durini, it was to work in his study or prepare singers. He was rarely able to take part in home life, which at that time was very active: there were visits from all sorts of people, who wanted to call themselves to Toscanini's attention, as well as his children's friends. Walter had started a bookshop in Milan, which he called "Poetry Bookshop", and was the first of the cosmopolitan Parisian type in Italy. Wally was a great social success owing to her beauty and wit. Wanda was young and still a student. She was predominantly an introvert and basically serious, but was as ironical and devastatingly frank as her father.

On the rare occasions on which he took a short walk, it was to meet some of his cronies, like the correspondent of *The Times* of London, Borsa, or the lawyers Broni and Patrocco, at the bookshop of Baldini and Castoldi in the Galleria, and exchange anti-Fascist news.

It required all Toscanini's flaming passion and vigorous perseverance to perfect the smooth working of the elaborate organization of the Scala. He succeeded in giving it the stability and discipline of a repertory opera company without falling into the errors of the German *Spielplantheater*, with its inflated bureaucracy, its careerism, and its sloth.

The general framework was rigid, but it might be called an elastic rigidity, because it was continually reviewed and revised; the essential substance of the performances remained the same year after year, but they were always subject to experimental changes, so that, each time, there was an element of the unforeseen. It should be noted that this is a characteristic Toscanini formula: a mixture of study and improvisation, precision and flexibility, punctilious rigidity with inspiration and untiring invention. His principle was that "there are never repetitions, but all performances are first performances". He managed to impregnate his collaborators with this method. He demanded the strictest discipline, unfailingly regular attendance, and absolute punctuality. All of them had to remain within reach, because, he said, "In the theatre nobody knows what may happen."

His creative attitude to his work in the theatre is illustrated by his remarks to a violinist during a rehearsal of the overture to *Traviata*. One phrase was not exactly to his liking, and eventually he burst out: "But, can't you read what it says? It's quite plainly written down." "It reads *lamentoso*," answered the player. "Well, weep then, *weep*, in the name of God!" exclaimed Toscanini. That is the essence of the theatre: everybody must be able to weep, or to laugh, or to tremble, or to die; all, not only singers and instrumentalists, but those who paint the forest or the castle or design the costumes, the stage-manager and the chorus-leader, the prompter and the carpenters—all, from the highest to the lowest, concerned in the production must share the emotions of the characters and the drama. Without all that, there can be fine performances, but never true *theatre*.

Not all the men in the Scala were of exceptional ability. They were held together, however, and animated by this spirit, and formed an unique ensemble, even measured by present-day standards. The most important member of the team, after Toscanini,

was the director-general, Angelo Scandiani. He had two pro-
fessions: he was an engineer and a baritone. Strangely enough, he
had taken part in 1903 in the performance of the third act of
Parsifal conducted by Toscanini as an oratorio. Later on the
engineer predominated increasingly over the baritone. His principal attributes were modesty, a conciliatory spirit, and prompt-
ness and accuracy at his work. Physically he was condemned to
an excessively sedentary existence because of heart disease, and he
died fairly young. His secretary was Anita Colombo, who was
young, intelligent, and extraordinarily energetic. Starting in a
minor post dealing with publicity, she gradually extended her
influence over the whole organization. When Scandiani died in
1930 she was promoted to the post of director-general. That a
woman should occupy a post of such responsibility was unheard
of at that time in Italy. Moreover, as a friend and faithful adherent
of Toscanini, she was suspected by the Fascists; and so she was
forced to resign after one year.

Another authority in the Scala was the chief scenic and stage
designer, Cavaliere Luigi Sapelli-Caramba, known as "the magician". He was one of those people who had been born with a
pencil in his hand. He had started sketching on the marble table-
tops of the bohemian cafés in Turin, became a cartoonist, and
then, from designing for operetta companies, in time became the
most able and versatile designer of theatrical costumes in Italy,
and owned a dress-making establishment which supplied costumes for the illustrious Duse. Once this lady summoned
Caramba by telegram to observe the colour of a certain lake at a
certain hour of the afternoon, so that he could copy it exactly for
a costume. Toscanini put him in supervisory charge over all the
complex stage machinery and scenic effects at the Scala.

Next in importance was Giovacchino Forzano, the producer,
who was a dramatist and film-producer. He was eloquent, picturesque, bombastic, and "a sharp one".

Next in the managing team came the director of scenic effects
proper, Giovanni Ansaldo, a plump, gentle man with white
moustaches. He spent his days brooding over the best way to

reproduce a cascade, or an avalanche, or a storm at sea. If his
effects were occasionally vulgar and even puerile, they invariably
delighted the gallery.

Lastly, and most important of all, was the general staff of assistants—Panizza, Gui, Lucon, Calusio, Votto, Ghione, Santini, and
Vittore Veneziani, the chorus-master.

Undoubtedly the most striking feature of Toscanini's reforms,
the outstanding feature of his achievement, was the training of
singers. Whatever controversy there might be about Toscanini's
other qualities, he was indisputably the greatest producer of voices
that the world has ever seen. Between 1900 and 1930 all the finest
singers in the world passed through his hands and were, to a
greater or lesser extent, influenced, taught, or actually formed by
him. To give some examples: in the first Scala period, Burzio,
Carelli, Storchio; Scotti, De Luca and Caruso; not to mention
Borgatti, the unequalled Wagnerian tenor. Then at the Metropolitan there were Farrar, Bori, Alda, Alma Gluck, Eames. He
was always impressing on his orchestra the importance of not
overwhelming the singers on the stage: "The public's come to
hear *them*—if they don't hear *them*, they don't hear the opera."
He was equally insistent that his singers should be good actors.
His tenacity was tireless, his patience was unwearying, and he
almost used hypnotism when it came to making the singers
identify themselves completely with the characters they were
portraying. Of course he could not have done it without intelligent performers: but there is no doubt that he formed some of the
outstanding interpretations of our times, such as the Jael of Tess,
the Nanetta of Ines Maria Ferraris, or, most impressive of all, the
Falstaff of Stabile, so perfect that Stabile became Falstaff and
Falstaff Stabile. One day in 1930 Mariano Stabile met Calusio by
chance in the Galleria. The latter asked him casually if he would
sing Falstaff for an impresario friend of his, in a provincial theatre.
Stabile refused indignantly, as he considered himself dedicated
solely to dramatic parts. Calusio begged him to change his mind,
as a personal favour, and offered to give him two hours free coach-
ing every morning. Stabile finally consented, and began to take

such an interest in the part that he pressed Calusio to let him sing for his friend the impresario. Calusio kept him dangling for weeks on the excuse that the impresario was on tour and might return at any moment. Finally Stabile lost patience, and Calusio told him that the impresario had arrived and that an audition was fixed for the next day. On the following day they were walking together in the Galleria. Calusio put his arm through Stabile's and walked towards the Piazza della Scala. On the way Calusio said quietly: "You know, I'm not taking you to sing in front of an impresario, but in front of Toscanini."

When he heard this terrible name poor Stabile, jovial, paunchy, and easy-going, felt himself swooning like a virgin in one of Walter Scott's novels at the sound of the trumpet which heralds the arrival of the knight at the castle. Calusio had to hold him up and almost carry him into the Scala. There, he was unceremoniously ordered on to the stage, which was still under repair. Stabile sang two pieces and then stepped down and introduced himself to Toscanini, who said to him: "Very good, very good. But you sing with too much measure, too metronomically." Stabile answered: "Maestro, I did not come for Falstaff. I only came to see if I have enough natural qualities to be able, one day, to sing with you."

This was the beginning of a period of endless study, first with Calusio, then interminable sessions with Toscanini, in which verse by verse, syllable by syllable, the whole part was minutely analysed in its vocal and psychological substance. In this connection the story is told of a friend of Signora Toscanini who, on a visit to her house, heard the phrase about the anchovy sung over and over again *ad nauseam* in the maestro's study—(". . . two pheasants . . . an anchovy . . ."). Eventually she invited the Signora to go out and have tea with her. After taking their time over tea in a café, the first thing they heard when they arrived back in the house was, ". . . two pheasants . . . an anchovy".

Stabile could write a book, almost a treatise, on the art of interpretation, recapitulating the story of each phrase like that extremely difficult "*Vado a farmi bello*", about which Toscanini said:

"You must find me a note which is exactly like a smile. Make it light, make it heavy, accent it as you wish, but it must *smile*." This was how they finally arrived at that legendary falsetto, for which, complained Stabile, an ass of a journalist criticized him two years ago, thinking that he went falsetto because he had lost his voice!

Another typical creation of Toscanini's was Nessi. Nessi was little more than a member of the chorus when Toscanini discovered him and, divining the possibilities in the little man with the quavering voice and a great facility for clowning, took him in hand. He succeeded in making something unique of him: an operatic character actor, a singer specially trained to portray with subtlety all those secondary characters which are usually allotted to bit-players. Nessi was incomparable, as anyone will agree who has seen him play Bardolph in *Falstaff*, the lamp-lighter in *Manon*, the beggar in *Boris*, the painter in *Louise*, and a hundred other inimitable character sketches.

Perhaps Toscanini's ideal singer was Pertile, whom Signora Carla had discovered one evening in the arena at Verona. Toscanini was looking for a Faust, and took him on at her suggestion. Pertile was later a professor of singing at the Milan Conservatory, but his name was so indissolubly bound up with the Scala that subscribers would still telephone him from time to time. He was the most adaptable and versatile of all Toscanini's singers: today a lyric tenor, tomorrow an heroic tenor, today Werther and to-morrow Manrico—all of them equally natural and perfect.

A good example of the maestro's patience and kindness to his singers was the case of Toti Dal Monte, who had such a triumphant success in "*Caro nome*" in *Rigoletto*. Toti always remembers her first piano rehearsal in the famous red room of the Scala. After she had finished "*Caro nome*", Toscanini said: "You sang that perfectly, but remember that Gilda is a woman in love, like Desdemona and Aida. She is not made of sugar and water; she suffers and weeps. You, too, must feel prostrated by grief." In this way he taught her his great discovery of separating the notes, not by pauses, as had always been done before, but by very short

panting breaths, exactly like a woman who loves and desires.
Toti was obsessed by *"Caro nome"*, and was convinced that
she could not sing it without drinking a little water beforehand.
But she did not dare say so to Toscanini. When she finally
plucked up her courage to do so, Toscanini answered: "Why
not?" And every time this point in the performance was reached,
he made the short pause necessary for Toti to go and drink her
glass of water. Toti was unique! On the threshold of the atomic
age, she was the last prima-donna of "bel canto", the last human
nightingale, a voice of 1830 miraculously resuscitated a hundred
years later. She is still singing, gives concerts, teaches, and lives in
Venice in a palace on the Grand Canal like a Doge's wife.

There were, naturally, a number of new operas in the repertory
of these seasons. Their number, however, was restricted, and
Toscanini was accused of ill-will towards the new composers.
His attitude was justified by the fact that none of the new operas
have survived, with the exception of *Deborah and Jael* of Pizzetti.
His programmes were almost always made up of his old favour-
ites, together with *The Magic Flute*, *Orfeo*, *Fidelio*, *Boris*, and
Ariadne and Bluebeard.

The two culminating events of this decade at the Scala were the
productions of *Nerone* and *Turandot.*

We have already described the endless delays in finishing
Nerone, which obsessed Boito for so many years after the success
of his first opera, *Mephistopheles*. *Nerone* had been announced as
the great novelty on the programme of the Scala for the season
1901–2, and again for the 1907–8 season. In 1912 there were
rumours that it would finally be performed in 1913, at the Scala
during the festival season dedicated to Boito's old friend, Verdi.

Boito read a complete draft of the opera to Giulio Ricordi. All
he had to do was to write out the full score—eight months, two
hundred and forty days, so many pages per day—and the opera
would be finished. Ricordi was so confident that he engaged
Caruso. Boito left for Lake Garda and shut himself up at Sirmione
to work. First, he was not satisfied with the paper. The ordinary

paper used by Ricordi's other composers did not suit him: the pages were too large. Ricordi had special paper sent from Paris, 32 × 40 cm. Boito changed his mind: he wanted 30 × 40 cm. Then there was the question of the stave-lines. Boito asked for three samples with twenty-four, twenty-eight, thirty-two lines respectively. Meanwhile he had found out that the sample of French paper was not suitable: it blotted when corrections were made. Finally, after endless delays, Ricordi sent him a package of paper which succeeded in fulfilling all his requirements. Weeks later Ricordi received a letter from Boito, broken-hearted, explaining that he had come to the conclusion that his knowledge of music and orchestration was inadequate, and that he would have to study from the beginning again before he could finish the opera.

A year or two later Toscanini came into his study and found a bulging envelope on his piano. Boito had sent him the score of the first act of *Nerone*, with a request to return it in two months. He promised to send him the second act at the end of that time. Toscanini was delighted, and immediately sat down at the piano and played it over. As page followed page he became more and more uncomfortable and disappointed. The drama was sustained and the music was warm and vigorous and never fell below a high spiritual level; but the instrumentation was execrable. It was ill-organized and unbalanced, typical of a dilettante composer inadequately instructed in technique. Toscanini, worried and bewildered, did as usual: kept silent. However, exactly two months later a servant arrived with a letter from Boito asking for the score. Toscanini took it back in person. They sat down at the piano together and Toscanini tried to explain what was wrong, and promised to orchestrate a passage of it himself to make his explanation clear. Unfortunately, Toscanini was called away and was then too busy to be able to carry out his promise. Hence, Boito's impression that their points of view were irreconcilable.

Nevertheless, Toscanini continued to express the opinion that the musical substance of the opera was magnificent, and to state that he preferred it in many ways to the best of Puccini's works.

L

Boito listened to him in silence; it did nothing to dispel Boito's
basic inferiority complex about *Nerone*. Soon afterwards Boito
fell ill and was taken to a nursing-home. Toscanini hurried to his
bedside, but nothing was said about *Nerone*. Boito never left the
nursing-home, and died there on June 10, 1922.

Immediately after his death all his friends were determined that
Nerone should be performed. The prime mover in the matter was
his friend, Luigi Albertini, managing director of the *Corriere della
Sera*, whom Boito had named his heir and executor. Toscanini
had difficulty in making Albertini understand that *Nerone* could
not possibly be performed in the score written by Boito. He suggested a second opinion from a friendly expert, and the score was
submitted to a mutual friend, the maestro Vincenzo Tommasini.
He was a philologist and distinguished musician, who had composed an opera, *Medea*. He proved to be in entire agreement with
Toscanini.

There was nothing for it, therefore, but to go over the whole
score and re-orchestrate *Nerone* from start to finish. This was not
the first time that Toscanini had undertaken a task of the kind.
He had done the same thing in Turin with an opera of Natale
Canti, *Savitri*, before performing it at the Regio, and with the
Oceana of Smareglia before producing it at the Scala during the
1903–4 season. The revision of *Nerone* was far more laborious
and took him and Tommasini from the autumn of 1922 to the
winter of 1923. For two months in the summer they went off together to a little village above Bellagio, in a delightful setting in
the middle of the mountains.

Finally, the long-awaited first performance was fixed for April
1924. For months beforehand, all the technical resources of the
Scala were concentrated on preparing the production, which was
supervised by the sculptor, Ludovico Pogliaghi, who was a mine
of erudition. Boito, infected with the aesthetics of archaism, had
been determined to have every detail of the period of Nero repro-
duced with absolute fidelity, and some of his stage directions were
highly technical and very obscure. The climax of the enormous
and elaborate settings was when an authentic chariot was drawn

on to the stage by four white horses and driven through a mob of hundreds of extras. An extensive publicity campaign about this unprecedented production aroused the public to a fever of expectation. People fought to get seats. The first night was an enormous success; but the opera was too monumental and too difficult, and was practically never given again except by Toscanini later in the same year in Bologna. It stands as a mausoleum in a desert: imposing, beautiful, but unworshipped.

Turandot was another posthumous performance. It is a strange coincidence that Toscanini, in a period of less than two years, was called upon to render this last service of friendship to two great Italian musicians of the period.

Poor Puccini! The public, who had seen him successful and acclaimed for thirty years, had no idea of the inner sadness of his last years. His last opera, *Turandot*, was never finished. His other operas had been composed with calm and unhurried steadily progressing work. He wrote *Turandot*, however, in anguish, anxiety, with a feeling of working against time, and painfully.

This ultimate, unhappy period of his life began with the unsuccessful career of his *Trittico*, which was also a cause of great friction between Toscanini and him. Puccini had one day read to Toscanini the libretto of *Tabarro* (one of the three episodes in *Trittico*), and Toscanini made no concealment of his feeling that it was the worst kind of grand guignol melodrama, in extremely bad taste, and unworthy of Puccini. Nevertheless, the composer went ahead with the work, and Toscanini went to the first night in Rome in 1918. Afterwards, finding the critic Vasco in the foyer, enthusiastically praising *Tabarro*, Toscanini declared: "Well, I do not like it at all." This was reported to Puccini, who was mortally offended, and for a long time afterwards would not see Toscanini.

Puccini's last years were also embittered by the negative and almost contemptuous attitude towards him of the younger generation of Italian musicians and critics. That they should think and say of him that he was just a talented melody-maker, an empiricist, an able music merchant, without any real culture and without anything essential to say, drove him almost to desperation.

He was further exasperated by the extraordinary success of Pizzetti's *Deborah and Jael* at the Scala in 1922. Pizzetti had been one of his most scathing and intelligent detractors, and his opera represented a developed reaction against the "interrupted lyricism" of which he had accused Puccini. Furthermore, Toscanini liked the opera and enthusiastically supported it.

One evening, coming out from a performance of *Deborah*, Gaianus, who was then music critic on the *Resto del Carlino*, noticed a solitary figure at a table at one of the cafés in the Galleria. On looking more closely, he recognized Puccini. He joined him, and they sat talking until two in the morning. Puccini poured out his grievances: his bitterness because of the *Turandot* fiasco, his disappointment at the general lack of appreciation of his work. At one point in the conversation he made the following naïve and moving statement: "When you come to Viareggio, I will show you my scores of Debussy, Strauss, Dukas, and others. You will see how worn they are, because I have read, re-read, analysed, and made notes all over them. . . ." He, the composer performed more than anyone else in the world, was trying to make excuses for himself.

When Toscanini went to Viareggio on September 7, 1924, to come to some agreement about *Turandot*, he found a saddened and aged Puccini.

Once when I was alone with him at a rehearsal of *Manon*, Puccini wanted me to accompany him to Toscanini's dressing-room. He dragged me along the passage excitedly, urging me to praise the execution and to tell him that it had been great ("He will not admit it," he added, "but he loves it"), and when we reached the room he pushed me in front of him because he was obviously afraid of facing, alone, this growling panther who was prowling up and down the dressing-room. It was the famous revival of *Manon* in 1923. On the evening of the first night Puccini was as excited and happy as a young man of twenty.

So the arrival of Toscanini was to him like the moment in
which the result of a lottery is declared, the moment in which the
number is drawn which will decide whether we have won or lost.
This visit was an immense consolation to him, as is shown by the
letter which he wrote immediately afterwards to Adami: "Toscanini has just left. We are in perfect and sympathetic agreement
and, finally, I can breathe freely. This is the end of a nightmare
in which I have been living since April" (the nightmare: Toscanini's opinion!). In a postscript he added: "The little which I
played Toscanini made an excellent impression."

Puccini still had the problem of that duet, which after the death
of Liú remains dramatically cold and pleonastic. It was this
problem which had prevented Puccini from finishing the opera.
At the end of September he went to Milan to read to Toscanini
the parts which had not been played at Viareggio. They installed
themselves in one of the small rehearsal rooms of the Scala.
Puccini was profoundly depressed, and obviously very ill. Toscanini was greatly moved by the sad state of his old friend and
turned the leaves for him with touching solicitude. This was the
last time Toscanini was to see Puccini. On November 4 Puccini
left for Brussels to be operated on and died. Before the operation
he asked if there was any news from Toscanini; not knowing that
Signora Toscanini had actually been sent to visit him, and was on
her way.

It was in a solemn mood, therefore, that Toscanini undertook
the fraternal duty of producing *Turandot*. Franco Alfano was
chosen to score the final duet, for the curious reason that he had
in the past intended to write a *Turandot* of his own. On the first
night, however, Toscanini decided to cut this addition. When he
reached the exact beat at which Puccini had left the score un-
finished, Toscanini stopped the orchestra, turned to the audience,
and made the first and last public speech of his life. He said
roughly the following words: "Here, at this point, Giacomo
Puccini broke off his work. Death on this occasion was stronger
than art."

Giuseppe Albini, who happened to be lunching that day at

Toscanini's house, says that the maestro hardly spoke, and did not eat a morsel of food. In front of him on the tablecloth stood a portrait of Puccini, at which he gazed from time to time. There was in his make-up an unexpected, latent vein of old-fashioned sentimentality.

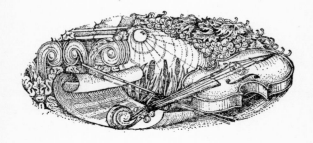

CHAPTER XIV

A Distressing Interlude

WHILE everything was proceeding smoothly inside the Scala, outside the clouds were gathering. A storm was brewing. As in the fourth part of the *Pastoral*, the unchaining of the elements is preceded by a melody, repeated twice, a petulant, bombastic, most un-Beethovian melody was echoing throughout Italy: *Giovinezza, Giovinezza*.

The first flash of lightning struck the Scala in 1923. One evening a group of young blackshirts was shouting and singing in the Piazza della Scala. They noticed that the Scala was illuminated. There were shouts of "Scala . . . Toscanini. . . . Ah! ah! that's the man—no?—who said that he would never conduct *Giovinezza*! Let's go and see if it's true." They rushed into the theatre in a body, burst into the auditorium and filed down the central gangway shouting: "Anthems! anthems!" Toscanini was conducting the third act of *Deborah and Jael*. Because of the disturbance the lights were put on. Toscanini stopped conducting and turned round. The spokesman cried: "Maestro, we want you to play *Giovinezza*." Toscanini, his face black as thunder, replied: "But the orchestra does not know it. We do not play improvisations." The young men then addressed themselves directly to the nearest players and asked them if they knew how to play it. When they received a negative reply, they declared that they would be satisfied if a single member of the orchestra would get up and play it. Toscanini then lost his temper, shouted "No, no!", flung down his baton and left.

Toscanini denied that he engaged in anti-Fascist polemics at this period. He claimed that he never meddled in politics and, from a personal point of view, this was true. Probably if Fascism had remained a normal political party and if he had liked Mussolini, he would never have been involved in these issues. He became anti-Fascist for two main reasons: because he could not bear to see people beaten up in cold blood; and because he could not stomach the napoleonic poses, the arrogance, the megalomania, and the pseudo-Roman profile of the Duce. It was a personal, human reaction which became political because, once it was laid down that Mussolini was infallible, any citizen who disagreed automatically became a political adversary—and a felon.

Nothing illustrates his attitude better than his conduct in the pitiable case of Giuseppe Gallignani in the same year, 1923. Gallignani was director of the Milan Conservatory, an excellent musician, adored by his pupils and a man of sterling qualities. One day, out of the blue, with suspicious suddenness, he was dismissed from his post by a telegram from the Minister of Public Instruction, who was then Giovanni Gentile. Gallignani was so overwhelmed that he committed suicide by throwing himself out of a window. The same day Toscanini sent a violently worded telegram to Mussolini holding the Government, and the Minister in particular, responsible for the tragedy which had deprived music and the Italian school of a noble fellow-citizen and a first-class teacher.

The funeral was on December 16. It was a grand funeral, with the Prefect, the Mayor, all the notables, heads of institutions and schools, associations, uniforms, flags, and chanting priests. When the coffin was lifted into the hearse, it was followed by an enormous wreath with gold lettering on the ribbons: "From the Minister of Public Instruction". Toscanini shouldered his way through the crowd, shouting, in a voice hoarse with fury: "Take that wreath away at once!" He then seized it himself, and flung it into the road with all his might. Nobody in the procession dared to touch the crushed and soiled wreath, and it was left lying on the roadway. At the cemetery, while the representative of the municipality was making his speech, Toscanini noticed a professor from the conservatory, who was said to have instigated a campaign of slander against Gallignani in Rome, hastily scanning some sheets of paper. Toscanini hurled himself at the man, shouting: "No, you are not going to speak!"—tore the papers from his hand, threw them on the ground, and stamped on them. It was long remembered as an unusually eventful funeral.

Neither of these storm signals was followed by any consequences. In fact, there were signs that the atmosphere might be clearing. The Council of the Scala invited Mussolini to inspect their labours. At the reception in the foyer, Mussolini made a point of taking Toscanini's arm. Subsequently there was a move to have Toscanini made a senator. Mussolini consented and told his secretary to include his name on the next list. Fortunately, the plan fell through, because someone remembered the affair of the Fascist hymn. Knowing Toscanini's hatred of titles and honours, one can imagine his face if he had been told that he had been appointed a senator under Fascism!

In 1925 on January 3 Mussolini made a speech which marked a turning point in the history of Fascism. With the connivance of the King, he suspended all the democratic guarantees which govern freedom in a modern state. All parliamentary opposition was abolished and the Fascist party seized possession of the State and the country. Toscanini took the hint and accepted a contract with the Philharmonic of New York. He did not abandon the Scala, but alternated his seasons of opera at the Scala with cycles of concerts in America.

On December 28 of that year he was to embark at Cherbourg, after getting under way a Scala season which included *The Mastersingers*, *Cena delle Beffe*, and *Cavaliere di Ekebú*. On the evening of the 27th he received a telephone call from the Prefect to say that Mussolini was in Milan and wanted to see him before his departure for America. Toscanini muttered an inaudible reply, hung up, and determined not to go. An hour later another call came from the Prefect. The members of the Council became alarmed and pointed out to him that, in his official capacity as head of the Scala, he could not possibly refuse an invitation from the head of

the Government. Finally they managed to bundle him into a
motor-car, but as soon as it reached the *Prefettura* in the
Via Monforte, Toscanini jumped out of the opposite door and
ran off. His friends caught him and almost carried him into the
building. Mussolini indulged in pompous generalities about
Art, Glory, Fatherland, Beauty, etc., with not a word about
politics. Toscanini answered in monosyllables; indeed, hardly
spoke.

It may seem strange that this cold war between Toscanini and
Fascism never came to a head, but both sides in fact had every
reason to avoid a crisis; Toscanini did not want to leave the Scala,
and Mussolini, for reasons of prestige, wanted to maintain the
level of excellence there that only Toscanini could ensure. The
extraordinary fact was that Toscanini succeeded, throughout this
period, in maintaining the complete independence of the Scala,
almost as if it enjoyed extraterritorial rights. Right up to the
time of Toscanini's departure, no portrait of Mussolini was ever
hung inside the Scala, even after every other responsible post in
the management had been given to a Fascist. Even after the
liquidation of the monarchy and the collapse of both Parliament
and Senate; even after the last stronghold of liberalism, the *Corriere*, with Albertini's resignation, had fallen into the hands of the
enemy; banks, industry, trade unions were under the strict control of the party; nevertheless, the Scala continued to lead its own
life, as if nothing had happened.

In 1931 occurred the most dramatic incident of Toscanini's life.
The scene was Bologna. It was the twentieth anniversary of the
death of Giuseppe Martucci, who had been the high priest of
music in Bologna. Besides being an apostle and educator in
music, Martucci had been a symphonic composer of some merit.
Two commemorative concerts of his works were organized, and
Toscanini was asked to conduct them. In January 1931 Giuseppe
Lipparini, an eminent Bolognese poet, had been sent to Milan to
discuss details. Toscanini prepared the programmes. The first
was to include the First Symphony and some minor compositions,

including the *Canzone dei Ricordi*, which was to be sung by
Favero; the second was to include the Second Symphony and the
Violin Concerto in B flat, which were Martucci's best works and
which Toscanini himself preferred. The soloist was to be Arrigo
Serato. The first concert was fixed for the first Sunday in May.
In April Toscanini had an attack of neuralgia in the arm and, on
medical advice, the concerts were postponed and the final dates
fixed for May 14 and 16.

Toscanini arrived in Bologna on May 8 to start rehearsals. He
had been fond of and admired Martucci, and his widow, to whom
Toscanini was devoted, still lived in Bologna. The orchestra
was by no means brilliant; the second violins, in particular, were
weak. After a week's rehearsals, however, he had whipped the
orchestra into shape and was satisfied.

The evening before the first concert, the Bologna newspapers
announced the inauguration on the morrow of the May Fair. It
was to be opened by no less a celebrity than His Excellency
Costanzo Ciano. All the Fascists in Bologna were mobilized to
welcome him. A grandiose programme for the great day was
announced, which included, "9.30 p.m.—Concert of the Maestro
Toscanini at the Municipal Theatre, graced by the presence of
His Excellency Ciano and His Excellency Arpinati".

The same day, after the afternoon rehearsal, the first violin
Campaiola, who had been brought especially from Rome, edged
up to Lipparini and asked what was to be done about the anthems.
It seemed obvious to him that the concert would have to be preceded by the Royal March and *Giovinezza*. Lipparini, an easy-
going fellow, felt his blood run cold at the idea of making this
proposal to Toscanini. Campaiola made a suggestion; at the entrance of the Fascist leaders, he would get up and sign with his
bow to the orchestra to strike up the anthems. Then, when Toscanini appeared, the concert would begin. Lipparini repeated this
suggestion to Toscanini, just then mounting the steps of the stage.
Toscanini pulled off his hat and flung it down the steps, then
screwed up the overcoat he was carrying over his arm, and threw
that down too. "Enough of these buffooneries!" he shouted.

Toscanini declared that if the anthems were played, he would refuse to conduct the concerts.

Lipparini, terrified, ran to see Arpinati, who at that time was the overlord of Fascism in Bologna—not for long, as events proved, because he quarrelled with Mussolini and came to a bad end. Arpinati was furious and said that the anthems must certainly be played. Lipparini then went to put the matter in the hands of the Prefect, Guadagnani.

This was followed by a period of intense official activity: proposals and counter-proposals from Prefect, federal secretary, vice-secretaries, generals, in turn. Toscanini had shut himself up in his hotel, the Brun, at the bottom of Via Bassi, one of the most aristocratic and exclusive hotels in Italy.

The debate spread to the more rowdy and fanatical elements of the rank and file. The seat of the Fascist Federation was the beautiful Fava palace, where, in the courtyard of high arches in mellowed brick, Arpinati, to draw in the people, had opened a restaurant, a café, and a barber-shop. In the café, during the afternoon, the hot-heads had agreed that if the anthems were not played, the concert would be stopped.

The hour of the concert was approaching. To complete the picture, it is necessary to describe Bologna on such a festive day in May. It was invaded by huge crowds of visitors; flags were flying, bands were playing in all the principal thoroughfares. The surrounding hills were in full blossom. The towers soared into the sky like blades flashing in the sun. The whole city of age-old, mellow red brick seemed an immense, colourful furnace.

At dusk, as a last resource, someone suggested that Signora Carla should approach the Fascist leaders in person and explain the maestro's point of view. It was already nine o'clock. But at that moment all the Fascist bigwigs were still at San Luca, a hill near Bologna, where they were inaugurating a funicular railway, and afterwards enjoying a banquet. All the notable Fascists, big shots and little shots, red in the face and shining with perspiration, were eating and drinking amidst great hilarity, when they heard that Signora Toscanini had arrived. They had completely forgotten about the concert. Was it really necessary to abandon the feast, the wonderful *cappelletti*, the chicken breasts cooked in the inimitable Bolognese fashion, the sparkling Lambrusco wine, and submit to two hours of deadly music? The decision was unanimous; as the maestro himself was insistent, their Excellencies would respect his wishes and, to solve the invidious dilemma, would give up the idea of attending the concert. . . . Toscanini was informed, and duly left his hotel to go to the theatre.

In the city, however, the young Fascists had not dined. They were parading, like famished young wolves, around the theatre. When Toscanini's car arrived at the stage door, a small crowd was waiting for him. It is probable that there was no premeditated plan to attack him. But an argument started as soon as Toscanini stepped out of the car. The back row pushed. Eugenio Muggiani, who was with the maestro, pushed back those in front, in an effort to protect him. The crowd became heated. First insults, then blows were exchanged. Muggiani was belaboured and sent staggering away from the car. The chauffeur, the faithful Emilio, covered the maestro, pushed him back into the car and succeeded in carrying him away at full speed. Toscanini had been struck on the temple and the upper lip, which was bleeding. The Fascists improvised a procession and, with the federal secretary Ghinelli in evening dress at their head, marched through the city, shouting and whistling, to the Hotel Brun, where Ghinelli told the maestro's friends that they would be well advised to see that he left the city if they wanted to avoid trouble.

To this day, nobody knows who struck Toscanini. Ghinelli himself was accused of being one of the aggressors. His fate was similar to that of Arpinati. He was disgraced soon afterwards and became an anti-Fascist. In 1943 he fled to Naples to enrol in the Corps of Liberation, was arrested, then released, then arrested again, tried, dismissed as "an immaterial party" and died of heart disease, swearing to the last, to his friends, that he had never touched the maestro.

CHAPTER XV

Peripatetic Music

TOSCANINI's name had acquired a legendary and international prestige by this time. There were repercussions of the Bologna episode all over the world, and the outrage caused universal indignation. Toscanini himself was wounded and bitter. It was not the physical injury—which he considered of no importance, inflicted by a set of stupid and misguided young men—that wounded and infuriated him, but the attitude of the Government. The day after, he had sent a telegram of protest to Mussolini. There was no answer except that, two days later, his passport was taken away from him—to be almost immediately returned. On the same day a laconic official communiqué was issued which stated that "a citizen" had slapped the maestro as a result of his refusal to play the national hymn. There was not a word of regret, and the text was carefully calculated to present Toscanini as an anti-Italian.

Toscanini was even more painfully affected by what he considered the cowardly attitude of some of his friends. Innumerable people visited him to express their sympathy and indignation, even outside the restricted circle of his intimate friends. But some, to whom he attached importance, stayed away. The Government had issued a warning that any open expression of solidarity with Toscanini would be considered an act of hostility to the regime. The house in Via Durini was watched and the names of all visitors were taken; his telephone was tapped, and there were signs that his letters were being opened.

Toscanini brooded, perhaps excessively, over what he regarded

as a betrayal on the part of these friends. One of them in particular had pretended to be away from Milan. Toscanini telephoned
him, heard his friend's voice, and slammed down the receiver with
an oath.

This was the period of Toscanini's life which could be called
the period of festivals. After Bologna, it was impossible for him
to continue working in Italy. He had already resigned from the
Scala in 1929. After eight years of unremitting labour, even his
iron constitution was feeling the strain. He felt physically and
morally exhausted. The strain had been aggravated in recent
years by the necessity of working with men of completely un-
sympathetic opinions and ideas. When he announced his resignation, he had specified that he did not intend to conduct any more
opera (except occasionally at the *Festspiele* in Bayreuth) but to
concentrate on concerts. In that year he had been appointed director in charge of the Philharmonic (previously he had been associ-
ate director), which had absorbed the New York Symphony
Orchestra. This work in New York, however, did not take up
his whole time; at this moment, when he was no longer able to
bear the heavy responsibility of running an opera-house, and was
compelled to work outside his country, there providentially
opened a new field of activity for him: the great international
music festivals, then becoming popular.

The idea of a musical Festival held once a year was inherent in
the Bayreuth *Festspiele*. Wagner's idea of an annual pilgrimage of
music-lovers was conceived in 1872, when the mayor of Bayreuth, Feustel, and his friend the banker, Theodor von Muncker,
made it possible to build the theatre. After the war Salzburg took
up the idea and organized a Festival, lasting a week, of dramatic
art which was to be complemented by music, exhibitions of pictures, cultural congresses, etc. The original idea emanated from
the eclectic and subtle brain of Hugo von Hoffmansthal and the
more robust energies of Max Reinhardt. Salzburg possessed in-
comparably greater architectural and scenic attractions than Bayreuth, in its flat and dusty valley. The success of the Salzburg

Festival was immediate and enormous, so much so that a large number of other places began to copy Salzburg; at the present time the festival fan can, if he has the means, wander from festival to festival, dramatic, musical, or cinematic, from early spring to late autumn, without a break.

So, during the next ten years, between 1929 and 1939, Toscanini was continuously on the move: from New York to Bayreuth, from Bayreuth to Paris, from Paris to Salzburg, from Salzburg to Vienna, from Vienna to Tel-Aviv, from Tel-Aviv to London, from London to Budapest, from Budapest to Lucerne. He was now established, as a conductor, in a class entirely by himself.

The first of his expeditions, both in order of time and importance, was to Bayreuth. In May 1929, when Toscanini had been with the Scala Orchestra in Berlin, Siegfried Wagner had approached him and invited him to come to Bayreuth. Siegfried Wagner was by no means a genius, in spite of his mother's efforts to have him hailed as "conductor, poet and composer" (in this connection, there are two curiously obsequious letters from Cosima Wagner to Mahler); but he was a competent man of the theatre, and Toscanini considers him a good producer. It was owing to his efforts that Bayreuth was modernized and rescued from the closed circle of old-fashioned managers and conductors who claimed to be the only men capable of interpreting Wagner's thoughts. The whole cumbersome bureaucracy of Bayreuth was hostile to the "sacrilegious" idea of inviting an Italian conductor. Siegfried, however, swept aside all these obstacles, welcomed Toscanini with open arms, and actually opened to him the doors of Wahnfried, the famous villa in which Wagner had spent his last years and where he was buried. Toscanini was put into Wagner's own apartment, worked in Wagner's study, and played on Wagner's piano: an unheard-of concession. In the first year, 1930, Toscanini conducted *Tannhäuser*, which had not been performed at Bayreuth for eight years. He revived the second edition of the opera, which Wagner had prepared in Paris, and therefore included the Venusberg scene. In the same year he also conducted *Tristan and Isolde*.

Shortly afterwards poor Siegfried died, and his wife, Winifred, invited Toscanini for the next year's Festival, promising to reinforce the orchestra, which Toscanini had found somewhat weak, with elements from the Berlin State Opera. The following summer Toscanini repeated *Tannhäuser* and added *Parsifal*; this shocked and frightened the superstitious traditionalists, as *Parsifal* had never been conducted in Bayreuth except by Karl Muck, who was venerated like a high priest, practically Amfortas incarnate, at Bayreuth, wore a frock-coat and gold spectacles, and who had just died. On this occasion Winifred made Toscanini a valuable present: a small autograph manuscript by Wagner, a few unpublished bars, written a few days before the composer's death and forgotten inside a score of *Tristan*; a very simple phrase, meditative, poignant with resignation, a melodic fragment vaguely reminiscent of Schumann.

The Bayreuth cycle was not an annual one. There were two seasons running, followed by a year of preparation. Toscanini had conducted there in 1930 and 1931; in 1932 the theatre was closed and it was taken for granted that he would go back in 1933. On January 30 of that same year, however, Hitler was proclaimed Chancellor of the Reich. Winifred immediately approached Hitler and persuaded him to write in person to Toscanini and confirm the invitation. Toscanini treated Hitler's letter as he treats all inconvenient correspondence: he let it lie. Some time later he answered with a short note declining the invitation, without giving any precise reasons. Toscanini was most reluctant to sever his ties with Bayreuth; the place was sacred to him for its memories of Wagner; and the theatre was his ideal: there was no applause, and the conductor, buried in a mysterious cave, invisible to the audience, was never called on to the stage and never saw the face of a single member of the audience. The Wagners and the Wagnerites were equally sorry to lose Toscanini; the well-known critic and Wagner commentator, Baron von Wolzogen, expressed their sentiments in a letter which is still in existence.

The periodic cycles of concerts which Toscanini conducted in Paris were almost in the nature of personal Festivals. Toscanini

M

had been to Paris in 1932 to conduct *Iberia* at a Debussy memorial concert. The idea of a regular cycle of concerts in Paris was due to Luigi Riboldi, an Italian lawyer who had fallen in love with the theatre and become an impresario. The two cycles of 1932, both at the Théâtre des Champs-Elysées, were a Franco-Italian Festival (Pizzetti, Respighi, Debussy, Berlioz, Dukas, Ravel) and a Wagner Festival. Toscanini returned to Paris each year up to 1936.

Throughout this period, however, the Festival of Festivals was Salzburg, in which Toscanini took part from 1934 to 1937. This Festival, which had originated as a drama Festival, included more and more music each year. Later, when the Festival organizers had come to a permanent arrangement with the Philharmonic Orchestra of Vienna, and particularly after Toscanini's first season, music became the predominant attraction.

During the first two seasons Toscanini concentrated on training the orchestra, which was uneven and unused to systematic rehearsals. He found the leader of the violins (Arnold Rosé) of great assistance. Besides playing for the Philharmonic, he had his own quartet. He was a typical product of the old musical tradition of Vienna, a gallant gentleman and an excellent companion. Toscanini not only improved the quality of the music but also widened the scope of the programmes. Largely because of him, Salzburg was packed not only with music-lovers but also with international celebrities of all kinds. It was probably the highest culmination of European culture: the farewell performance of a civilization about to die. And this solemn artistic occasion was always thronged—from the Bar Europa to the Bazar Café, the tables were crowded and one could find poets and princesses, famous professors and illustrious snobs, elbowing stars like Marlene Dietrich or pestiferous international blue-stockings, impoverished noblemen, international crooks, and swarms of beautiful women.

The season lasted six weeks. The first year Toscanini lived in the Hotel Europa, but afterwards rented a villa at Liefering, a few miles from the town, which he infinitely preferred. When he

could be persuaded to leave his retreat, it was to meet Bruno
Walter or Stefan Zweig, or have a meal at the Restaurant Trauber
with his faithful Milanese followers: Ansbacher, Amman, Gius-
sani, Polo and others.

The friendship between Zweig and Toscanini was a strong
one, but it had a pathetic and unlucky ending. They met for
the first time at the beautiful eighteenth-century villa which
the poet owned on the Kapuzinerberg. Zweig showed the
maestro his wonderful collection of original manuscripts and
souvenirs: Beethoven's desk was among them. He handed Toscanini, smiling, a score and said: "There is a work of a famous
composer, probably the only one you never knew." It was
an unpublished symphony by Nietzsche. Toscanini read some
pages at the piano, then he gave it back saying, "I do prefer
Wagner."

Zweig and he were very fond of each other. Zweig became
a fanatic of the maestro, and the preface to Stefan's biography is
his brilliant literary account of the attachment. When Austria fell
into Hitler's hands and Zweig had to flee from his home, leaving
his books and everything he loved, the friendship with Toscanini
remained as a comfort to him. In 1937 Zweig was in Nice when,
one morning, coming down from his room, he learned that Toscanini had arrived the night before in the same hotel. So they met
again. Just then, however, Zweig had fallen in love with his
secretary, Lotte Altmann, and later he was divorced from his wife
and married Lotte. Toscanini violently took sides with the former
wife, Friederike. To a mutual friend who tried to justify Zweig,
he shouted: "A man can take a mistress, but he must have only
one wife all his life." For the same dogmatic conception of
married life, which he held not so much on religious as on Italian
traditional grounds, he later broke with Heifetz, when the violinist
had a divorce. He even ill-treated poor old Busch when he, as a
widower, married again! So Zweig and Toscanini parted in
coolness. And when the tragedy came, and Zweig committed
suicide, Toscanini wept, but again did not approve of him. He
thought Zweig should never have surrendered. He should not

have given the hated tyrant this satisfaction, but withstood and lived to see his punishment.

Among Toscanini's major successes at Salzburg were *Falstaff*, *Fidelio*, the *Mastersingers*, and the *Requiems* of Verdi, Mozart and Brahms. While at Salzburg he also gave several concerts in Vienna. In October 1934 he accepted Schuschnigg's invitation to conduct Verdi's *Requiem* in commemoration of Dollfuss, assassinated by the Nazis on July 25 of that year. And in 1937 the Viennese asked him to conduct a concert in honour of his own seventieth birthday.

Hitler annexed Austria on March 12, 1938, and Toscanini immediately severed his connections with Salzburg, although he had undertaken to conduct *Iphigenia in Aulis*, *Boris*, and the *Barbiere* for the Festival in the following summer. Toscanini seemed to be fighting a series of rearguard battles, first Bayreuth and now Salzburg had been rendered untenable by the onward march of the totalitarian hordes. In 1938 he had to fall back on Lucerne. We are apt to forget that Lucerne is a Wagnerian citadel second only to Bayreuth; Wagner, who finished the instrumentation of *Tristan and Isolde* there in 1859, came back again in May 1866, to join Cosima. There they lived, at the Villa Tribschen, until 1872; Eva and Siegfried were born there. Here, thanks to the enthusiasm of the musical section of the population, led by Toscanini's friends, the city president, Zimmerli, and Colonel Pfyffer, the last notable concerts of the pre-war era were organized, conducted by Busch, Ansermet, and Bruno Walter. Toscanini joined them there, and in 1938 and 1939 led the Festival, with two culminating events: Verdi's *Requiem*, given in the church of the Jesuits, a rococo ballroom of stupendous size, with vast expanses of white-and-gold plaster and Bohemian crystal chandeliers; secondly, the Tribschen concert, on August 25, 1938, in front of Wagner's villa, before a select audience of about a thousand people seated on the grass and on the neighbouring mountain-side.

The concert was to be broadcast, and elaborate precautions had been taken to ensure an undisturbed performance. The steamers on the lake were stopped during the concert, and all cattle had been evacuated from the neighbouring houses. Appropriate measures were also taken to silence chickens and other animals. Nevertheless, as the Overture to the *Scala di Seta* opened with the violins whispering softly, a bird started singing loudly on a laurel bush in the garden! And of course it was heard by radio audiences all over the world. This was a.great day—in fact a religious rite for Toscanini. He did not conduct; he might, more correctly, be said to have officiated. And when, at the end, three pretty Swiss girls in national costume came and offered him flowers, the gesture appeared so out of place to him that he was extremely unpleasant to them. "I am not a ballerina!" he shouted. The girls were so frightened that one of them actually broke into tears.

Toscanini's Palestine concerts could also be considered as one of his rearguard actions for liberty. In 1936, Hubermann, who had formed an orchestra at Tel-Aviv, went to New York to seek financial support and to arrange for broadcasts. He needed above all somebody with a big name, and Royal of the N.B.C. had advised him to approach Toscanini. To Hubermann's surprise, the maestro agreed to go to Tel-Aviv that very year. Toscanini's decision was partly motivated by his indignation at the rich Jews of New York, who had been niggardly in their contributions to Hubermann. In 1936 Toscanini also took the Tel-Aviv orchestra on a successful tour in Egypt. He went back to Tel-Aviv in 1938, when there was already fighting between the Jews and the Arabs. Toscanini and his wife were living in a house lent to them by a friend and he had to go through the Arab quarter to reach it. Toscanini paid no attention to the firing and was not molested in any way. In fact, when the Toscaninis were without bread because of a Jewish fast, they went to buy some in the Arab quarter and were treated with great respect.

One evening in Tel-Aviv he gave a concert especially for the peasants. The women arrived with their babies on their backs and presented him with the first oranges of the season. On the same occasion a public presentation of an orange-grove was made to him. His admirers insisted on him travelling through Jerusalem in a tank—a somewhat useless precaution, as Toscanini would not go inside the vehicle, but sat outside to enjoy the view.

His Festival period ended in 1939, when he conducted Beethoven overtures, symphonies, and the *Missa Solemnis* during the London Music Festival in June of that year.

From October 1938 Toscanini had become, for all practical purposes, an exile. Throughout that year there had been a campaign of hatred against him in Italy. In March, at the instigation of Farinacci, the Fascist Press had been calling for the Government to "take measures against" Toscanini. Plain-clothes policemen dogged his footsteps and went to the length of taking the numbers of the cars which left Italy to convey people to his Festivals. This procedure was hastily dropped when some of the cars were found to belong to the Princess of Piedmont, the widow of Marconi, and a number of titled Fascists. The Italian consul at Zurich, a fanatical Fascist called Gemelli, declared openly that Toscanini should be put against a wall and shot. Finally, his passport was withdrawn, on the pretext that he "had no reason to leave Italy".

His son, Walter, was at that time employed by the publishing house of Mondadori, and in connection with certain formalities he had become friendly with an official at the police headquarters of Milan. This man rang Walter up and made an appointment to see him in a bar. Walter found the man looking perturbed, and was given an advance hint about his father's passport. Toscanini and his wife decided to hand over the passport, but they said that they must insist on finding out whether the passport would be returned in time for the N.B.C. concerts, for which Toscanini was due to leave in a few weeks. Meanwhile, Walter was called to the Questura and told that his father would have his passport returned if he would sign an undertaking not to express unfavourable opinions about the Fascist regime when he was abroad. As Toscanini had already engaged a stateroom on the *Ile de France*, he had to be told about this interview. Walter (who had actually prepared a plan of escape by seaplane from Lake Maggiore) then began pulling strings, and thanks to Mario Borsa, who was the London *Times* correspondent, and Gottlieb Wernli of the *National Zeitung* of Basle, a Press campaign was set on foot in Switzerland, America, and most other countries; and it caused such a scandal that Mussolini, to save face, ordered Toscanini's passport to be restored to him. These are the facts of this passport affair, which should dispose of the claim in Ciano's diary that Toscanini got his passport owing to Ciano's magnanimity.

Toscanini took the Simplon Express to catch the ship at Cherbourg. At Iselle, the Italian frontier station, he presented his passport, only to be told that he could not continue the journey without special permission from the Milan police. This turned out to be a silly mistake, and it was dealt with by telephone; but meanwhile the train had left, and the next train would not get him to Cherbourg in time to catch the boat. He telephoned to the head office of the French Line in Paris, and they immediately assured him that the ship should not leave without him. And they duly instructed the captain of the *Ile de France* to delay his departure for three or four hours, until Toscanini arrived on board.

Toscanini made a pious pilgrimage to Parma before leaving Italy for good. He called on his aunt Cesira, his only remaining relative of the older generation: his mother, Paola Montani, had died in 1924. He revisited the Conservatory, and found a photograph of himself on the wall—although at that time his name had been taken off the street. There is a street in Parma named after Toscanini—the Viale Toscanini, which was renamed the Viale Marconi after the Bologna incident in 1931, regained the name of Toscanini in July 1943, lost it again in September 1943, and so on. There is a tail-piece to this story: when the Viale had first been opened, an enterprising bar-keeper called Riccardo Furlotti had opened a *Bar Toscanini*, in the best position, with a view of the bridge and Oltretorrente. When the name of the street was changed, Furlotti received an official letter requesting him to change the name of his bar. This was followed by a threat a few days later: if he did not change it, he would lose his licence, so then Furlotti painted out the name Toscanini, but did not replace it with any other name. Some time later a minor police official told him that His Excellency the Prefect was outside and wanted to see him. The Prefect asked him sternly why he had not put up another name for his bar. Furlotti said, "What am I to call it?" and the Prefect said, "Anything you like! Go on, think of something!" So Furlotti grudgingly painted up the name Impero. On July 25, 1943, to Furlotti's delight, he was able to put back Toscanini's name. In September the name had to be eliminated once more. The wise bar-keeper—thinking, rightly, that it was only a question of gaining a little time—did not bother to paint out the name, but merely pulled a creeper across it. Nowadays, if you go to Parma, you can stroll down the Viale Toscanini, and have a drink in the Bar Toscanini.

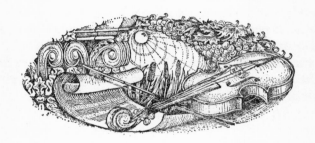

CHAPTER XVI

The Conquest of Space

In May of the same year, while he was on holiday at the Isolino, Toscanini had been visited by Samuel Chotzinoff, the pianist, Jascha Heifetz's accompanist and brother-in-law. He came, at this providential moment, like a modern, middle-aged Ariel, on behalf of the N.B.C. to ask Toscanini to conduct its new Symphony Orchestra.

Apart from sporadic broadcasts, like those of his Salzburg and Lucerne concerts, the maestro had made regular Sunday broadcasts with the Philharmonic from Carnegie Hall over the C.B.S. network, from 1930 until he left the Philharmonic in 1936. He left in a fit of pique, because the management had invited Sir Thomas Beecham as guest-conductor without consulting Toscanini. This incident is typical of Toscanini, his strong likes and dislikes, his quickness to take offence, his sudden reactions, and his obstinacy in adhering to the consequences of such reactions. In the case in point, the incident was trifling, but once he had made up his mind to leave the Philharmonic, nothing would shake his decision. Unlike his departure from the Metropolitan several years before, he remained on friendly terms with the Philharmonic, and actually suggested his successor, John (later Sir John) Barbirolli.

Another typical case of this impetuosity was his grudge against Stravinsky. This arose from a conversation with Tommasini, who reported Stravinsky as having said that Verdi was impotent. "But didn't you slap his face for him?" shouted Toscanini. From that day onwards he cut Stravinsky dead. He would not even speak to him when they were on board ship together in 1939 on the way to New York. His attitude towards De Sabata was somewhat similar. When De Sabata, in 1930, annoyed by the audience's cool reception of his ballet *The Thousand and One Nights*, indignantly walked out of the Scala, Toscanini had sent two telegrams from America imploring him to stay. The second one, in particular, was lengthy, concerned, and affectionate. De Sabata did not answer these telegrams, nor did he go near Toscanini on his return to Italy. This was enough to estrange Toscanini permanently. They never met again until very recently, when De Sabata was appointed artistic director of the Scala. Toscanini went to a rehearsal, and the two great conductors had a long chat together in the empty auditorium.

The rupture with Pizzetti was even more curious. The cause was not very clear, even to Pizzetti. Probably it sprang from political antipathies; there had been an exchange of letters; it became slightly acrimonious, and that was enough for the maestro. One evening, years after, in 1947, when Toscanini happened to be in Milan, *Deborah and Jael*, which had not been performed for years, was to be broadcast. Toscanini listened in, and was, as of old, gripped and moved by the music. During the interval his daughter, Wally, came downstairs to tell her father that Pizzetti was upstairs, if Toscanini wanted to see him. Wally, who is exceptionally good-natured and hates to see people at loggerheads, had hoped to be able to engineer a reconciliation in this manner. Toscanini categorically refused to see him. He liked his music, he loved *Deborah*; but see a man who had offended him, never!

His Sunday broadcasts with the Philharmonic had been appreciated by an extremely wide public, as was demonstrated by the fact that hundreds of thousands of grateful letters were showered upon him.

When Toscanini left the Philharmonic, Columbia made it known that they would gladly forward to the maestro any letters which listeners wanted to send him. It is true that the habit of writing a radio letter to an admired artist is a widespread practice in America. But this time it was an avalanche. Columbia made a selection from the innumerable thousands of letters, put them in five enormous leather-bound albums, and presented them to the maestro. On re-reading them today they still constitute a singular and impressive documentation, an impressive testimony to the habits and the spirit of America. They are not the usual flowery, banal letters. The tone is simple and sincere, simultaneously reverent and familiar, and is a tribute to the writers as well as to the recipient of the letters. Each one of them expresses gratitude in a strictly personal manner; five Germans from Paris, Illinois, say that they write to him from their "poor solitary house lost in the vast Middle West"; the gentleman from Vacherie, Louisiana, who sends the maestro a photograph of his delightful old Colonial villa so that he can see the place where his concerts were faithfully listened to every Sunday, "among flowers and birds listening too". One good fellow, on paper headed Roslyn Window Cleaning Co., in a burst of enthusiasm, proclaims: "Only God and Beethoven are waiting for you!"—without apparently noticing that, if the maestro had taken him at his word, he would be bound without delay for the other world. (It is remarkable how many commercial houses wrote letters; it is doubtful whether in Italy a single businessman would have taken the trouble to write!) But the spirit, or rather the essence of this plebiscite, repeated in one form or another in almost all the letters, is epitomized in these words of a lady listener in Indianapolis: "Your departure is a serious loss for me. Life had begun to mean something richer and more profound than it had been before." In no other country in the world would it be possible to envisage such an exchange of confidential letters between a multitude and an artist. Symphonic music had always been broadcast in America; how can one explain these particular concerts having been able to make such a profound impression, so as to become for millions and millions of listeners a spiritual integration of their lives?

It was this fact which Chotzinoff and Sarnoff (General Sarnoff who later organized the whole signal network for the Normandy invasion) were astute enough to take advantage of. Up to this time Columbia (C.B.S.) had enjoyed a virtual monopoly of broadcasting classical music. The N.B.C. were now determined to challenge Columbia; but to do this they had to have something bigger and better. Why not a special orchestra, a first-class orchestra which would be called by the name of N.B.C.? This exceptional orchestra must have an exceptional conductor, preferably one who had some legitimate title to be called "the greatest conductor in the world". This conductor was Toscanini; and also, by chance, he was free. Hence Chotzinoff's journey to Italy, with an offer which Toscanini promptly accepted.

The inaugural concert took place on Christmas Eve, 1937. For this momentous occasion Toscanini had chosen the magniloquent Concerto Grosso in C minor by Vivaldi, the Symphony in G minor by Mozart, a companion work to the Symphony in E flat and to the *Jupiter* (all written in 1788 for the same concert), with its fascinating alternation of melancholy and sprightliness; finally Brahms's First Symphony in C minor, with its powerful initial dissonances, which Toscanini constructed like the arches of an immense portal, and the restless chromatism of the first movement subsiding gradually, through the plaint of the pizzicatos, the flute pastoral of the *Scherzo*, to the four enormous superposed steps of the *Finale*.

The N.B.C. claimed that twenty million radio sets had been turned on to listen to that concert in North America alone (the N.B.C. covers Canada through the C.B.C.), without counting the millions of overseas listeners who were able to tune in on the programme through the five international short-wave stations linked up with the N.B.C. Toscanini had conquered space, and from now on was to conduct for invisible and immeasurable audiences, and not for limited ones that had paid for their seats.

In fact it involved an entirely new technique of symphonic expression. This required not only a continuous and gradual adaptation of technical methods—for example in the placing of the microphones, in the composition and distribution of the instrumental groups (he was always experimenting with new acoustic effects; as, for example, the occasion when he put the chorus outside the hall in a corridor)—but also often required a new valuation of the terms of expression, an adjustment of colours and volumes, a special accent of the phrasing. It is remarkable that it should have been Toscanini, the oldest working conductor, who realized this ultra-modern concept of a great orchestra organized and trained solely for broadcasting.

It was necessary for this perfect orchestra to have a perfect home. Thus was born the famous Studio 8-H, so perfect that as soon as it was completed it had to be rebuilt! It was situated in the R.C.A. skyscraper of the Rockefeller Center, on the eighth floor, and was semi-elliptic in shape. At that time Studio 8-H was not only the largest broadcasting studio in the world, but also had the most perfect technical equipment.

Meanwhile the dictators were spreading their tentacles. Mussolini had become Hitler's vassal. Poland had been swallowed up. On September 27, 1939, Warsaw fell. On October 14, 1939, Toscanini started his new season, and between October 28 and December 2 gave a series of six concerts dedicated to Beethoven.

On April 9, 1940 Denmark and Norway were invaded, on May 10, Belgium, Holland, and Luxembourg. Toscanini's reactions to these tragic events were, in part, reflected by his programmes during those years. There was a nostalgic return to the voices of the past, voices of his youth, like Bazzini (*Saul*, in a concert given in January 1939); Martucci (Second Symphony in March 1940); even his beloved Bolzoni (Minuet and Serenade in June 1943), Mancinelli (*Fuga degli Amanti* in June 1944), and Catalani on a number of occasions.

On May 14, 1940, the broadcasting studio shut down, and Toscanini was sent to South America by the N.B.C. on a good-will tour. He was there on June 17, when he heard the news of the fall of Paris.

After Pearl Harbour (December 7, 1941) and America's entry into the war, Toscanini, besides his broadcasting activities, conducted charity concerts. From then till the end of the war he gave about twenty concerts, for the Italian Benevolent League, for the Roosevelt Hospital, for child welfare, for the Infantile Paralysis Fund, for the Red Cross, the War Bond drive, etc. Of

these, the most successful one was the concert in aid of the Red
Cross. This was a mammoth affair, in Madison Square Garden,
May 1940, organized by an influential committee headed by La
Guardia and Dewey, which realized the fantastic sum of $100,000
and broke all records for charitable concerts.

For the sake of charity he even had a film made: *The Hymn of
the Nations*, a cantata composed by Verdi in 1862, with text by
Arrigo Boito, for the inaugural ceremony of the great London
Exhibition. It is a composition for chorus and a vastly reinforced
orchestra. Everybody was astounded when he agreed to do this
film. His avoidance of the limelight and hatred of personal
publicity were well known and accepted facts. Besides, he had
been known to refuse fabulous offers ($250,000 in one case) to
appear in Hollywood films.

Although Toscanini took no part in active politics during the
war, he did not dissociate himself from his fellow emigrants. He
was a member of the New York anti-Fascist group, the Mazzini
Society. But when this Society split and Salvemini, Borgese, and
Pacciardi seceded, leaving Sforza and Tarchiani with the rump,
Toscanini's sympathies were with the former.

Toscanini's likes and dislikes were accentuated by the un-
settled atmosphere due to the prolonged hostilities. He fought a
sort of private war of his own, waging offensives and contracting
alliances. One of his idiosyncrasies was his hatred of Churchill,
whom he believed had once entertained Fascist sympathies. He
respected Roosevelt, but "did not like his face". His abhorrence
of Fascism was equalled by his abhorrence of the institution of
monarchy. He remained particularly incensed against the house
of Savoia, for he considered that, in betraying his trust to the
Italian people, the King of Italy had betrayed him, Arturo Toscanini, personally. He had obstinately refused to meet the Princess Maria José during the Festival period, although this poor
lady was a passionate and cultured musician. She must have had
an intellectual *beguin* for him, and on one occasion sent a score
of the Verdi *Requiem* to him at Lucerne with a request for his
signature. Toscanini refused, flatly, and Signora Toscanini

had to return the score to the Princess, with a big bunch of roses.

On this subject Toscanini went so far against his inclinations and habits as to write a political article in *Life*. He did so because of his fear that the Allies, after getting rid of Fascism, were treating with and would bolster up the hated Savoia monarchy. Essentially, his article was an impassioned plea for a direct understanding between the Italian and American peoples, circumventing the monarchy. It directly and violently attacked the King and Badoglio.

When the news arrived in April 1944 that not only was there not to be a Republic, but that republicans like Sforza, Tarchiani, and Omodeo had sworn obedience to an interim monarchical government, Toscanini signed a manifesto (with Salvemini, Borgese, and Don Sturzo): "We do not demand that the American and English armies should force republican principles upon Italy. But we do demand that they cease to support the Monarchy as a temporary expedient during their occupation." This was to be Toscanini's second and last public political pronouncement.

CHAPTER XVII

A Revolution in Hats

IN 1939 Toscanini, realizing that his exile would be prolonged indefinitely, felt tired of hotel life and decided to set up house in America.

He found a large furnished house to let at Riverdale on the crest of Independence Avenue, which runs along the tail of Manhattan. It had a big garden and a view across trees and lawns down to the majestic, metallic Hudson River, and, by chance, it bore his mother's name: Villa Paulina. He lived there with his family for two years and then moved to the Villa Freeman, a little further along on the same hillside. The drive from Rockefeller Center to Riverdale took at least forty minutes, but, after a tiring day, Toscanini found the drive along the river a good form of relaxation— once clear of Broadway. The road crossed the Harlem River over the Hudson Bridge. His chauffeur Luigi's standard joke was that the authorities should inscribe Toscanini's name on one of the pylons of the bridge out of the proceeds of the innumerable 10 cent toll payments disbursed on his behalf. Toscanini became so attached to Riverdale that when the Villa Paulina came up for sale he decided to buy it.

Villa Paulina can hardly be described as an architectural master-piece. It is a cross between a Swiss mountain chalet and a late Victorian mansion. But it is a comfortable and friendly house. The centre of the house is a vast drawing-room, dominated by an enormous staircase which mounts to a circular landing. Signora Toscanini's apartment was to the right and his to the left. The latter consisted of two large rooms. His bedroom occupied the left corner of the façade. His study was in front, overlooking the river. The two rooms being connected by a small corridor, the walls of which were covered with autograph scores (Berlioz, Mendelssohn, Hugo, etc.). To the left of his study door, as one entered, was his grand piano; in the centre, facing the balcony, his writing-desk. The walls were covered with paintings and photographs—one of Debussy, several of Brahms, and one of Cosima Wagner. A little further on there was Wagner's last portrait, with an attestation of authenticity inscribed on the back by Wagner's friend, Gross, who gave it to Toscanini in Bayreuth. There was a little faded photograph which is marked *Val Seriana, August 1913*, with the inscription: "Toscanini, with love from Grubicione". It shows Grubicy in profile, wearing a straw hat, his corpulent person contrasting with the slender Toscanini, wearing his usual boat-shaped felt hat with upturned brim. On the opposite wall were the Grubicy paintings. There was also a vivid sketch of an interior by his granddaughter, Sonia, the daughter of Wanda and Vladimir Horowitz. The other corner of the room was lined with bookcases containing books and scores: all the works of Verdi, Wagner, Puccini.

Beside the piano there is a double cage of canaries, a small compartment for the parents and a larger one for the fifteen children. These are the maestro's favourite friends, and he was never annoyed if they sang while he played. He was particularly proud of mother canary's reproductive capacities.

For finally there was peace. Twenty days before the Italian armistice, for the last concert of the season, Toscanini included in the programme the final chorale of the *St Matthew Passion*: "In tears of grief, dear Lord, we leave Thee. . . ." Innocent, pastoral notes; grief consoled; thanksgiving rendered.

Yet Toscanini had no illusions that there was going to be very much consolation or true thanksgiving about the armistice. It was by no means a true peace; but it meant that at any rate he could see the members of his family from whom he had been separated; even his granddaughter, Emanuela, whom he had last seen as a baby. That year (1943) he made no attempt to go back to Italy himself.

N

It was still practically impossible for the family to reunite. Walter, who acted as secretary and manager for his father, and superintended all the recording business, resided in America. He married Cia Fornaroli, a very gentle woman who had been first ballerina at the Scala, and a great one; she died recently. The second daughter, Wanda, had also settled in America, married to Vladimir Horowitz. A beautiful and clever woman, she has, more than the others, the features and the fiery, outspoken character of her father; and a story is told that, on the occasion of one of the fabulous banquets given by Reinhardt at his castle in Salzburg, whilst Toscanini was sitting among the other guests next to Mrs. Thimig, Wanda appeared with a moustache and wearing her father's jacket and hat, and all the guests stared in silence, as if they were bewildered by a magician's trick. The elder daughter, Wally, lives in Milan. Very beautiful, too (she has her grandfather Claudio's eyes, long, lustrous, faintly almond-shaped), very charming and droll in her own way, with no sense of order, but generous, she has friends everywhere, and represents the social side of the family. She married Count Emanuele di Castelbarco, and their daughter married recently Duke Acquarone, son of the former Italian Royal Household Minister.

On July 25, 1943, Italy liberated herself from Fascism. Next morning long strips had been pasted across the façade of the Scala with the words: "Long live Toscanini" and "Come back, Toscanini". This had been done by a Milanese lawyer, Franco Dameno, one of Toscanini's most fervent admirers, who would probably have been happy to live the rest of his life on a desert island with nothing but Toscanini records. When the Fascists returned, behind the Germans, Dameno was arrested, had most of his teeth kicked out, and was flung into jail. By this time the Scala had been severely damaged by bombs in an air-raid on August 16, 1943.

The damage was not confined to fire—the offices, store-rooms, and services, including the archives, had been burnt out. There had been a direct hit on the auditorium, which was in ruins, and the stage had been saved only by the metal safety curtain. The reconstruction of the Scala was entrusted to Ghiringhelli by the Socialist mayor, Greppi, immediately after the end of the war. Ghiringhelli was an industrialist, with special experience of the leather trade. He was a great lover of opera, however, and volunteered to superintend the reconstruction. Thanks to his organizing experience and banking resources, this was completed in the record time of six months.

In April 1946 Toscanini arrived back from America, via Paris. He did not stop in Milan, as his house in the Via Durini was requisitioned, but went straight to his property at Ripalta Guerrina, near Crema, about thirty miles from Milan. Signora Toscanini had bought this property some years before; but strangely enough, for it was very reminiscent of nearby Busseto, it never appealed to him and he made only brief visits to it. This was almost the first time that he had slept in the house. At Ripalta he waited impatiently to be able to see his beloved Scala again. He telephoned to Ghiringhelli every day, but there seemed to be endless delays. Finally, Toscanini could wait no longer, drove into Milan, and walked into the Scala. It was still full of workmen, and the auditorium was in darkness. Toscanini walked up the middle gangway and stood there alone, surrounded by his memories and revelling in the feel of his beloved Scala. Nobody, except Ghiringhelli, knew he was there. By an extraordinary coincidence, the electricians were testing out the new circuits and, just at that moment, made all the switches to test the house lights. Suddenly, for the first time, the whole auditorium blazed with light: and there in the middle, alone, stood the little dark figure of the maestro. He clapped his hands two or three times to feel the acoustics, and said, simply, "Good."

The inaugural concert, on the evening of May 11, 1946, was perhaps the most impressive occasion in the Scala's honourable career of a century and a half. The packed audience was delirious with excitement. Toscanini had chosen a completely Italian programme. In the second part there was the entire third act of *Manon*, and in the third the Prologue to *Mephistopheles*. But the soul, the essence of the concert was in the first part: the stupendous prayer from *Moses*, the gratitude of a liberated population expressed in song; the chorus of *Nabucco*, a great remembrance of the *Risorgimento*; and the *Te Deum* of Verdi, a religious culmination and the best of auguries for the future.

It was a popular concert in the Italian sense of the word. Toscanini intended it to appeal to the people, the humble people of the streets. That evening the concert-hall had been connected up with loudspeakers placed outside about the Piazza della Scala and in the great Piazza del Duomo. Seated on the steps, on the pavement, perched on railings and on refuse bins, a dense crowd listened rapturously: humble folk from the overcrowded dwellings nearby, from the Porta Romana, from the Porta Genova, the Porta Lodovica, and the Porta Ticinese, all the bombed suburbs. They were workmen, artisans, small shop-keepers; whole families with their children, young mothers with their babies asleep in their arms.

The Italo-American Association, which had its luxurious quarters in a palace on Via Moroni, organized a great reception to be held after the concert in honour of Toscanini. The *élite* of fashion and wealth, together with the distinguished members of the committee, were all there, and of course it did not occur to them for a moment that Toscanini might not come. They waited for him, chatting elegantly of stocks and shares, sports models, and the monarchy, and watching the entrance. At long last Wally arrived, to make her father's excuses. He would not come.

Though Toscanini was happy to be back in Italy, his character had not changed; and the usual frictions and misunderstandings ensued. Even before the concert there had been a heated discussion on the subject of a speech. Greppi, the Socialist mayor, had expressed his desire to make a short introductory speech. Greppi was a man of the highest integrity, respected by all; he had, moreover, lost his only son, Mario, brutally slaughtered in public by a gang of Nazi-Fascists. Toscanini was reluctant to refuse Greppi's request, but was incapable of giving way on a matter of principle. He was determined that the evening should be one of nothing but music, and set his face against the intrusion of any other factors, political or otherwise. It astonished Toscanini that Greppi and his friends could not understand his point of view. Greppi, on the other hand, could not understand why Toscanini was so unreasonable as to object to the first magistrate of the city pronouncing a few words of welcome on such an occasion. It was an *impasse*. Mutual friends attempted a compromise; they tried to arrange for Greppi to broadcast his speech just before the transmission of the concert. Greppi, who was deeply offended, refused, and did not even attend the concert. It arose from the same old difficulty: that of reconciling Toscanini's touchy scruples and the requirements of official life.

Two years later, when Toscanini returned for the Boito commemoration, the squabbles and pin-pricks began again. Even as he came down the gang-plank from the liner, when a photographer exploded his magnesium flash in Toscanini's face, there ensued a classic bout of fisticuffs between Walter and the photographer.

On the thirtieth anniversary of Boito's death, Toscanini organized a solemn memorial performance, in which he gave the third act of *Mefistofele*, and the third and fourth acts of *Nero* in their entirety with costumes, scenery, and choruses. It was his first return to opera for a long time. In the same year he conducted a concert at the Scala for the benefit fund for the orchestral players of the Scala. There was considerable criticism of both these programmes on the score of their being "old-fashioned".

When he returned in the summer of 1949 there were no incidents to disturb his tranquillity. He was able, finally, to take possession of his beloved Isolino, renting it back from its tenants. The Isolino of San Giovanni is a minute island opposite Pallanza, on Lake Maggiore. It is a beautiful spot, with the villa, on two floors, facing away from the shore and looking over the wide panorama of the lake with the mountains in the distance. The garden is sub-tropical, with rippling lawns, a profusion of trees, and a riot of flowers. A gravel-walk goes down to a little sandy beach, shaded by a clump of ancient weeping willows.

He divided the summer of 1949 between resting at the Isolino and two concerts: the first, already mentioned, for the benefit of the players, and the second, three days later, in Venice to open the Music Festival.

He had just returned to New York, thoroughly rested, contented, and serene, when there arrived the bombshell of his nomination as senator. According to the new Italian Constitution, the President of the Republic has the right conferred upon him to appoint, as life-long senators, five citizens who "have rendered exceptionally distinguished services to their country". It is not surprising that one of the first names submitted for this honour to the new President Einaudi was that of Toscanini. When the proposal was announced, the maestro was filled with consternation.

The appointment upset him in two ways. In the first place, he had felt all his life a frantic horror for every kind of official responsibility or honour, and, as he said, what use would he be in the Senate, a musician who knew nothing about government or politics? They ought to leave the making of laws to those who knew how to make them. Secondly, he had not forgotten that the manifesto he signed in 1944 ended with Burckhardt's saying that "*émigrés* should never return": Toscanini was determined never to accept any kind of reward for anti-Fascism. Therefore, after hours of worry, he declined the honour in a telegram to the President which began:

> "It is an old Italian artist, much disturbed in spirit by your unexpected telegram, who addresses himself to you and begs you to understand that this appointment of Senator for life is in profound contrast with his feelings and his way of life and that he is obliged to decline this honour with infinite regret."

This refusal gave rise to new misunderstandings. Most Italians saw in it a new proof that Toscanini was estranged and no longer cared for his country. He had refused in 1944 to become President of the Scala. He had refused to preside over the committee

for Verdi's memorial year. Now he refused to be a Senator—this
was going too far!

Traces of this resentment were evident in the reception that the
audience gave to Toscanini's concert at the Scala in June 1950.
He had come especially to conduct Verdi's *Requiem*, and, although
the gallery was enthusiastic, the applause from the stalls and boxes
at the beginning of the concert and after the first part was dis-
tinctly tepid. Nevertheless, a few minutes later all this quarrelling
and suspicion was forgotten in the divine surge of the music. The
conclusion of the concert was triumphant.

A new phase of Toscanini's career is linked up with the emer-
gence of a new technique, the modern "open sesame" or Merlin's
mirror of the cathode ray and the electronic tube: television. On
March 20, 1948, Toscanini and his orchestra were televised for
the first time. The concert consisted entirely of Wagner. His
success, as one might expect, was phenomenal, and from that time
onwards he was asked to give regular commercial television performances. In the spring of 1949, when Toscanini conducted the
whole of *Aida* with soloists and choruses, in two sessions, it was
calculated that there were about ten million people watching the
opera, without counting the enormous number who must have
listened in on the radio. So the same man who played in the first
performance of *Otello*, in Verdi's presence, linked Verdi with the
electronic age.

It was also in 1949 that the executives of the Rockefeller Center
planned a great surprise; an Atlantic–Pacific tour of Toscanini
and the N.B.C. Orchestra. This tour had two main objects. First,
to present the orchestra in person. There are about three hundred
and fifty symphonic orchestras in the U.S.A., thirty of which are
major ones and well known, especially the Philharmonic, the
Boston and the Philadelphia. All of them, of course, play in
public. This was not the case with the N.B.C. Orchestra, which,
until the advent of television, had only been seen from time
to time by selected audiences allowed into the studio. The
second reason was because of the increasing competition in the

gramophone-record world. The tour would be the best way to advertise Toscanini's records, particularly the forthcoming "L.P." ones.

Toscanini was somewhat apprehensive of this tour. It was to begin only six days after the end of the N.B.C. season. This had concluded with *Falstaff*, which had been exhausting for Toscanini, who realized that the whole responsibility for the success of the tour would rest on his shoulders. The original intention of the organizers was that Toscanini should confine himself to two programmes.

However, ten days before they were due to go, the maestro decided that in spite of the extra work required, they would have to have four different programmes, or both he and the orchestra would get bored. He decided on two new ones; and the next day completely altered them. Then he decided that they would after all have to have six programmes, and it took a great deal of work and confusion before these were settled. The organizers—who had to provide the scores, get programmes printed, etc.—were now in a panic, and when Toscanini was at last safely on the train, the whole N.B.C. heaved a sigh of relief. One day more and he would certainly have decided it was necessary to do eight programmes.

There is some controversy on the subject, but it is believed that Atlanta was the city which will go down in history as the site of the great revolution in Toscanini's hats. To the amazement and consternation of his orchestra, he appeared one morning, not with his eternal boat-shaped black felt hat, but with a magnificent pearl-grey one. He remembered that the last time he had been in Atlanta, twenty-nine years previously, he had likewise bought a new hat—a panama, which was then the fashion. "I wonder what sort of hat I shall buy," he said, "if I come to Atlanta again in another twenty-nine years."

He is said to have conducted even better than usual that evening. In the Overture to the *Scala di Seta*, the flying violins on the fourth minim were brought to an almost shuddering stop, like the sudden pulling-up of a herd of mythical colts. And at the end of

the Brahms First Symphony one of the players in the orchestra
was heard to mutter as he walked off the stage: "God, I never
thought that even he was capable of conducting like that!"

The orchestra was to have another shock. At seven the next
morning, when the train stopped at the station of Mobile, the
players, who were all in shirt-sleeves because of the semi-tropical
heat, saw Toscanini appear in a dressing-gown of crimson silk
with facings of electric blue—a gift from Sarnoff. Ghignatti, the
French horn-player, who had known Toscanini from the Scala
days onwards and had never seen him except in a black suit and a
dark bow tie, nearly fainted.

The members of the N.B.C. Orchestra formed a select and
pleasant company. Mishakoff, the first violin, who had arrived in
America with Piatigorski, is a well-known concert-player and his
name is associated with his string quartet, which is one of the best
in America. The leader of the second violins, Remo Bolognini, is
a well-known concert-player in South America and one of Isaye's
last pupils. The next second violinist, Guillet, also had his own
quartet, and worked with Ravel for a long time. The trumpet-
player, Glantz, is undoubtedly one of the finest in the world.
There were no less than three composers of genius: Carlton
Cooley, the first viola, who, according to Toscanini, knows
everything there is to be known about music; the 'cellist, Alan
Shelman, whose Concerto for 'Cello and Small Orchestra was
heard by the author at the Philharmonic, its texture rich and exquisite, and Boris Koutzen. Almost all nationalities were represented. As well as Mishakoff, the bass-bassoon player, Reines,
was Russian. Besides Bolognini and Ghignatti, Vito, the harpist
(from Marsico Vettere Potenza); Paolo Renzi, the oboeist (a
Roman), with his son Paolo, the flautist; Cerina, the horn-
player, from Salerno; and the violinist Ciompi, from Emilia, were
all Italians.

The special train consisted of twelve enormous pullmans,
which carried 125 people and $250,000 worth of instruments, for
six weeks, for 8,000 miles, across twenty-four states and stopping
at twenty towns. It was a real ambulant Festival. In eleven of

these cities the day of the concert was proclaimed by the mayor as "Toscanini Day". In others, as for instance Baltimore, the police had given orders for his car to be driven with the klaxon blaring continuously, so that, when he went out, the rest of the traffic should stop or pull on one side, as if the President himself were passing.

CHAPTER XVIII

The Empty Podium

WE have seen that in 1950 Toscanini was still an unbeaten octogenarian, alert, full of energy, honoured and cherished by millions. Then on March 1, 1951, something happened that made him say, "Since the first of March I have not been the same man." There had been insidious prodromal symptoms for some time: a sense of discomfort in the right leg, culminating in severe pain, which was diagnosed as circulatory obstruction. Various forms of treatment were prescribed for him in New York, including daily exercise at home on a stationary bicycle. On March 1, as he was pedalling, he was suddenly stricken with pain; he did not collapse, but managed to drag himself to the bathroom, where his family found him sitting on the edge of the bath, evidently not clear in his mind as to what had happened.

Fundamentally, he had been extremely fit all his life, and still at eighty-four he was showing few signs of his real age: the hair flowing back from his temples was whiter, but his cheeks were as pink as ever, and the skin of his face bronzed and firm. The flash of his eyes was veiled only by the heavy lenses which he now had to wear. He had become slightly less slim, and did not carry himself quite so erectly; nevertheless his summer guests at the Isolino were glad to see that he clambered up and down the cliff paths as nimbly as far younger men.

He used to ascribe his strong physique to two things: first, the fact that conducting always made him sweat freely, thus stimulating the circulation; secondly, that he has always been a sparing eater. His resistance had always been superb; and of course so had his muscular control. De Luca once told how he was talking to Toscanini while the latter was shaving with an open razor. The lights failed; when they went on again, De Luca was horrified to see that the maestro had finished shaving himself in the pitch darkness. Toscanini could not perceive anything odd about it; there was no danger of cutting himself. You cannot do that without perfect physical balance.

For some reason, people were always avid to know about his diet, although in fact Toscanini never had any special diet. There was a legend in the States that he lived on nothing but soup; and one playful friend once persuaded some reporters that he existed entirely on goats' milk, from goats that were kept specially for the purpose on the roof of the Rockefeller Center. He used in fact to eat very little—although his family sometimes whispered that he made up for it in the privacy of his room, where he always kept plenty of milk, biscuits, and fruit. It is certainly true that when he was working he would very often forget his meals; and his preference was always for simple food. Like any good northern Italian, he was fond of *minestra*—which is not soup in the English sense, but a filling dish.

He never touched wine until he was thirty, and until late in life never much liked it. He had a life-long horror of drunkenness. He would often have a glass of red wine with his meals, but champagne was always his favourite drink, and half a glass of it is all that he would ever touch in the intervals of concerts or rehearsals. He never liked tobacco. In all these ways, away from the theatre, Toscanini was always a man of quiet and normal habits. It was only in his music that he was not normal; therein lay his divine madness. Otherwise he was easy-going, domestic, and friendly. He was even sociable, for all his hatred of snobbery and grandeur—which was indisputable; there was nothing he hated more than fashionable receptions, at which he always behaved in such a shy and gloomy manner that it reinforced the legend of his eccentricity. Even in New York, in the greatest days of his fame, he was rarely seen in "high society"; and it may be symptomatic that among the many "conquests" that have been

attributed to him, there has never figured the name of a woman
of fashion.

He preferred to stay at home: the Toscaninis always kept
open house, and received a constant flow of visitors against their
own special background of an exceptionally united and intimate
family, that yet often seemed disorganized and even quarrelsome.
It was always a gay and unexpected house; and there, among
friends of his own choice, the maestro was at his best, and would
talk for hours, chattering, arguing, fuming, and of course endless-
ly reminiscing. Here his extraordinary memory provided constant
fascination for his listeners. One day in 1954—he was eighty-
seven then—he was complaining that many of today's best-
trained young singers lack the strength and dramatic feeling of
their predecessors. As an example, he described the tenor Mozzo
making his debut in an opera called *Stella*, by one Manzocchi, at
the Regio at Parma, when Toscanini was still training there; and
he outlined the whole libretto, and described all Mozzo's quality
and action, as if he had been listening to the opera only the previous evening.

From 1948 onwards Toscanini's life was divided between his
two homes: Riverdale during the concert season, from October
to April; and Via Durini in Milan for the remaining months, with
holiday periods at the Isolino. Musically, he was never really
happy to be far away from the Scala for too long: and it was in
Milan that the true background of his musical life lay. Although
he never assumed an official position, he continued to take a
fatherly interest in the Scala. Those who disliked him accused
him of unwarranted interference in matters which were not his
concern, but the truth was that his opinion was continually being
asked on every sort of question. An example in point was when
one of Verdi's early operas, *Oberto, Conte di San Bonifacio*, which
Verdi himself had repudiated, was to be included by the Scala in
the Verdi Centenary Programme. He sent a fulminating telegram
of protest to Ghiringhelli and broke with him for a year. He was
also furious when the Scala recently produced *Carmen* in French,
obliging Italian singers to sing in French. Toscanini was always

set against "this new mania" of singing operas in their original language. The Italian theatre-goers, he said, will not be moved if Don Jose sings *"Fermant mes paupières"*. They want him to sing *"Carmen te lo giuro"*, and only then will they thrill to it.

His interest in Italian musical life continued to be tireless. He had a constant flow of visitors: the rising composers, Menotti, Veretti, Mortari; conductors both young and old, Votto, Gavazzeni, Sanzogno, Giulini; the new star performers, Tagliavini, Di Stefano; and every time that he went to a performance as a spectator, performers and staff at the Scala, on hearing that the maestro was there, were immediately put almost into a state of electrical tension. Something more: he had a soft spot for young singers struggling to get a foothold in opera. He took to giving, secretly, private auditions for those young people. Voices were for him like horses to an old racing man; he never got tired of them, he could not do without them.

With less exacting work to do, at home in his old house with his family round him, he enjoyed a new fulness of companionship and social life; and, as always, his friends rejoiced in his vivid, shrewd, and entertaining talk. It was always full of prompt wit, of which one or two public sallies deserve recording. To the great Landowska, for instance, sighing to him, "Oh, cher maître, je voudrais jouer une fois avec vous, et je mourrais heureuse,"— "Eh bien, madame, ne jouez pas avec moi, et vivez heureuse." And another time, at Lucerne, when a great and celebrated soprano kept missing one note in the *Requiem*, in the interval he jumped up on to the stage, and, to her alarm and the onlookers' horror, rushed up to her with his hands stretched out like claws towards her vast and heaving bosom, crying in broken English, "Oh, if only that were all *brains*!"

And then came March 1; and the physical trouble was not the only one of that period. In the previous summer, while he was at the Isolino, Chotzinoff suddenly announced his arrival. Chotzi (as he is nicknamed) came from New York with the invidious task of breaking it to the maestro that, as the R.C.A. had decided to equip the whole of Radio City for television, his old studio 8-H would no longer be available. The symphonic concerts would therefore have to be transferred to Carnegie Hall or Manhattan Center, whichever he preferred. Toscanini, with his diabolical touchiness, felt that this was the thin end of the wedge. He said nothing to Chotzinoff, except that he preferred Carnegie Hall, but he voiced his anger to his wife, and that in no uncertain terms. Things got worse when, back in New York, Chotzinoff cabled to say that Carnegie Hall was no longer available, and that the maestro would therefore have to transmit his concerts from Manhattan Center.

Now, Toscanini had always hated that particular hall; not only because of its bad acoustics, but because its atmosphere was distasteful to him. His first instinct was to cable that he would conduct at Carnegie Hall or not at all; but he realized that this was not the time to bring another hornet's nest about his head. He arrived in America unusually depressed, and refused to see Sarnoff, President of the N.B.C. The emotional disturbance had made his leg worse, and a period of intensive treatment seemed necessary. Thus, the first cycle of autumn concerts was held without him. A special memorial concert had been fixed for January 27, 1951, at the Carnegie Hall, at which he was to conduct Verdi's *Requiem*. He was determined that once he set foot on the rostrum of Carnegie Hall, they would not be able to dislodge him; and in fact, the next cycle began there. The old fighter won his point once more.

Alas, his triumph was to be a short-lived one. On Saturday, February 17, 1951, before the scheduled concert began, the announcer broke the sad news to his millions of listeners that on medical advice the maestro would not be able to conduct any more concerts that season, after the present one. He conducted this concert with his usual fire and *brio*, but he walked with difficulty and had to lean on the rail of the rostrum. The last item on the programme was the almost symbolical one of the *Enigma Variations* by Elgar.

In the meanwhile in Milan, his wife, who had been ill for some time, took a sudden turn for the worse. In April she collapsed with a serious attack—a cardiac infarct. The family, who had kept the maestro in daily touch by letter all the time, now telephoned him, and he took a plane the same day, filled with anxious foreboding and sure that he would arrive too late. Temporarily, however, Signora Carla made a miraculous recovery, so that her husband was able to be with her for some weeks. She then passed into a coma and died peacefully.

During this sad and trying period Toscanini's reaction was unexpected, for the catastrophe seemed to stimulate all his reserves of physical strength. For weeks on end he practically refused to go to bed. He dozed occasionally in an armchair or at a table with his head on his hands. In the end, grief and exhaustion together caused a serious attack in his leg and he also felt that his sight was going. He kept prophesying his own death. First he said that he was going to die in July, the month in which his mother had died. Then he said that he would die at the same age as Verdi, eighty-seven. In this state of mind, he took to going out in the middle of the night and wandering around the neighbouring streets, always choosing those which were darkest and most deserted.

Something became evident to everybody at that time, that those who understood him best had always known: the strength and depth of his attachment to his wife, and his dependence upon her. Part of the legend about him had always proclaimed his great success with women, his many conquests—though it was ever a puzzle to his close friends how a man who was continually at work, in the concert hall or in his study, or else in the company of his wife and family, could justify his reputation as a great lover. Signora Carla was constantly at his side, on journeys, on holidays, as his secretary, as his dresser. For most of his career she had handled all his business, defended his privacy, and been invaluable in the diplomatic handling of any awkwardnesses due to his outbursts of temper. She fanatically adored her "Tosca" (as she called him) and fanatically took care of him; and it would never have occurred to him to be disturbed because she had not read

Leopardi or Carducci, and sometimes spelt Bach "Bac"; for far deeper bonds of sympathy and human contact united them.

At this point, one can now perhaps without indelicacy breathe a word or two concerning the romantic side of Toscanini's life. Agile, well-proportioned, with the lines of his face full of energy, yet at the same time gentle and regularly formed, with limpid yet fiery eyes, his physical attractions were indisputable. But he had another quality, which to women is seductive above all: that gift for virile dalliance, of giving each woman the feeling that at that moment he lived only to admire *her*, to understand her, to dedicate himself to her. Toscanini made all women feel that, even those in whom he had no possible further interest, shopgirls or charladies. He was in fact highly susceptible to women: but there was always the underlying concern about hurting his wife, and that faith in the sanctity of the family, which meant that all his love-affairs were beset with complication, worry and inhibition.

The names are of no matter: to repeat them would be hardly seemly towards the women who are dead, or tolerable for those still living. Two however can be mentioned. One is that of Krusceniska, who, the maestro once told a friend, was the only woman with whom he was madly in love who refused him, preferring a solid, restful landowner husband. The other is that of Rosina Storchio: by whom he had a son; whence sprang the one real tragedy of his life. Frances Alda has already recorded the miserable scene that occurred during the stormy première of *Madam Butterfly*, when, Storchio's pregnancy being already apparent, at one moment somebody in the audience shouted out, "Do you see Toscanini's child?"

The baby was very pretty, with great black eyes and the unmistakable brow; but alas, he was a poor remnant of humanity, completely palsied and speechless, and all the devoted care of his unhappy mother was of no help. And so at sixteen years old, just as he was born, deficient and pretty, he died.

There is a pathetic story in this connection, which shows how deep a scar this tragedy left upon the maestro's heart. Before moving the boy's body to Milan, to that tomb in the Monumentale

o

where she now rests with him, Rosina Storchio had interred her
son in the little cemetery of S. Fedele, near Como. Grubicy,
moved by her grief, painted a small picture of the tiny walled
burial-place in the country, with the graves lying in the sun, and
beside one of them the weeping figure of a woman in mourning,
Storchio. On Grubicy's death, this picture went with many of
his others to the painter Benvenuti, a great friend of both Toscanini and Grubicy. Benvenuti has told me how, many years later,
one day there arrived by car, at his remote house in the mountains above Leghorn, Toscanini and his wife. As they walked
round the house, talking of Grubicy and other old friends, Benvenuti noticed that the maestro seemed very agitated. While Benvenuti talked with Signora Carla, he roamed around, picking up
frames and canvases, peering into corners. Benvenuti knew that
he was looking for *that* picture, but he did not dare to speak of it,
and neither did Toscanini. Shortly afterwards he left.

In speaking of Toscanini's love-life, one should not of course
forget that practically numberless community of his impassioned
but platonic admirers, devoted to his cult, Toscaninian vestals,
surrounding him even in his old age with a dedicated aura of
music-loving ecstasy and *amitié amoureuse*. During the war, a
group of Italian ladies actually formed a fan-club, called "The
Waves of Love", which met to listen, in solemn unity, to his
N.B.C. transmissions or his latest recordings.

Toscanini was faced, after the death of his wife, not only with
bitter loneliness, but also with the brooding question, which had
hung over him since March 1: was he still able to conduct? Carla
Toscanini died on June 20. During the weeks which followed, the
rumour spread abroad that he would not take up the baton again,
that he had ended his career. But, for him, conducting was as
natural as breathing; and nobody voluntarily stops breathing; it
seemed inevitable that he would either take up his work again, or
die. He had always been inflexible in his strict requirements of
others, and had implacably retired any singer or player who was
no longer capable of giving a perfect performance. He knew very

well that to be a good conductor you must be in a state of perfect physical fitness; it is a hard job, even an athletic one. (Cantelli, naturally a slender man, used to say that a few years of it enormously developed his chest.) He felt it necessary to subject himself to a searching test; but he could not very well go back to New York and ask them to arrange a test to see if he was still capable of conducting. Fortunately, the right occasion arose. He had arranged to do a recording, the proceeds of which were to go to the Verdi Home of Rest. He decided to conduct for the recording, with the Scala Orchestra, on August 6, 7, and 8.

They were to play a suite from *Vespri Siciliani* and the two preludes of *Traviata*. The recording was kept secret, and strict orders were given that no outsiders were to be allowed in the studio. Poor Toscanini was a bundle of nerves. After five minutes, however, he felt a new man, in full possession of his faculties, and this was evident to everybody. His tempo was still his own prodigious tempo. His gestures were the same, perhaps not quite so free, but always decisive, and immediately clear to the orchestra, even in the most subtle inflections. His ear was as infallible as ever. The first part of the music was timed five times on two different days and gave exactly the same results, the maximum variation being from 4 minutes 18 seconds to 4 minutes 19 seconds. At the end, the orchestra applauded. He spent the whole afternoon rehearsing, recorded the next evening until late at night and completed the recording on the third evening. For various reasons, the records were unfortunately not released. He was entirely reassured, returned to America in September, and presented himself punctually on November 3 for the first concert. He conducted as erect as ever, and scorned the support which had been thoughtfully put around the rostrum. He had not conducted the orchestra for eight months; he stopped it after the first few beats, to make the characteristic remark, "Wake up, you sluggards!"

In the 1951–2 season he conducted twelve concerts between November and March. In the following season, 1952–3, he conducted fourteen concerts, as well as two in July and August, and a Wagner concert at the Scala. In 1953-4 there were eleven concerts. All this does not include his many recording sessions. He had started in 1944 on recording complete operas and choral works, and by 1952 he had completed *Fidelio*, *Bohème*, *Traviata*, *Otello*, *Falstaff*, and the *Requiem*.

The first recording that Toscanini ever made was at Camden, during the tour of 1921. The orchestra stayed at Philadelphia for a week, expressly for this purpose, and the recordings were made in a church that the Victor people had fitted up as a studio. The technique of recording was far from perfect, and one of Toscanini's players remembers him flinging down the disc of *A Midsummer Night's Dream* and shouting, "That is all wrong. It is not my tempo and not my attack!" The experience put him off recording for many years, until his wife, good business woman that she was, persuaded him back to it by bribing him with a painting he particularly coveted. He could earn 40,000 Lire from a single disc—as much as a whole year's salary at the Scala.

He started recording for the N.B.C. in 1938. The technique was very much improved, but he would not yet admit that records could be anything but a poor substitute for "live" music. There were other disastrous incidents: Toscanini recorded seven major symphonies for the Victor company, with the Philadelphia Orchestra, but after endless rehearsals, and an epic scene between Sarnoff and his executives, and the expenditure of thousands of dollars, they were never issued for sale. The new High Fidelity methods finally dissipated his old mistrust, and after 1950 his contribution to recorded music mounted swiftly.

His choral and operatic recordings presented the N.B.C. technicians with a formidable task. To get the maestro's final approval for a recording was never easy. In the first place, he would allow only one single microphone in the studio: otherwise, he says, the mixer in the control cabin is the real conductor. Nevertheless, every detail must be clearly perceptible—and with only a single sound source, this is of course no easy matter. His ear had to be able to distinguish every note: "Where is the piccolo?" he might ask at a certain point; and then each of the series of recordings of the piece would have to be listened to, until the elusive piccolo could be heard. And then that beat would have to be extracted from its tape, and inserted in the other, without up-setting the balance. And even then the dynamics would never be good enough for Toscanini: the pianissimo passages never soft enough, the fortissimo never *really* fortissimo. To crown his career, Toscanini set himself this task—to establish a canon of his last recorded performances, passed as perfect by himself, an imposing collection to carry his name and transmit his art.

In January 1954 he conducted *Un Ballo in Maschera*, and any-one who has heard it will probably agree that this is the very finest of all Toscanini's opera recordings: a fresh, powerful, and intoxicating performance. Only two months after this he was in-formed that the N.B.C. had decided to disband the orchestra, and that they could therefore dispense with his services.

Of course, there always lie behind such decisions many factors which are not apparent to the outside observer; it is indisputable that the orchestra was a heavy financial burden to the N.B.C., and, with Toscanini's precarious health, an increasingly risky in-vestment. Nevertheless, it is difficult to sympathize with the summary treatment of the old maestro by such an immensely wealthy corporation. It would not have ruined them to keep him on a little longer; to dismiss him was certainly to terminate his career, and posterity is now denied the recordings he was con-templating, of *Trovatore* and *Rigoletto*.

His farewell concert was fixed for April 4, 1954—a Wagner programme. His retirement was announced only a day or two before it; it had been agreed that officially the maestro would take the first step, with a letter of resignation to Sarnoff: "And now the sad time has come when I must reluctantly lay aside my baton. . . ." The draft of it lay on his desk for two weeks before he could bring himself to sign it.

The concert was a solemn, awe-inspiring occasion. The audience at Carnegie Hall must have felt that they were present not only at a concert, but also at the last act of a human drama. In the middle of the concert, for a few beats, a terrible thing happened to Toscanini: he lost control. He put his hand to his eyes, and made a few feeble and meaningless gestures with his baton. The orchestra was so well-trained that it was able to carry on with hardly a falter, but the audience had noticed, and the atmosphere of emotional tension was indescribable. Toscanini pulled himself together and finished the concert, but at the end he did a thing unprecedented for him: he did not wait for the last chord, but put down his baton and left the rostrum just before it. No one was allowed into his dressing-room; it became known, later, that he had given way to tears. For the next few days he stayed at home and remained quite silent. Some time afterwards, when one of his daughters asked him what he had felt on that occasion, he answered, touching his chest over his heart: "An infinite sadness in there."

He left America without saying goodbye to anybody, not even the orchestra. Later, when the N.B.C. Orchestra was disbanded, most of its members formed a new "Symphony of the Air Orchestra". Before their first concert they cabled Toscanini that they intended to pay him tribute, by playing without a conductor. And so in fact they did, at Carnegie Hall on October 27 of that year, and played with such superb balance and spontaneity that they might have been a chamber ensemble. And so in a way that empty podium was Toscanini's last triumph.

That year, 1954, was the first in which he did not return to America, and the first Christmas he had spent in Italy for many years. He had retired from conducting; but that did not mean that he was going to be idle. He went on with the perfection and editing of his recordings.

In 1952 at Via Durini he had first started working with a young friend, Sandro Cicogna, an engineer, industrialist, and musician, on the task of re-recording and revising the older recordings which he had not finally approved. They started with the Fourth and Ninth Symphonies of Beethoven, and went on to the Verdi *Requiem*. The maestro would only allow any recording to be published after giving his own written warrant. For the *Requiem*, instead of the usual "O.K." he wrote "Viva Verdi."

His state of health much improved during the winter of 1954–5. The Piccola Scala, a small lyric theatre on the lines of the *Kammerspiel*, had been built behind the Scala, and Toscanini planned to conduct the opening performance, at Christmas 1955, with *Falstaff*. Thus, he hoped to fulfil an approximation of his dream of conducting *Falstaff* once more at Busseto. He was so elated at the prospect that on the day he discussed the plan with Ghiringhelli his blood-pressure rose from 140 to 205. (It is true that tests made in previous years had shown that his pressure always rose by leaps and bounds whenever he listened to music.) He plunged into the details of the production with all his old zest. The stage-director was to be Luchino Visconti, to whom Toscanini said: "You are young; think up something new and especially beautiful for the sets and the production. I am an old man, I can only visualize it in the same old way." Toscanini's inaugural performance was announced in the papers.

As the months of that winter passed by, his general health remained good, but his sight was failing. He became more and more convinced that he would not be able to conduct *Falstaff*, after all. This, and the growing difficulty he encountered in finding solitude, ever more necessary to him, in the flat which he shared with his daughter Wally in Milan, and the insistent appeals from Walter that he should return to the U.S.A. to get on with the recordings, finally decided him to return to Riverdale in February. And of course, once he was in America, there was no need to find an excuse for not conducting at the Piccola Scala!

His return to Riverdale was a sad one. He came back to America as a simple private citizen, like a man in retirement. There began for him a last, sad, exile: exile from the orchestra, from that marvellous sonorous universe in which he had lived and worked and breathed for seventy-five years. And at the same time there began for him a new period of rear-guard action, fought against old age. All his life, he had had a proud, almost morbid, shame and horror of illness or feebleness. He had now come to the extreme point, beyond which life becomes purely vegetative. It was agonizing for his companions to look on at that desperate struggle; to see him continually at watch against himself, alert to catch the least sign of decline, testing to see if he could still hear the tick of that clock from that armchair, if he could clearly distinguish that object at that distance. Heroic, altruistic, he would accept no help, even when it was necessary, and would rebuff any sign of pity. He was so jealously determined to do everything for himself, that his family secretly made a spyhole in the wall of the bathroom; for if he had been overcome by some trouble while he was in there, he would never have called for help. His sight, affected by the circulation, declined faster than his hearing. He had to give up reading scores and books, and this was a terrible loss for him. Finally, the few last dear faces could no longer be distinguished. It was this isolation of blindness that spared him later, on the eve of his death, a dreadful blow, when Cantelli, the young conductor whom he particularly cherished, died in a crash at Orly.

However, his ear, that superhuman ear, remained active. From his armchair, through a specially placed system of loudspeakers, he used to listen to the run-throughs of recordings organized by Walter in the sound laboratory below in the basement of Villa Paulina. There a small band of ardent technicians devoted themselves to revising and re-recording the old performances, cleaning them of blemishes, cutting out coughs and other noises before they put them on the tape; and under the maestro's direction, using a technique of "cutting" similar to that in film-making, producing a definitive collection of his great performances. (As an example of the extraordinary refinement to which this technique has been brought, it can be stated that from the performance of a Brandenburg Concerto given by the Philharmonic in 1938, there were extracted no fewer than 240 coughs!)

Observing the astonishingly regular sequence of cause and effect that governed Toscanini's whole career, one might conclude that herein lay the reason for which he did not die, as he logically should have done, after that last concert, on April 4, 1954. He had his recordings to complete. He had to complete that collection of interpretations which must stand as the final memorial of his work.

From 1954 to 1957 he supervised the final revision of certain essential performances, some of them made up from material recorded during his period with the Philharmonic: the *Requiem* of Verdi, the *Requiem* of Cherubini; Strauss's tone poems, *Death and Transfiguration*, *Till Eulenspiegel*, and *Don Quixote*; *Harold in Italy* by Berlioz; *Hary Janos* by Kodaly; Act IV of *Rigoletto* (published in the collection "Verdi and Toscanini"); the Brahms Double Concerto, the Third Symphony of Schumann. The last work that he completed was the final revision of *Aida*, recorded in 1949; which completes his operatic series, and will be published posthumously. Once again, the extraordinary symmetry: with *Aida* he began his career, with *Aida* it ends.

In his last years the attacks of thrombosis recurred at intervals, one exceptionally grave one in July 1955, from which he made an astounding recovery. A warning, on Christmas Day 1956, had no immediate sequel. It was on New Year's night that the attack was renewed, this time implacably. He had enjoyed the New Year dinner with his family and friends, appearing more calm and cheerful than usual. He ate well, and was even merry. He had with him at that time, besides his children, his granddaughter Emanuela, who was married the previous spring, and had come to bear her first child in her grandfather's house. The party went on until three o'clock. In the night he had a first haemorrhage, and overcame it. He had a second one, and overcame that. It took nine of them to vanquish that formidable frame. He survived, unconscious, for another sixteen days.

He died the same death that Verdi had died: the great man whom all his life Toscanini held as his model. Toscanini lay now as fifty-six years earlier he had seen the old man lie on his deathbed in the Hotel Milan: his eyes closed, already cut off from the living, the only sign of life, the strained panting in his broad chest. So that the noise of the carriages should not penetrate to Verdi's room, the municipality of Milan had spread the surrounding streets with straw. This time there was no need: snow covered the slopes of Riverdale.

Index

218